Improving Primary Mathematics Teaching and Learning

Improving Primary Mathematics Teaching and Learning

Edited by
Mary McAteer

Mc
Graw
Hill   Open University Press

Open University Press
McGraw-Hill Education
McGraw-Hill House
Shoppenhangers Road
Maidenhead
Berkshire
England
SL6 2QL

email: enquiries@openup.co.uk
world wide web: www.openup.co.uk

and Two Penn Plaza, New York, NY 10121-2289, USA

First published 2012

A catalogue record of this book is available from the British Library

ISBN-13: 9780335246762 (pb)
ISBN-10: 0335245761
e-ISBN: 9780335246779

Library of Congress Cataloging-in-Publication Data
CIP data has been applied for

Typeset by Aptara Inc., India
Printed in the UK by Bell and Bain Ltd, Glasgow.

Fictitious names of companies, products, people, characters and/or data that may be used herein (in case studies or in examples) are not intended to represent any real individual, company, product or event.

MIX
Paper from
responsible sources
FSC
www.fsc.org FSC® C007785

The McGraw-Hill Companies

Contents

List of contributors

Mike Askew is Professor of Primary Education at Monash University, Melbourne. Prior to that he was Chair Professor of Mathematics Education at King's College London. Internationally regarded as a leading expert on primary mathematics education, he has directed many research projects including the influential 'Effective Teachers of Numeracy in Primary Schools', 'Raising Attainment in Numeracy' and 'Mental Calculations: Interpretations and Implementation'. He was deputy director of the five-year Leverhulme Numeracy Research Programme, examining teaching, learning and progression in number from age 5 to age 11. His most recent book is *Transforming Primary Maths* (Routledge 2012).

Sue Bailey is a senior lecturer for a Primary Mathematics Specialist Teacher programme at Edge Hill University, and a Primary Mathematics Consultant with Lancashire County Council supporting schools and leading training courses. Previously she worked for almost 20 years in primary schools where she held positions of Mathematics Subject Leader and Deputy and Acting Head Teacher; she has a MA in Education Management. She has also contributed for three years to the development of the Every Child Counts programme led by Edge Hill University in partnership with Lancashire County Council.

Elizabeth Carruthers is head teacher of Redcliffe Children's Centre, Nursery School and Research and Professional Development Base in Bristol. She has worked in all phases of education, which includes being a local authority Foundation Stage adviser and a numeracy consultant with the National Numeracy Strategy. Her research interests are in Early Years education, wild forest experiences for children and the pedagogy of children's mathematical graphics. She has published mainly on the subject of children's mathematical graphics. She is presently studying for a doctoral degree at the University of the West of England.

Victoria Grinyer is an associate tutor working for the Mathematics Specialist Teacher programme at Edge Hill University. She trained and began her teaching career in Oxford and has taught in two primary schools. She was part of the Senior Leadership Team and was the mathematics coordinator in her last teaching role. She has a Masters degree in Education and has always had a strong interest in children's mathematical thinking.

Alice Hansen is an educational consultant and director of Children Count Ltd. Prior to this, she worked in higher education as a principal lecturer in mathematics education and as the programme leader for the Primary Postgraduate Certificate of Education with Qualified Teacher Status (QTS) programme at the University of Cumbria. She has worked in a wide range of primary schools in England and abroad. Her research interests include Early Years and primary children's mathematical thinking and how information and communication technology (ICT) can be used to enhance teaching and learning.

Mary McAteer is director for a Primary Mathematics Specialist Teacher programme at Edge Hill University, having previously worked for more than 30 years as a school teacher, primary mathematics, science and technology consultant, and programme lead of an MA in Education. She has a particular interest in forms of practitioner research. Her most recent publications are 'Theory generative approaches in practitioner research', in J. Adams, M. Cochrane and L. Dunne (eds) (2011) *Applying Theory to Educational Research: An Introductory Approach with Case Studies* (Oxford: Wiley Blackwell) and 'Action Research in Education' (BERA/Sage Research Methods in Education commissioned series). She is a member of the Collaborative Action Research Network (CARN) Coordinating Group.

Lynne McClure works with and for teachers and their students. She has taught mathematics and/or mathematics education in primary and secondary schools, and in further and higher education institutions. She previously lived in Scotland, combining course leadership at Edinburgh University with consulting to government departments, universities, local education authorities and numerous schools both in Scotland and abroad. She is a member of the Advisory Committee on Mathematics Education, council member of both the Mathematical Association (MA) and the Association of Teachers of Mathematics (ATM) and edits the *Primary Mathematics* journal for the Mathematical Association. Her research interest is in appropriate curricula for able young mathematicians and she has published widely on the subject. She became Director of the award-winning NRICH project at Cambridge in March 2010 (http://nrich.maths.org).

Effie Maclellan is Research Professor in Education at the University of Strathclyde. Before coming to Strathclyde, she worked for many years as a class teacher and a head teacher in mainstream primary education and in special education. Her PhD was an empirical investigation into how young school-aged children use the rich conceptual knowledge that they bring to school to develop the formalisms of addition and subtraction as these are typically understood. The overall thrust of her research and scholarship is in learning, teaching and assessment but within that she retains an enduring interest in mathematics education.

Suzan Nelson is an associate tutor for the Faculty of Education at Edge Hill University, working on the Mathematics Specialist Teacher programme. A former Head of Department and Behaviour Manager at Prescot School, she has experience of teaching a variety of subjects including mathematics at a number of secondary schools. Suzan holds teaching qualifications in English, Drama, Personal, Social, Health and Economic Education (PSHEE), Citizenship and Careers, and was formerly an adviser for the PSHE Association. She also has a Master's in Victorian Literature and holds the National Professional Qualification for Headship (NPQH). She is currently undertaking research for a PhD in the reasons for youth unemployment.

Carol Rushworth-Little is employed by Worcestershire County Council as a specialist learning support teacher (mathematics specialism), working for the Learning Support Team, Children's Services. She previously taught mathematics and ICT in secondary schools and a tertiary college for 13 years before moving into primary education where she had responsibility for mathematics coordination, and for special needs and inclusion. She has a particular interest in dyscalculia, and her MA dissertation research focused on teachers' and pupils' perceptions of indicators of dyscalculia. She has written the Worcestershire Diagnostic Assessment Test, used to identify areas of mathematical strengths and weaknesses of pupils within the authority. She also works as an independent author of mathematical training materials for an educational publishing company.

Steve Sherer has over 30 years' experience of working in a range of primary and secondary schools, teaching all age groups from Foundation Stage to A level, including roles as mathematics subject leader. He is currently employed as a senior lecturer at Edge Hill University, Lancashire, where he works on postgraduate professional development courses, including the Numbers Count and Mathematics Specialist Teacher programmes. He has a particular interest in the use of creative approaches to learning and teaching.

Ian Thompson taught for 19 years before moving into teacher education at Christ Church College, Canterbury and then at Newcastle University, where he began researching children's mental and written calculation strategies and their understanding of place value. He has written over 140 articles, conference papers and book chapters, and edited three books for Open University Press: *Enriching Primary Mathematics Teaching* (2003), *Teaching and Learning Early Number* (2nd edn, 2008) and *Issues in Teaching Numeracy in Primary Schools* (2nd edn, 2010). He was seconded to the National Numeracy Strategy for two years and in 2002 became an independent mathematics consultant. He is currently Visiting Professor at Edge Hill University.

Vivien Townsend is a former primary school teacher, mathematics adviser and e-learning adviser for a local authority. She currently works as a freelance consultant, supporting primary schools with mathematics and ICT. She sits on the joint primary subcommittee of the ATM/MA and is a co-opted member of the ATM General Council. She regularly holds continuing professional development (CPD) sessions for both experienced teachers and those new to the profession – including presenting workshops at ATM conferences – and leads challenge days for pupils. Her research interests include active, creative approaches to teaching mathematics, and the use of blogging software.

Maulfry Worthington has taught for many years in the 3–8 age range, has been a National Numeracy Consultant and has lectured on Primary and Early Years mathematics and Early Years education, and is currently undertaking doctoral research into the genesis of mathematical semiosis in early childhood (VU University, Amsterdam). She has co-authored a number of texts with Elizabeth Carruthers, including *Understanding Children's Mathematical Graphics: Beginnings in Play* (Open University Press, 2011), and following the Williams Review, they were commissioned to write *Children Thinking Mathematically* for the Department for Children, Schools and Families (DCSF 2009). They have won national awards for their work and are co-founders of the international Children's Mathematics Network (www.childrens-mathematics.net.)

Acknowledgements

We gratefully acknowledge the support of many people in the production of this book:

Fiona Richman and Laura Givans for their editorial advice and support.

Our families, friends, colleagues, and students for support and opportunities to share and shape ideas.

The various teachers and pupils who have participated in the research studies.

Particular thanks are due to:

Ronit Bird, 'Dyscalculia Toolkit' (reproduced in Chapter 7 with permission from SAGE Publications).

All the staff and children of Redcliffe Children's Centre and Maintained Nursery, Bristol, for the case study of Shereen in Chapter 11 and many other rich examples and insights. Case studies 11.2 and 11.3 are featured in Carruthers and Worthington (2006).

Our thanks go to Karen and her head teacher who agreed to the conversation documented in Chapter 12 and understood that it would be used for educational writing.

Sarah and Emily Rushworth, Patrick McLaughlin.

The Edge Hill Extended MaST Team.

Introduction

This book grew from our shared passion for teaching and learning mathematics in primary schools. Our experiences as university tutors, consultants, researchers and practitioners in the field make us continuously question what good mathematics teaching is and how we, in our various roles, can and do support its development. We are diverse in both practice and voice, and so while chapters are structured in order to provide some stylistic and epistemological congruence, it is our hope that the individual voices remain strong and vibrant, and bring the work alive for you.

We have each drawn on our own and on other research and scholarship to illustrate and explore specific issues in practice, in order to present both a practical and a theoretical perspective. In this way, we hope to present not simply a 'guide to practice', but more a 'guide to understanding and developing practice'. Throughout the book, we invite you to reflect on practice-based issues, your own beliefs and values, your (perhaps as yet unarticulated) theoretical stance, and the conceptual and theoretical underpinnings of practice. For this reason you will see some diversity within the book, you may come across ideas you disagree with (and we hope you do!), and you may find yourself asking some questions about things that you previously took for granted. While discussion of issues such as 'mathematical ability', 'mathematical processes and procedures', 'pedagogical appropriateness', features to some extent in the chapters that follow, their discussion in full is beyond the scope of this book, but may, and should inform your own reflections on and explorations of your practice.

The book is designed to be used as a reader, suited to the needs of trainee teachers, practising teachers, teacher educators, and others involved in mathematics education. Part 1 provides a brief contextual overview of current issues in mathematics education in the United Kingdom, and paints a backdrop against which to consider the teaching and learning issues of part 2, and the professional development issues of part 3. The book need not be read in its entirety, cover-to-cover, although part 3 presents a developing story where Chapters 10, 11 and 12 are probably better read in sequence. Chapter 13 provides a more generic overview of the role of professional development in supporting improved practice in the teaching of mathematics.

The book's production comes at a time of major change in relation to the curriculum, and also in terms of teacher initial and continuing education. While chapters do make links to the National Curriculum, their content and approach has been chosen to reflect issues in mathematics teaching which are of real concern to teachers, and are, and will continue to be important in the early learning experiences of primary school children.

Part 1

Primary mathematics teaching today

1 Primary mathematics teaching today

Introduction and context

Mary McAteer and Suzan E. Nelson

Mathematics matters

Why is skill in mathematics important? Why should we not just accept that some people 'don't get it'?

Before addressing these questions, it is necessary to clarify the language and terminology used. It is important to note that the term 'numeracy' is not interchangeable with the term 'mathematics' (although often portrayed as such in the media). It is, however, a central and fundamental part of mathematics, and in general, those who exhibit difficulties in numeracy are likely to have difficulty across the whole discipline. While one result of poorly developed numeracy (and mathematics) might be lack of progress at school, there are clear indicators that its impact is much wider, and indeed more serious than this. A functional level of numeracy is an essential life skill, and those who fail to achieve this level of competency will find themselves challenged in many aspects of life, from shopping to reading a bus timetable. Effective mathematics teaching and learning is clearly a key part of early education.

The current situation in mathematics teaching and learning

Pupil attainment

The attainment of English pupils in mathematics is, according to the Royal Society of Arts (RSA) (Norris 2012: 4), 'at best stable, or even in decline' (although Ian Thompson, in Chapter 10, questions this analysis) and yet using numeracy skills is something we take for granted each time we try to calculate the special offer deals, pay our bills, measure out the ingredients for a recipe or reckon an aggregate sports score. It lies at the heart of much of the modern technology that forms such a big part of our lives (mobile phones, computers, calculators, even most modern cars). It is in high demand from employers as many jobs require the ability to analyse spreadsheets and data sets (Hastings 2006) – and this now includes all teachers:

> Basic numeracy and quantitative skills are increasingly necessary in all jobs and life-skills, for tasks including budgeting and data-handling. And the changing nature of the international economy means that maths skills and knowledge are in higher demand than ever.
>
> (Norris 2012: 4)

In 2005, primary school test results showed that schools in England were still far short of the government's target of 85 per cent of 11 year olds reaching the required level in English and mathematics with improvements of just 1.3 per cent in mathematics. And in 2008, 78 per cent of 11 year olds reached the expected level 4 in mathematics – a rise of just six percentage points since 2000, and an increase in the gap between attainment at 7 and at 11. The league tables for 2011 show that 1310 primary schools in England fell below the expected standards (Standards and Testing Agency 2011).

The Trends in International Mathematics and Science Study (TIMMS 2007) survey reveals England lying in seventh place both for grade 4 (Year 5) and grade 7 (Year 8) behind Hong Kong, Singapore, Japan and Taipei in both stages. This at least has shown an improvement since the previous TIMSS, which placed England tenth. The Organization for Economic Co-operation and Development (OECD) league tables for 2009 places the UK twenty-seventh with Shanghai, Singapore, Hong Kong, Korea, Taipei and Finland occupying the top six slots (OECD 2009).

In December 2011, Schools Minister Nick Gibb compared England to three regions and countries around the world – Massachusetts (the highest performing US state for mathematics), Singapore and Hong Kong – and expressed concern at the over-reliance on calculators in English schools, signalling that it contributed to poor mathematical skill development. Singapore's success was achieved through enhancing teacher expertise and curriculum coherence – the former by impressive Continuing Professional Development (CPD) and the latter by 'approving' text books and teaching materials (Oates 2010).

Public concern about low levels of mathematics attainment, poor teaching and mathematics anxiety can also be seen in headlines such as 'Poor numeracy is blighting Britain's economic performance and ruining lives, says a new charity launched to champion better maths skills'

(Burns 2012a), 'Pupils should learn maths by using it' (Burns 2012c) and 'School maths lessons: Pupils scared to ask for help' (Burns 2012b).

Alongside these concerns about pupil attainment, there were similar and linked concerns expressed about teacher expertise.

Teacher expertise

In March 2003, Charles Clarke, then Secretary of State for Education and Skills, said:

> It is a combination of deep subject knowledge and a range of appropriate teaching and learning techniques which make for the most powerful interactions between teachers and pupils. Enhancing subject specialism therefore needs to be seen not as an end in itself, but as a way of bringing about excellence in teaching and learning to improve standards in our schools.
>
> (Charles Clarke, cited by Williams 2008: 8)

This increasing emphasis on subject specialisms became particularly important in primary schools where it was noted that less that 3 per cent of postgraduate trainee teachers have a mathematics-related degree. It is interesting to note that this lack of specialist mathematics knowledge in primary school teachers is not a new phenomenon. As far back as 1959, in an article reprinted by the *Times Educational Supplement* (TES) in 2011, the then new chief education officer for Surrey, a Mr A.M. Baird, was quoted as saying that 'until recently, academic standards in maths [for trainee teachers] had been too low' (TES 2011).

In order to address the problem of lack of teacher expertise, a review of mathematics teaching in Early Years settings and primary schools was commissioned following Gordon Brown's (2007) identification of primary mathematics teaching as a key focus for his Government. This review had the specific purpose of identifying effective mathematical pedagogies, provision for all, effective early intervention for those identified, the appropriate range of conceptual and subject knowledge in mathematics for primary aged pupils (including the ways through which Initial Teacher Training (ITT) and continuing professional development could secure that), effective design and sequence of the mathematics curriculum, and finally, the ways in which parents and families could be best supported in order to help their children develop in mathematics. The outcome of this process resulted in the Williams Review (published in 2008), which highlighted the 'importance of a young child's ability to count, calculate and work confidently with mathematical ideas' (Williams 2008: 5) and recognized the role that teachers have in this development. Teachers' skills and fluency in the subject need to be such that they have the 'confidence and flexibility' (Williams 2008: 5) to be a good teacher of mathematics and extend the children's knowledge, skills and understanding. Mathematics as an academic discipline is unique in that it combines both practical applications with abstract concepts. Effective mathematics teaching involves teachers in crafting these together in a complementary and meaningful way.

The impact of poor mathematics attainment

Recent studies show that the impact of poor numeracy is far reaching. In *The Long Term Costs of Numeracy Difficulties*, the Every Child a Chance Trust (2009) stated that the UK government's 2003 Skills for Life survey (in which over 8,000 adults in England had mathematics skills tested) found that 15 million adults were judged to have numeracy skills at or below entry level 3 (equivalent to the skills expected of an 11 year old) and that 6.8 million had skills at or below entry level 2 (the standard expected for a 9 year old). The report summarized that:

- About 15 million adults in the UK have very poor numeracy skills.
- One in six companies currently have to provide remedial mathematics classes for their employees.
- Each year over 30,000 11 year olds (over 5 per cent of their age group) leave primary school with numeracy skills at or below the level expected of the average 7 year old.
- Numeracy failure carries high social costs – the proportion of the prison population with very poor numeracy skills, for example, is even greater than the proportion with poor literacy skills.

Numeracy failure starts early and, if not dealt with, becomes embedded. Studies conducted by the Centre for Research on the Wider Benefits of Learning (Duckworth 2007) show that those who are very low attainers in mathematics at 7 years are likely to remain so at 11. Children leaving Key Stage 1 at 7 years old without having mastered the most basic numeracy skills will in almost all cases be identified by their primary school as having special educational needs (SEN) and be placed on the 'School Action' or 'School Action Plus' stages of the national SEN Code of Practice. 'By the age of 11, 34 per cent of children with very poor numeracy skills will have Statements of special educational needs' (Every Child a Chance Trust 2009: 10).

The educational effects of numeracy problems include high rates of truancy and a greater risk of exclusion at secondary school (a higher percentage than would be expected) and a greater likelihood of ending up as not in employment, education or training (NEET) once they leave.

Added to this, numeracy difficulties are also linked to increased health risks and an increased risk of involvement with the criminal justice system. Furthermore, a 1997 report for the Basic Skills Agency found that 58 per cent of those with poor numeracy and competent literacy were likely to be found in the low wage bracket. This compares with just 30 per cent of those with competent numeracy and poor literacy (cited in Hastings 2006). A 2011 Skills for Life Survey produced for the Department for Business, Innovation and Skills showed that almost 25 per cent of participants achieved below entry level 3 in numeracy. Carol Taylor, the National Institute of Adult Continuing Education (NIACE) Director for Research and Development, expressed her concern at the 2011 figures, saying 'One in six of the adult population ... are seriously disadvantaged as employees, citizens and parents' (Taylor 2011).

The government now recognizes the importance of mathematical skills to England's economic future: 'Science, Technology, Engineering and Mathematics (STEM) industries are becoming increasingly central to economic competitiveness and growth and will provide many of the jobs of tomorrow for young people' (Norris 2012: 4).

Parents also recognize this. Extra mathematics lessons account for more than half of all private tuition outside school hours.

The implications for teachers

In a 2004 report into post-14 mathematics, Adrian Smith pointed out that in order to compete in the global economy, the UK needed more specialist mathematics teachers with better continuing professional development (Smith 2004), a point echoed four years later by the Williams Review (Williams 2008).

Laurie Jacques, speaking at the time in her capacity as director for policy and quality at the National Centre for Excellence in the Teaching of Mathematics (NCETM), argued that the low numbers of mathematics specialists entering primary schools clearly has an impact on mathematics leadership:

> in a lot of schools they have acquired the [mathematics subject leader job] because no one else would take it on. As a result it has become a management rather than a leadership role; they do the admin and resources bit well, but they don't necessarily focus on teaching and learning.
>
> (Carrington 2010)

The National Audit Office (cited by Ward 2008) found that the biggest factor in whether pupils went to secondary school enjoying mathematics was whether they had been taught the subject by an enthusiastic teacher at primary level. Celia Hoyles, director of the NCETM, called for more and better subject training for teachers (Neumark 2010), saying that people are often put off mathematics at school, but good teachers can open up the door to understanding, and foster a more positive relationship with mathematics in children.

Also supporting the need for specialist mathematics training for primary school teachers was the production by the Office for Standards in Education, Children's Services and Skills (Ofsted) in 2009 of the report *Improving Practice in Mathematics Teaching at Primary Level*, citing the fact that for many teachers, their knowledge of mathematics stopped at the course they studied at 16, and that while they might work hard to develop the skills they need to deliver to their classes, they fail to appreciate the wider view of the mathematics curriculum (Ofsted 2009: 12).

The Williams Review (2008) concluded that, given the changes in the methods of mathematics teaching, it was the teacher, rather than the parents, who would have the most influence over the learning outcomes. It further confirmed that just 13 per cent of primary school teachers (at that time) had a mathematics specialism, and a key recommendation was for 'the presence of a Mathematics Specialist in every primary school, who will champion this challenging subject and act as the nucleus for achieving best pedagogical practice' (Williams 2008: 1). This, the third of the ten recommendations, was the catalyst for a National CPD programme, the Mathematics Specialist Teacher (MaST) programme, which started in January 2010.

In November 2011 Ofsted's report on primary mathematics reiterated many of these findings: that high quality teaching 'secures pupils' understanding of structure and relationships in number'; that successful schools swiftly recognize problems and equally quickly apply suitable interventions and that 'clear, coherent calculation policies and guidance' support staff and pupils in the development of mathematics skills (Ofsted 2011). Furthermore, such schools 'recognise the importance of good subject knowledge and subject-specific teaching skills' and aim to develop staff's knowledge appropriately.

Michael Gove, MP, said at the Advisory Committee on Mathematics Education:

> mathematical understanding is critical to our children's future. Our economic future depends on stimulating innovation, developing technological breakthroughs, making connections between scientific disciplines. And none of that is possible without ensuring more and more of our young people are mathematically literate and mathematically confident.
>
> (Michael Gove, cited in Ofsted 2011: 4)

Efforts are being made to address the problem; several programmes have been launched in the last few years to enhance the mathematical skills and knowledge of existing primary school teachers.

The continuing professional development (CPD) context

In recent years CPD initiatives have been developed to both support and encourage serving teachers to engage in award-bearing CPD programmes. Pitched at postgraduate level, they have provided opportunities for teachers to undertake periods of rigorous reflection on practice, small-scale practitioner inquiry projects, and develop strong understandings of theory–practice relationships. Changes in funding arrangements since the mid 1990s resulted in the development of closer links between schools and universities as organizational rather than individual need became the driver for programmes. Partnerships through which university faculties of education worked alongside groups of schools, local authority clusters or other collectives began to emerge. The years between 2006 and 2011 saw the introduction of the funded postgraduate professional development (PPD) initiative through which teachers in England were subsidized to access master's level professional development programmes. Programmes such as the Master's in Teaching and Learning (MTL) in England (short-lived though it was), the Chartered Teacher Pathway in Scotland, and the current development in Wales of a Master's in Educational Practice all bear out both the desirability and the potency of highly contextualized professional development. In addition, their designation as master's level courses, rather than traditional 'INSET' (in-service training) programmes, which tended to train teachers in the use of specific resources or approaches (normally being completed in one-day or half-day sessions), suggests that the academic rigour is a valuable feature of them.

Despite recent changes in legislation and funding, the focus still remains on high quality professional development for practising teachers (in many cases linked to a specific subject or pedagogic focus). While the PPD funding stream was discontinued in 2011, there remained an emphasis on good quality CPD provision. The introduction of the National Scholarship Scheme in 2011, which called for applicants who wanted to 'use this money for Master's level development, or other highly valuable opportunities, such as subject specific seminars', was as a direct result of the Schools White Paper, *The Importance of Teaching* (Department for Education (DFE) 2010). Master's level professional development continues to be a central strand in educational initiatives and policy-making.

Recent initiatives in the teaching of mathematics

It is against this backdrop that we can begin to explore a range of recent initiatives in relation to the teaching of mathematics.

Every Child Counts

Every Child Counts was launched by the Every Child a Chance Trust in November 2007. Its aim was to develop a numeracy intervention scheme using highly trained teachers to teach children on a mainly one-to-one basis for around 12 weeks. Between 2007 and 2010, over 14,000 children received support. In 2009–10, 7820 children received specialist one-to-one teaching in numeracy.

The gains made by the 7820 children taught were assessed using a pre- and post-intervention mathematics test that provides standardized scores and a Number Age; this showed that they made an average gain in Number Age of 14 months in 21.5 hours of teaching – over four times the 'normal' rate of progress. They made an average standardized score gain of 15 points, taking them from well below average into the average range. Of the participating children, 91 per cent increased their confidence and attitude to mathematics, and 72 per cent achieved nationally expected levels in mathematics in National Assessments at the age of 7 years. Interestingly, the greatest gains were made by the lowest attaining children at point of entry to the programme.

Chartered Mathematics Teacher

The Chartered Mathematics Teacher (CMathTeach) is a professional recognition of excellence and experience in mathematics subject knowledge and pedagogy. Launched in 2009, its aim is to 'reflect the balance between teaching skills (pedagogy) and mathematics knowledge that is necessary for a professional teacher to educate and inspire today's students' (CMathTeach 2009).

It is intended to classify a teacher as being at the forefront of the profession, exhibit standards of professional excellence across mathematics teaching in the twenty-first century, and recognise them as at the same level as a Chartered Mathematician.

Primary Mathematics Specialist Teacher Programme

The Primary Mathematics Specialist Teacher Programme (MaST) began in 2010 after being piloted as Fast Track the previous year. Providing participants with a Postgraduate Certificate in Specialist Primary Mathematics and Mathematics Specialist Teacher status, it consists of a two year course covering subject knowledge, fit-for-purpose pedagogy, and working with colleagues in their school (and schools in the case of small schools) to provide effective professional development through classroom-based collaborative professional activity. Its aim is to develop teachers so they can implement improvements in the teaching and learning of mathematics for all children. During the programme, teachers improve their mathematics subject knowledge, extending their understanding of mathematics concepts and curriculum progression. Added to this, the development of a strong repertoire of teaching and leading strategies, ensures that they improve their competence and confidence to teach mathematics and also to lead their colleagues in schools.

Conclusion

This brief overview of a highly complex historical and cultural context highlights the importance of high quality mathematics education for all children, identifying its particular significance for primary school children. Its purpose is to map, rather than interrogate the terrain – that is the remit of later chapters. It describes a changing landscape, and one which begs many questions in its navigation. Not least among these questions is the nature of the evidence base on which change is made. Some of the research and reports cited in this contextual overview are the focus of question and critique in later chapters of the book. The notions and practices of teacher initial and continuing education and training are, at the time of writing, in a period of major transition. What does seem certain though, is that teachers will continue to be held accountable for pupil learning and performance. Clearly, the role of primary school teachers in building secure foundations is a key part of this. If through their improved subject knowledge and pedagogical skills they can begin to build a culture of success in, and indeed enjoyment of, mathematics in schools, then perhaps slowly but surely the gains will be evident not only in test scores, but also in society in general.

References

Burns, J. (2012a) Poor numeracy 'blights the economy and ruins lives'. BBC News, 2 March. Available at www.bbc.co.uk/news/education-17224600 (accessed 23 May 2012).

Burns, J. (2012b) School maths lessons: Pupils 'scared to ask for help'. BBC News, 5 March. Available at www.bbc.co.uk/news/education-17258668 (accessed 23 May 2012).

Burns, J. (2012c) 'Pupils should learn maths through using it'. BBC News, 14 March. Available at www.bbc.co.uk/news/education-17356465 (accessed 23 May 2012).

Carrington, L. (2010) Training for primary school maths specialists: To raise standards, specialists are needed to teach maths from an early age, starting with the new Mathematics Specialist Teacher Programme. *Guardian*, 18 January. Available at www.guardian.co.uk/do-the-maths/teaching-drive (accessed 26 January 2012).

CMathTeach (2009) *What is Chartered Mathematics Teacher Designation*. Available at www.cmathteach.org.uk (accessed 23 May 2012).

Department for Business, Innovation and Skills (BIS) (2011) *2011 Skills for Life Survey: Headline Findings*. BIS Research Paper 57. London: BIS.

Department for Education (DfE) (2010) *The Importance of Teaching: Schools White Paper*. CM 7980. London: The Stationery Office.

Duckworth, K. (2007) *What Role for the 3 Rs? Progress and Attainment during Primary School*. London: Centre for Research on the Wider Benefits of Learning.

Every Child a Chance Trust (2009) *The Long Term Costs of Numeracy Difficulties*. London: Every Child a Chance Trust.

Every Child a Chance Trust (2010) *Impact Report 2009/10*. London: Every Child a Chance Trust.

Hastings, S. (2006) Numeracy. Available at www.tes.co.uk/article.aspx?storycode=2216489 (accessed 23 January 2012).

Neumark, V. (2010) The challenges of learning and teaching maths. *Guardian*, 18 January. Available at www.guardian.co.uk/do-the-maths/learning-and-teaching-maths (accessed 26 January 2012).

Norris, E. (2012) *Solving the Maths Problem: International Perspectives on Mathematics Education*. London: Royal Society of Arts.

Oates, T. (2010) *Could Do Better: Using International Comparisons to Refine the National Curriculum in England*. Cambridge: University of Cambridge Examinations Syndicate. Available at www.cambridge assessment.org.uk/ca/digitalAssets/188853_Could_do_better_FINAL _inc_foreword.pdf (accessed 30 January 2012).

Office for Standards in Education (Ofsted) (2009) *Mathematics: Understanding the Score: Improving Practice in Mathematics Teaching at Primary Level*. London: The Stationery Office.

Office for Standards in Education (Ofsted) (2011) *Good Practice in Primary Mathematics: Evidence from 20 Successful Schools*. London: The Stationery Office. Available at www.ofsted.gov.uk/resources/good-practice-primary-mathematics-evidence-20-successful-schools (accessed 23 May 2012).

Organization for Economic Cooperation and Development (OECD) (2009) *Viewing the United Kingdom School System through the Prism of PISA*. Available at www.oecd.org/dataoecd/33/8/46624007.pdf (accessed 30 January 2012).

Smith, A. (2004) *Making Mathematics Count: The Report of Professor Adrian Smith's Inquiry into Post-14 Mathematics Education*. London: The Stationery Office.

Standards and Testing Agency (2011) *2011 National Curriculum Assessments Review Outcomes (Provisional)*. London: DfE.

Taylor, C. (2011) *NIACE Response to the 2011 Skills for Life Survey*. Leicester: National Institute of Adult Continuing Education (NIACE). Available at www.niace.org.uk/news/niace-response-to-the-2011-skills-for-life-survey (accessed 23 May 2012).

Times Educational Supplement (TES) (2011) 16 October 1959: 'Education depends on high standards for trainee teachers'. Available at www.tes.co.uk/article.aspx?storycode=6070603 (accessed 23 January 2012)

Trends in International Mathematics and Science Study (TIMSS) (2007) TIMSS overview. Available at http://nces.ed.gov/timss/ (accessed 6 February 2012).

Ward, H. (2008) Poor results for primary maths. Available at www.tes.co.uk/article.aspx?storycode=6005404 (accessed 23 January 2012).

Williams, P. (2008) *Independent Review of Mathematics Teaching in Early Years Settings and Primary Schools: Final Report*. London: DCSF. Available at http://dera.ioe.ac.uk/8365/1/Williams%20Mathematics.pdf (accessed 10 December 2011).

Part 2

Teaching and learning in primary mathematics

Part 2, comprising Chapters 2–9, presents and discusses contemporary issues in teaching primary mathematics. Illustrated by case studies from the authors' own research projects, each chapter makes broad links to the mathematics curriculum (notwithstanding its dynamic nature) drawing on the general themes and principles that continue to be relevant to teachers.

The chapters are structured to provide you with:

- An introduction to the topic
- Chapter aims
- The mathematics curriculum and children's learning
- Conceptual and theoretical perspectives
- Case studies with commentary and prompts for reflection
- Summary
- Further reading

However, the order in which they appear may vary so as to be congruent with the needs of the topic being discussed. You will notice, that despite their differing focal areas, there is a strong and common theme of children's cognitive development in relation to mathematics (rather than technical competence), and a deep and meaningful engagement with children's own articulations of their learning needs.

2 Using children's mathematical misconceptions to support teaching and learning

Alice Hansen

Introduction

This chapter aims to enhance teachers' understanding of children's misconceptions and to help teachers to see them as a tool for developing children's mathematical understanding and improving attainment. Taking a social constructivist approach, the chapter explains how children construct their own concepts, which include 'misconceptions' or 'naive conceptions'. By taking this approach, the chapter emphasizes how misconceptions are a naturally occurring aspect of children's (and adults') mathematical conceptual development and therefore should be an expected outcome of children constructing their own knowledge. Once this has been established, the chapter considers how teachers can learn more about the misconceptions their pupils have by offering practical ideas for exploring misconceptions with children such as assessment for learning, analysing children's written work and summative assessment. Finally, it will identify broad strategies for how teachers might support children to address their misconceptions, such as creating a classroom culture that encourages talk and learning from each other as well as more practical ideas, such as preparing examples of possible misconceptions to present to children than can be addressed.

Chapter aims

This chapter aims to enhance your understanding of children's misconceptions by:

- Identifying what misconceptions are
- Discussing why misconceptions happen

- Considering how we can learn more about the misconceptions our pupils have
- Identifying what we might do to support children to address their misconceptions.

Conceptual and theoretical perspectives

Errors and misconceptions: what are they and how are they different?

Because errors and misconceptions exist regardless of a specific curriculum, this section will start by inviting you to reflect on an example of the work of two children when undertaking a simple addition task. Having done this, and further explored a case study from practice, I then consider how revealing and sharing misconceptions supports the development of effective pedagogy within the curriculum.

Reflection

Analyse Ishmal's and Frankie's work in Table 2.1. Think about which child seems to have made an accidental error, and which child may have a misconception that can be identified in their written work. Can you identify what the misconception is?

Table 2.1 Ishmal's and Frankie's sums

Ishmal	Frankie
1. $12 + 4 = 16$	1. $12 + 4 = 15$
2. $23 + 5 = 28$	2. $23 + 5 = 27$
3. $54 + 2 = 57$	3. $54 + 2 = 55$
4. $72 + 6 = 78$	4. $72 + 6 = 77$
5. $87 + 3 = 90$	5. $87 + 3 = 89$

Errors

Errors are commonplace in classrooms and are normally easy to spot. There are two reasons why errors happen. One is that the error was accidental. For example, from his written work above, it is possible to conclude that Ishmal appears to have made an accidental error in question 3 because he has correctly answered the other sums. When Ishmal was questioned about his work, he responded (pointing to the addend, the number 2): 'Oh, oops, I thought that was a "3"'.

Alternatively, errors can be driven by a misconception.

Misconceptions

Frankie answered all five sums incorrectly. Analysis of Frankie's written work shows she provided an answer that is one less than the correct answer each time. A consistent incorrect pattern of answers such as this is one way of seeing that a misconception exists. Indeed, on talking with Frankie about her work it was possible to understand how the error was occurring. To calculate 12 + 4, Frankie counted on four from *twelve*, instead of correctly from the next number, *thirteen*. She said, 'I put twelve in my head and then counted on four. 12, 13, 14, 15'.

Misconceptions occur in children, teenagers and adults of all ages regardless of their level of attainment, and not just in mathematics. Although errors are straightforward to identify, not all misconceptions will be evident to you or even the person who holds the misconception. It may be many years before a misconception comes to light and for everyone, many misconceptions will never be identified and/or addressed.

The relationship between errors and misconceptions

Figure 2.1 shows one representation of the relationship between errors and misconceptions. The Venn Diagram (Figure 2.1) shows an intersection of the sets {misconceptions} and {errors}, signalled by the arrow. These are the errors that occur as a result of misconceptions, or the misconceptions that are reinforced or created due to making the same error repeatedly.

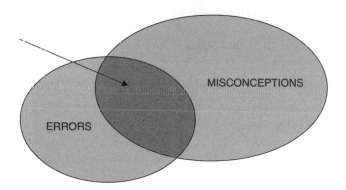

Figure 2.1 Venn Diagram showing the relationship between errors and misconceptions

	Error	Error
Misconception	An error is caused by a misconception. This is the same subset as the intersection in Figure 2.1	When a misconception exists but there is no error made or evident, it is not possible to address the misconception
~~Misconception~~	An error occurs, but is due to a mistake of some sort. This is easily rectified by the child	When a child is operating most effectively, they are not making errors and have no misconceptions about the specific study that negatively effect their learning

Figure 2.2 Carroll Diagram showing the relationship between errors and misconceptions

Another way to think about the relationship is using a Carroll Diagram, as in Figure 2.2. This representation provides four outcomes. The outcome that is the equivalent to the intersection in Figure 2.1 is the shaded set.

In both cases the errors made due to misconceptions are most interesting to teachers because the errors point to a misconception that can be addressed. This idea is revisited later in the chapter.

Why do mathematical misconceptions exist?

Now that we have broadly identified what errors and misconceptions are and how they are related, this section looks at why we all develop mathematical misconceptions.

Constructivist theories (Piaget 1953; Vygotsky 1978; Bruner 2006a, 2006b) explain the psychological view of learning as a learner constructing (rather than transmitting and receiving) their knowledge internally. Similarly, Noss and Hoyles (1996: 105) put forward the case for learning as the construction of a web of connections 'between classes of problems, mathematical objects and relationships, "real" entities and personal situation-specific experience'. They explain how learners use formal and informal resources to construct mathematical meaning by making and reinforcing links between these resources. However, a key extension of

Noss and Hoyles' (1996) notion of webbing and constructivist theory is that in webbing the resources can be internal (as for constructivist theory) or external (physical or virtual). Within any given situation, a learner will act within the situation using the range of resources they have access to. Noss and Hoyles (1996: 122) refer to this as *situated abstraction*. Of course, when the resources (internal or external) are naive or limited in any way, misconceptions will naturally emerge.

Let us take an example to illustrate this. A short time ago I met Harry, who was 9 years old. He was using a calculator to explore questions such as $5 \times 0.2 = \square$. He knew that

- $2 + 2 + 2 + 2 + 2 = 10$
- multiplication can be thought of as repeated addition
- $5 \times 2 = 10$
- the answer to 2×5 is equal to the answer to 5×2
- an array can be used to represent multiplication:

He could also recall all the basic facts to 10×10 at speed.

However, when Harry found the calculator informing him that $5 \times 0.2 = 1$, he was confused and asked his neighbour if his calculator was working properly. He had developed the misconception that *multiplication will always make the answer bigger*.

Reflection

Does this misconception make Harry's mathematics understanding deficient in any way? Are there any other experiences, or ideas about multiplication, you would have introduced Harry to prior to asking him to multiply using decimal numbers? Why / why not?

From the example of Harry it would not be accurate to describe his mathematical understanding as deficient in any way. After all, Harry's misconception is unsurprising when his experiences of multiplication to date have used positive whole integers and have indeed produced a bigger answer. Although it is likely that no one has instructed Harry that the answer to a multiplication question is always bigger, he has constructed that notion for himself from the plethora of examples he has seen and used. Indeed, Harry's response was typical in the class that day and the teacher had carefully planned the use of calculators in the lesson to elicit these kinds of responses from the children.

Simpson (2009) describes another example from her class:

> Shaun had successfully measured a number of pencils and had been able to record their lengths in order; he knew that 21.4cm was longer than 21.25cm. However, in another lesson later in the same week, he was ordering a list of numbers and stated that 13.65 was bigger than 13.7.
>
> (Simpson 2009: 15)

From the two examples, it is possible to see that learning is messy. At any moment, a child will move from thinking they understand a mathematical idea to finding that they need to know more. This can often be motivating for children as they desire to learn more about the world around them, and the role of the teacher is to effectively support their mathematical development by harnessing children's curiosity.

Can misconceptions be avoided?

The previous section explained how misconceptions are created as a by-product of children's conceptual development and are therefore an inevitable part of learning mathematics. However, in this section we will consider how the things you say and do as a teacher can inadvertently lead children to formulate misconceptions. So, although misconceptions are par for the course, you should be mindful not to teach additional misconceptions: there are enough potential difficulties or barriers to learning without you adding to the list!

What the teacher says

Case Study 2.1 provides an illustration of how one teacher unwittingly fuels some misconceptions in her classroom. Read the case study and consider how Simone approaches her teaching of primary mathematics.

Case Study 2.1: Simone's story

Simone has been a teacher for three years. She has worked with Key Stage 2 children during that time. At her request, the mathematics subject leader, Mike, has been given the opportunity to work with Simone over one term to support her mathematics planning, teaching and assessment. Through working with Simone, Mike identifies a number of examples where she has made comments to the children that could potentially reinforce misconceptions.

Mike produced the following list of examples in preparation for his discussion with Simone:

- 'Five take seven. You can't do that'
- 'Fives into three don't go'
- 'Add a zero when multiplying by ten'
- 'Look at these triangles . . .' △ ◣ △
- 'You can remember a rhombus by thinking of it as a square that has been sat on'

Commentary

Through the case study examples you may be able to see that Simone's mathematics pedagogical subject knowledge is poor. She also lacks confidence when it comes to teaching mathematics. As a result, her approach to teaching children is procedural and she has learnt over her three years of teaching that the children 'get the answer right' if they follow the rules and apply the tricks she teaches them.

Reflection

Revisit the statements Simone has made. Reflect on what future difficulties the children may meet if they learn the rules and tricks that Simone has modelled or encouraged them to apply. Use Table 2.2 to help you.

Table 2.2 Statements that cause potential later difficulties

Simone's statement	Future potential difficulty created
'Five take seven. You can't do that' 'Fives into three don't go' 'Add a zero when multiplying by ten' 'Look at these triangles . . .' 'You can remember a rhombus by thinking of it as a square that has been sat on'	

The first three statements are inaccurate. It is possible to take 7 from 5: the result is negative 2 (-2). So because the calculation can be done (although it may have been undesirable in the strategy Simone was teaching the class), it is misleading to suggest that it cannot be carried out. Similarly, 5 can be divided into 3, and the answer is 3/5, or 0.6. Finally, if one 'adds a zero' when multiplying a decimal number by 10 without paying attention to the place value of the digits, then the answer will remain the same (e.g. $2.34 \times 10 = 2.340$).

While the fourth statement about triangles is not incorrect, Simone is limiting the examples she is using with the children. Although she has produced right-angled, isosceles and equilateral examples, they are still all prototypical because the base of each triangle sits horizontally. It would be desirable for Simone to also show other orientations of the triangles.

Simone's final statement asks the children to think about shapes at only a visual level (van Hiele 1986) (i.e. 'a square that has been sat on'). By doing this, she is not encouraging them to consider the figure's properties or how rhombuses are defined. This potentially limits their ability to think about geometric definition. It also unwittingly makes children think of squares and rhombuses as two shapes that are unrelated to each other and this can inhibit later geometric reasoning (Hansen 2008). Undertaking the next reader reflection will help you to develop this idea.

Reflection

Visualize the diagonals of a square. What do you notice? You will probably notice that the diagonals are the same length, they are perpendicular and that they bisect. Now visualize the square turning into a different rhombus, a rhombus that is not a square. What happens to the diagonals? Which properties stay the same? Which change? Why? Now visualize the rhombus returning to a square.

You can repeat this visualization activity with other properties such as order of rotation or reflective symmetry.

Did the reflection activity help you to think of a square as a particular type of rhombus? That is, did you think about how a rhombus has two perpendicular bisectors, and that to be a particular instantiation of rhombus – a square – the perpendicular bisectors also need to be of equal length?

You may have found the task you were asked to complete in the reflection above challenging. Did you already know that there was a relationship between squares and rhombuses that could be explored through their diagonals? Or was this new to you? Perhaps you thought that there was no relationship between the two shapes except for the length of their sides remaining the same. This task may have revealed something that you didn't know, or perhaps even a misconception you hold yourself. If so, the reflection may have been a good illustration of how the tasks that children complete in the classroom can hide or reveal a number of misconceptions. It is to this very issue that the discussion now turns.

Tasks the children complete

In order for children to widen their 'fields of experience' (Ackermann 1991) or broaden their 'contextual neighbourhood' (Pratt and Noss 2002), it is important for teachers to think carefully about the tasks they present to children. The following illustration presents two tasks that share the same objective: to identify squares. Read through the tasks in Figures 2.3 and 2.4 and carry out the reader reflection that follows.

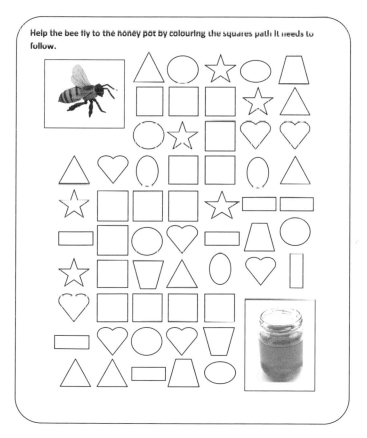

Figure 2.3 Sample worksheet

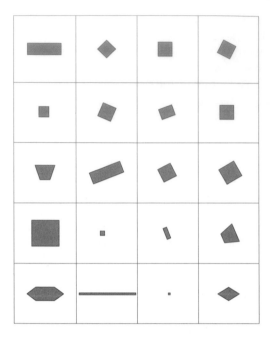

Figure 2.4 Sorting cards

The task in Figure 2.3 is similar to a worksheet that I recently saw.

The task in Figure 2.4 shares the same learning outcome. It asks the children to work in a small group (of two or three) to sort the shapes on the cards (see Figure 2.4) into two sets: Set A contains squares, Set B contains shapes that are not squares. The children need to feel confident that all the children in the group are convinced that each card is in the correct set by talking with each other about the reasons for their decisions.

Reflection

Think about what skills, knowledge and understanding a child needs to demonstrate in order to correctly complete the worksheet and the sorting activity. How are the tasks different?

Mason and Johnston-Wilder (2006) offer a most useful explanation of what to look for in a task:

> A relevant type of task involves situations that appear to give rise to contradictions or surprises. In these tasks, learners need to sort out what is happening, resolve differences of opinion or conflicting

explanations, and find some way to account for what is going on. Learners are called upon to explain things to each other and to locate differences and agreements in their explanations.

(Mason and Johnston-Wilder 2006: 64)

To what extent do the two tasks offer a context for children to explore, discuss and explain contradictions and surprises?

Reflect more broadly now. Think about the types of tasks you expect your own pupils to carry out. What do you notice about them? How do those tasks reflect your approach to learning and teaching primary mathematics?

In the reader reflection box you were asked to think about how the types of tasks you ask learners to engage with reflect your own pedagogy. This theme is developed in the following section as the discussion turns to addressing misconceptions.

The mathematics curriculum and children's learning: how can misconceptions be addressed?

Earlier in this chapter I discussed how misconceptions are an inevitable by-product of learning and as such they should not be seen as a negative aspect of learning. Instead they should be positively used to support children's cognitive development.

There are many ways to address children's misconceptions. The following discussion offers three principles that you can apply within whatever classroom context you find yourself in. What remains consistent throughout is the use of high quality tasks (refer to discussion above). The principles are:

- Developing a classroom (and school) ethos that celebrates the complexity of learning.
- Using misconceptions to support children's cognitive development.
- Planning an effective curriculum that allows for misconceptions to be revealed.

Developing a classroom (and school) ethos that celebrates the complexity of learning

In the previous reader reflection you were asked to think about the types of tasks you plan for your learners. The tasks you plan for your learners provide a window into your mathematics pedagogy. One key aspect of your pedagogy is how you foster a mathematical ethos and what happens in your classroom and school. After all, 'the quality of an education system cannot exceed the quality of its teachers and principals, since student learning is ultimately the product of what goes on in classrooms' (OECD 2010: 4).

This is an aspect that has been a focus of Ofsted research also: 'The most effective teachers ... cultivate an ethos where children do not mind making mistakes because errors are seen as part of the learning. In these cases, children are prepared to take risks with their answers' (Ofsted 2003: 18).

Yackel and Cobb (1996) identify how the teacher is instrumental in developing the class ethos. They refer to the class ethos in mathematics lessons as sociomathematical norms.

Sociomathematical norms

Sociomathematical norms are particular to mathematics lessons. They are 'normative understandings of what counts as mathematically different, mathematically sophisticated, mathematically efficient, and mathematically elegant in a classroom ... Similarly, what counts as an acceptable mathematical explanation and justification is a sociomathematical norm' (Yackel and Cobb 1996: 461). These are constrained by the 'current goals, beliefs, suppositions and assumptions' of the classroom participants (Yackel and Cobb 1996: 460).

The process of developing sociomathematical norms is *reflexive*: as you gain more insight into your pupils' mathematical development, you can adjust the sociomathematical norms. Sociomathematical norms are imperative within classroom discussion because they create the backdrop for the argumentation of mathematical ideas. As argumentation evolves, *taken-as-shared communication* is subtly adjusted because it continues to form the backdrop for discussion. This in turn brings about children's cognitive development.

Reflection

Research shows us that as children progress through school they learn not to ask questions, even when they do not understand (Boaler 2009).

How often do you encourage children to ask questions? Who do they ask questions to? Questioning and arguing about mathematics helps to develop children's ability to reason about mathematics. Think about your planning and teaching. When do the children use reasoning to justify their answers and defend their methods?

High quality talk in mathematics

Talking about mathematics has been highlighted and discussed for many years. The seminal report *Mathematics Counts* by the Committee of Inquiry into the Teaching of Mathematics in Schools (Cockcroft 1982) referred to the significant role of talk. Paragraph 252 provides one example:

> It is necessary to realise that much of the value of an investigation can be lost unless the outcome of the investigation is discussed. Such discussion should include consideration not only of the method which has been used and the results which have been obtained but also of false trails which have been followed and mistakes which may have been made in the course of the investigation.
>
> (Cockcroft 1982: para 252)

Note the reference to errors and misconceptions in this paragraph. Using misconceptions to support cognitive development will be discussed further in the next section.

Crucially, talk has remained at the forefront of policy-makers', researchers' and teachers' minds for many decades, yet regardless of this ongoing focus, talk in mathematics still remains an issue. For example, Ofsted's review of the National Literacy and Numeracy Strategies and their effects on the primary curriculum (Ofsted 2003) included a key finding that 'in too many lessons, teachers' talk dominates and there are too few opportunities for pupils to talk and collaborate to enhance their learning' (Ofsted 2003: 3).

Furthermore, in the first independent review of mathematics teaching in Early Years settings and primary schools since the Cockcroft Report, Sir Peter Williams identified that talk

> should extend to high-quality discussion that develops children's logic, reasoning and deduction skills, and underpins all mathematical learning activity. The ultimate goal is to develop mathematical understanding – comprehension of mathematical ideas and applications.
>
> (Williams 2008: 165)

Reflection

Think about the tasks presented earlier in Figures 2.3 and 2.4. Focusing on children's potential misconceptions related to squares, which task would be more effective in exposing these? How and why? Which gives rise to more opportunity for children to talk about what they know and don't know about squares?

Think about what sociomathematical norms might be evident in a classroom where the type of task presented in Figure 2.3 is typical compared to a classroom where the task in Figure 2.4 is typical.

Using misconceptions to support children's cognitive development

Earlier in this chapter I discussed the constructivist approach to learning and explained how making links between related ideas helps children build up a conceptual picture. Of course, this process also develops misconceptions which are an inevitable part of learning mathematics. This way of thinking about learning is advantageous to teachers. Seeing value in using misconceptions as a pedagogical tool to support cognitive development is widely espoused in the research literature. By teachers adopting 'a constructive attitude to their children's mistakes' (Koshy 2000: 173), children develop a coherent mathematical knowledge (Barmby et al. 2009). Drews (2011) explains how talking about misconceptions can help children to see themselves as successful learners who attempt more challenging work. The assumption behind promoting this approach is that teachers have good subject knowledge. This was illustrated in Case Study 2.1 of Simone.

Case Study 2.2 shows how Sheila, a Year 6 (10–11 year olds) teacher, helped her children improve their mathematical disposition as well as their confidence and readiness for the statutory tests at the end of their primary schooling by systematically introducing talking about errors.

Case Study 2.2: Sheila's story

Like most schools we have a bank of test questions from previous test papers. From Year 4 all the teachers include the odd question related to the topic the children are learning about into lessons. We agreed that this drip-feeding of questions in regular lessons would improve the children's confidence for the tests at the end of Year 6 because they have met many before the actual test, which most of them have been successful in working out.

For most children that works well, but I was really mindful of the children who would still continue to get incorrect answers. I thought that for some in my own class it was having the opposite effect to the desired one. So, over the first term I started to keep a record of inaccurate comments that children made or incorrect answers that they gave in written pieces. Then in the terms that followed, when we revisited the topics, I used some of the comments or wrong answers as a talking point to start off the main part of the lesson when I thought it was useful. I even made some up, thinking of what the children might do wrong. It was really successful. The key to its success was that the children were talking about the errors and possible misconceptions behind the errors. They were happy to talk about their mistakes. Over the year I saw a real shift in how we talked about maths. The children volunteered their own mistakes for discussion, wanting help from their peers about how to improve their understanding. There was also an improvement in the children's desire to want to check their independent work more fully, and also their stickability at a maths problem ... they were willing to try more avenues if the first ones they tried didn't work.

With the children's permission, I used their work in the first term the following year with the new class so I had something to use from the start. The maths attainment of the children in that class over that year improved at a greater rate than any class I'd had before. Now all the teachers from Year 2 and above use this approach in some maths lessons

Commentary

Sheila's findings reflect the work carried out by Mike Spooner. Spooner (2002) found that studying incorrect answers in past test papers provided an opportunity for greater openness on the part of children to explore and discuss their misconceptions.

Planning an effective curriculum that allows for misconceptions to be revealed

This final principle encourages you to think about how you can provide an effective class and school curriculum for misconceptions to be revealed. In this section we discuss curriculum content (using and applying mathematics) and curriculum assessment (assessment for learning).

Using and applying mathematics

The 2000 National Curriculum (Department for Education and Employment (DfEE) 1999) for mathematics contained a Programme of Study (PoS) called 'Using and Applying Mathematics'. This attainment target is embedded within the other three attainment targets – Number; Shape, Space and Measures; Handling Data – showing its importance within mathematics learning. Within using and applying mathematics, children should be taught problem solving, communicating and reasoning. Table 2.3 identifies the skills, knowledge and understanding required for using and applying mathematics.

Table 2.3 What 'Using and Applying Mathematics' involves

Problem solving involves	Communicating involves	Reasoning involves
• making connections • discussion • enquiry • planning • deciding • organizing • interpreting • reasoning • imagination, inventiveness, diverse strategies • investigation • justification • persistence • representations • trial and error	• accepting and giving feedback (including peer coaching) • ad hoc as well as more structured representation • calculations • demonstrating reasoning • diagrams • explaining methods and solutions • ICT • lists • making choices and decisions • pictures • resources • tables • using mental images and models • written skills	• creating • deduction • applying • exploring • predicting • hypothesizing • testing • classifying • explaining • finding patterns • inference • logic • making connections • mapping • organizing information • proof • reflection • trial and error

Source: Adapted from Hansen and Vaukins (2011: 13–25)

Reflection

Problem solving, communicating and reasoning are core to learning mathematics. Reflect on a mathematics lesson you recently taught. Use Table 2.3 to help you to consider what problem solving, communicating and reasoning you were explicitly engaging your children in. How could you focus on these aspects further with the children? How would a focus on these aspects support revealing and addressing errors and misconceptions?

Use and application, when systematically planned for and effectively facilitated, is a conduit for children to discuss and address their errors and misconceptions. What remain central tenets throughout are effective task choice and ongoing development of sociomathematical norms.

A crucial component of systematic planning involves clear and effective assessment. Therefore, in addition to thinking about the curriculum content that is on offer in your classroom and school, also consider how you use assessment for learning within the curriculum on offer.

Assessment for learning

Koshy (2000: 173) reminds us that 'as in real life, mistakes made in mathematical lessons can also be very useful. They provide us with very useful insights into children's thinking and mathematical understanding. Mistakes that are persistent can often highlight gaps in the child's knowledge'. Lee (2006) explains how using mathematical misconceptions can lead to creative approaches in assessment for learning strategies. In light of this, what role can children's errors and misconceptions play in assessment for learning, and how can assessment for learning address errors and misconceptions?

The Cambridge Primary Review (Alexander 2010) warns that although assessment for learning helps teachers to promote children's learning, 'it is difficult to shift teachers from reliance on specific techniques (the letter of AfL) to practices based on deep principles integrated into the flow of lessons (the spirit of AfL)' (Alexander 2010: 290). Indeed, Hargreaves (2005) identifies six different conceptions teachers hold of assessment for learning. These are:

1. *Monitoring pupils' performance against targets or objectives.* This focuses on a process the teacher follows.
2. *Using assessment to inform next steps in teaching and learning.* This focuses on what action the teacher needs to take next.
3. *Giving feedback for improvement.* This focuses on the teacher informing children how to take the next steps towards a given standard.
4. *Teachers learning about children's learning.* This focuses on children improving their future learning.
5. *Children taking some control of their own learning and assessment.* This focuses on children's learning processes.
6. *Turning assessment into a learning event.* This focuses on children's involvement in assessment.

Reflection

Write down your own definition of 'assessment for learning', then compare your definition to those conceptions Hargreaves (2005) found that teachers hold.

Which of Hargreaves' definitions might value children's errors and misconceptions most?

While it would be possible to answer that each of the six conceptions of assessment for learning could value errors and misconceptions, it is the final three that reflect the journey this chapter has taken you on. *Teachers learning about children's learning* is part of the reflexive process of developing sociomathematical norms in your classroom; *children taking some control of their own learning and assessment* and *turning assessment into a learning event* firmly centre children's talk within mathematics learning.

Summary

This chapter has focused on how you can use children's misconceptions to support learning and teaching. In summary, the chapter identified the difference between errors and misconceptions and how they relate to each other. It demonstrated that misconceptions exist as a by-product of learning and can be found in children and adults (even teachers!) alike.

Although misconceptions cannot be avoided, the teacher's role includes ensuring additional misconceptions are not created through the way they talk about mathematics. Teachers are also responsible for choosing and designing the tasks children undertake. Planning for tasks that encourage children's misconceptions to come to the fore is crucial for conceptual development. Underpinning everything is the ethos teachers foster in their classrooms and schools. Central to this should be high quality talk in mathematics and valuing the errors children make and misconceptions they exhibit as a core component of children's learning.

Further reading

Cockburn, A. and Littler, G. (2008) *Mathematical Misconceptions: A Guide for Primary Teachers*. London: Sage.
This thought-provoking book brings together a selection of writing about children's misconceptions and big ideas in mathematics such as zero,

place value and equality. It also looks at how children learn mathematical ideas and aims to develop your own mathematical understanding along the way.

Hansen, A. (ed.) (2011) *Children's Errors in Mathematics: Understanding Common Misconceptions in Primary Schools* (2nd edn). Exeter: Learning Matters.

This practical guide to children's common errors and misconceptions in mathematics provides a bank of common errors children 3–11 years of age make. It discusses learning theory and mathematical development in each attainment target of the mathematics curriculum to explain why the errors may have occurred. The teacher's role in understanding and addressing common misconceptions is also covered.

References

Ackermann, E. (1991) From decontextualized to situated knowledge: Revisiting Piaget's water-level experiment. In I. Harel and S. Papert (eds) *Constructionism*. Norwood, NJ: Ablex.

Alexander, R. (2010) *Children, their World, their Education: Final Report and Recommendations of the Cambridge Primary Review*. London: Routledge.

Barmby, P., Bilesborough, L., Harries, T. and Higgins, S. (2009) *Primary Mathematics: Teaching for Understanding*. Maidenhead: Open University Press.

Boaler, J. (2009) *The Elephant in the Classroom: Helping Children Learn to Love Maths*. London: Souvenir Press.

Bruner, J.S. (2006a) *In Search of Pedagogy, Volume I: The Selected Works of Jerome S. Bruner*. Abingdon: Routledge.

Bruner, J.S. (2006b) *In Search of Pedagogy, Volume II: The Selected Works of Jerome S. Bruner*. Abingdon: Routledge.

Cockcroft, W.H. (1982) *Mathematics Counts: Report of the Committee of Inquiry into the Teaching of Mathematics in Schools* (Cockcroft Report). London: HMSO. Available at www.educationengland.org.uk/documents/cockcroft (accessed 31 January 2012).

Department for Education and Employment (DfEE) (1999) *The National Curriculum*. London: DfEE.

Drews, D. (2011) Errors and misconceptions: The teacher's role. In A. Hansen (ed.) *Children's Errors and Misconceptions* (2nd edn). Exeter: Learning Matters.

Hansen, A. (2008) Children's geometric defining and a principled approach to task design. Unpublished doctoral thesis, Warwick University. Available from www.children-count.co.uk/images/PhD%20Final.pdf.

Hansen, A. and Vaukins, D. (2011) *Primary Mathematics across the Curriculum*. Exeter: Learning Matters.

Hargreaves, E. (2005) Assessment for learning? Thinking outside the (black) box. *Cambridge Journal of Education* 35 (2): 213–24.

Koshy, V. (2000) Children's mistakes and misconceptions. In V. Koshy, P. Ernest and R. Casey (eds) *Mathematics for Primary Teachers*. London: Routledge.

Lee, C. (2006) *Language for Learning Mathematics: Assessment for Learning in Practice*. Maidenhead: Open University Press.

Mason, J. and Johnston-Wilder, S. (2006) *Designing and Using Mathematical Tasks*. St Albans: Tarquin.

Noss, R. and Hoyles, C. (1996) *Windows on Mathematical Meanings: Learning Cultures and Computers*. Dordrecht: Kluwer Academic.

Office for Standards in Education (Ofsted) (2003) *The National Literacy and Numeracy Strategies and the Primary Curriculum*. London: HMI.

Organization for Economic Cooperation and Development (OECD) (2010) *PISA 2009 Results: What Students Know and Can Do – Student Performance in Reading, Mathematics and Science (Volume I)*. Available at http://dx.doi.org/10.1787/9789264091450-en (accessed 30 January 2012).

Piaget, J. (1953) *The Origin of Intelligence in the Child*. London: Routledge & Kegan Paul.

Pratt, D. and Noss, R. (2002) The micro-evolution of mathematical knowledge: The case of randomness. *Journal of Learning Sciences* 11 (4): 453–88.

Simpson, A.R. (2009) The micro-evolution and transfer of conceptual knowledge about negative numbers. Unpublished doctoral thesis, Warwick University. Available from http://go.warwick.ac.uk/wrap/2240.

Spooner, M. (2002) *Errors and Misconceptions in Mathematics at Key Stage 2*. London: David Fulton.

Swan, P. (2001) Dealing with misconceptions in mathematics. In P. Gates (ed.) *Issues in Mathematics Teaching*. London: Routledge Falmer.

van Hiele, P.M. (1986) *Structure and Insight: A Theory of Mathematics Education*. London: Academic Press.

Vygotsky, L.S. (1978) *Mind in Society: The Development of Higher Psychological Processes*. Cambridge, MA: Harvard University Press.

Williams, P. (2008) *Independent Review of Mathematics Teaching in Early Years Settings and Primary Schools: Final Report*. London: DCSF. Available at http://dera.ioe.ac.uk/8365/1/Williams%20Mathematics.pdf (accessed 10 December 2011).

Yackel, E. and Cobb, P. (1996) Sociomathematical norms, argumentation, and autonomy in mathematics. *Journal for Research in Mathematics Education* 27 (4): 458–77.

3 Children becoming expert symbol users

Maulfry Worthington

Introduction

This chapter explores semiotics as a significant aspect of teachers' subject knowledge and reveals its central role in children's understanding of mathematical notations. It argues that this meaning-making perspective can more effectively support children's early and developing use of the abstract symbolic language of mathematics (Williams 2008), deepening their understanding of calculations, problem solving and wider aspects of the mathematics curriculum as they move through school. Since both writing and 'written' mathematics are abstract symbolic languages, learning them can be complex for young learners.

Chapter aims

An important part of the Mathematics Specialist Teachers' programme (MaST) in England is for teachers to understand 'how children learn mathematics, progression in mathematical understanding and recording and mathematical language' (Edge Hill University 2012). This chapter aims to give you an understanding of the role of abstract symbols, appreciating children's active role in developing symbolic flexibility in mathematics. This will be developed in three key ways:

- Your reading will be supported with findings from research helping you recognize how, through meaningful social contexts, children's informal prior knowledge can be extended and developed.
- Key features of successful learning highlighted within the chapter will help you appreciate how they contribute to learning as children move through the primary school.

- You will develop your understanding of some aspects of effective classroom cultures that enhance children's understanding of this significant aspect of mathematics.

The mathematics curriculum and children's learning

Early Years Foundation Stage

The current Early Years Foundation Stage (EYFS) informs practitioners that 'effective implementation' includes valuing 'children's own graphic and practical explorations of Problem Solving, Reasoning and Numeracy' (Department for Education and Skills (DfES) 2007: 61). It emphasizes that children should:

- Create and experiment with symbols and marks
- ... show their understanding of number labels such as 1, 2, 3
- Begin to represent number
- Use own methods to work through a problem.

(DfES 2007: 64–8)

The *Independent Review of Mathematics Teaching in Early Years Settings and Primary Schools* (Williams 2008), widely referred to as the Williams Maths Review, made specific recommendations regarding children's understanding of abstract mathematical symbolism, devoting a significant section to *children's mathematical graphics* (Carruthers and Worthington 2006) in the chapter on 'Early Years' (although unfortunately omitting to emphasize its relevance to Key Stage 1 and calculations). One of the Review's main recommendations resulted in the publication *Children Thinking Mathematically* (DCSF 2009) that Carruthers and Worthington were commissioned to write. Carruthers and Worthington began by developing their pedagogy in the Early Years classes and settings in which they taught in the 1990s. To better support young children's developing understanding of the abstract symbolic language of mathematics they drew on principles of emergent writing, developing their research on *children's mathematical graphics* since the early 1990s.

Key Stages 1 and 2

In the current National Curriculum 'using and applying number' for Key Stages 1 and 2 is divided into sections headed *problem solving*, *communicating* and *reasoning* that include: 'Develop flexible approaches to problem solving... Make decisions about which operations and problem-solving strategies to use... communicate in spoken, pictorial and written form... using informal language and recording, then mathematical language and symbols' and 'explain their methods and reasoning when solving problems involving number and data' (DfE 2011). It is important here to emphasize that *recording* places the emphasis on mathematical symbols, notations as *products* and is a lower level of cognitive demand than *representing* mathematical thinking (as in children's own *mathematical graphics*).

For Key Stage 2, pupils should 'find different ways of approaching a problem in order to overcome any difficulties... organize work and refine ways of recording... use notation, diagrams and symbols correctly within a given problem... present and interpret solutions in the context of the problem' (DfE 2011). At the time of writing, both the EYFS and the National Curriculum are under revision and it is to be hoped that guidance for teachers on these aspects are given greater attention.

Children's development of mathematical knowledge and understanding

Ginsburg (1977) first documented children's difficulties with 'written' mathematics: subsequently Hiebert (1984) argued:

> many of the children's observed difficulties can be described as a failure to link the understandings they already have with the symbols and rules they are expected to learn. Even though teachers illustrate the symbols and operations with pictures and objects, many children still have trouble establishing important links.
>
> (Hiebert 1984: 501)

Hughes's (1986) seminal research into young children's difficulties with mathematics showed how children's own informal and intuitive representations play a significant role in 'translating' between their own representations and later 'school' mathematics. Hughes suggested that greater emphasis should be placed on children's early understandings by 'introducing symbols in meaningful communicative situations... If this idea can be communicated effectively to young children, it may have a profound effect on their subsequent mathematical education' (Hughes 1983: 172).

Many other researchers have explored the significance of symbol use in mathematics (e.g. Gifford 1990; diSessa et al. 1991; Bialystok 1992; Cobb et al. 2000; Brizuela 2004; Carruthers and Worthington 2005, 2006; Ernest

2006) acknowledging the centrality of children's own representations and written methods for mathematics.

Impact on understanding and achievement

Children's experiences in the Foundation Stage clearly impact on their confidence and achievement in mathematics. Foundation Stage Profile (FSP) point 8, 'use developing mathematical ideas and methods to solve practical problems', was particularly highlighted in the Williams Maths Review, emphasizing 'relatively few children' attain this point (Williams 2008: 41). Subsequently details of children's learning at the end of the Foundation Stage were published, showing the lowest levels of achievement for FSP point 8 were writing and *calculations* (DfE 2010).

Since both writing and 'written' calculations are abstract symbolic languages, it seems likely that children's difficulties with symbolic understanding may be at the heart of this problem: this can lead to children who 'may eventually resort to coping strategies that alienate themselves from an understanding of number' (Munn 1998: 70). Their confusion often becomes evident from 5 to 7 years, the point at which teachers demonstrate specific ways to 'record' and when increasing formalization of mathematical notations is assumed helpful. Evidence from Ofsted reports since 2002 (for example, Ofsted 2008) repeatedly highlights the lack of children's informal written methods in Reception classes and throughout the primary school and a need to strengthen the relationship between mental and written mathematics: they also raise concerns about the low levels of attainment with calculations, and in the area of 'using and applying mathematics'.

Conceptual and theoretical perspectives

Understanding, using and communicating mathematics

This chapter is underpinned by sociocultural and social-semiotic theory (e.g. Vygotsky 1978; Kress 1997) and is founded on our shared belief that all children can become confident symbol users and problem solvers in mathematics. 'Semiotics' describes the relationship between signs, meanings and cultures: this is the point at which this chapter begins. Mathematical symbols, written calculations and charts support thinking and enable children to explore and communicate ideas. Children's own symbolic representations mediate understanding: they are acknowledged as 'symbolic' or cultural 'tools' that can be used to resolve particular psychological problems (Vygotsky 1978), and are integral to mathematics.

Van Oers (2000) emphasizes:

> The invention, use and improvement of appropriate symbols are the characteristic features of the mathematical enterprise...the efforts of the pupils to get a better grip on symbols in a meaningful way should be considered one of the core objectives of education, especially in the domain of mathematics.
>
> (Van Oers 2000: 136)

Research evidence

Based on evidence from her research with young children, Munn (1998) reached two important conclusions: first, for young children, progress in understanding symbolic functions depends on both writing and on graphical representations of number that children explore in a range of contexts, and second, 'The important development is the *function* of the symbol – its role in the child's mental activity – and not in its form' (Munn 1998: 69, emphasis in the original).

Pape and Tchoshanov (2001: 124) propose that mathematical representations need to be thought of as tools for cognitive activity 'rather than products or the end result of a task'. Terwel et al. (2009: 28–9) argue that, first, graphical representation 'closes the gap between prior knowledge and the material [children] are involved with. Second, it provides opportunities for creative engagement and ownership of conceptually difficult material. Third, it enables students to exercise their 'meta-representational knowledge', which is expected to be of value in the creation of new representations.

The evidence from a substantial body of research shows that a significant and positive feature of children's engagement in developing personal representations to communicate their conceptual understanding, is their active involvement with such representations that can 'develop *a sense of knowledge ownership*, which makes students feel free to transform this knowledge as the situation requires' (Terwel et al. 2009: 28–9, emphasis added). Hoyles (2010) emphasizes that mathematical thinking depends on students being 'able to interact with abstraction', arguing that '*sym bols* shape how mathematics is expressed and "known"'. Like Terwel et al. (2009), Hoyles (2010) also emphasizes 'that students *take ownership* of mathematical processes' (Hoyles 2010: slides 2 and 3, emphasis in the original).

These features help pupils 'learn how structuring processes develop', enhancing their 'capacity to generate new solution processes and to transform a representation according to changes in the situation, facilitating the construction of solutions to relatively new and unfamiliar problems'.

Children are then 'in a better position to understand pictures, graphs, schemes, models, or similar intellectual tools and are more successful in solving new, complex mathematical problems on relations and proportions' (Terwel et al. 2009: 26–7, 41).

Becoming successful symbol users in mathematics

The philosophy underpinning *children's mathematical graphics* is rooted in the belief that children have a significant role to play in their learning, both in the understandings they bring and in their active engagement with graphical representations and symbols. From this perspective children's potential is realized through social contexts and in learning cultures rich in graphicacy and meaning making. The adults' role in this context is pivotal in children's learning. Adults create rich learning environments that include interactive displays of texts and children's graphics; adults model graphical representations and symbols for authentic purposes arising from children's play and everyday experiences. Above all adults show that they value children's thinking and their graphical marks and representations by taking a close interest in their meanings and ideas.

Rather than drawing, maps, writing and mathematical notations being isolated 'activities' separated from personal meaning, or 'products' embedded in teacher-planned tasks, graphicacy becomes an integral and significant aspect of children's and adults' daily experience. In graphically and meaning rich contexts, children *choose* to use symbolic representations to support and communicate their thinking. As the following case studies show, immersion in such contexts supports powerful individual and shared understandings of the abstract symbolic language of mathematics, leading to flexible use of calculations and problem solving.

Children's understanding of symbols and their functions are central to this perspective and align well with FSP point 8 'use developing mathematical ideas and methods to solve practical problems' and 'using and applying number' of the National Strategies. In our joint research we studied young children's marks, symbols and graphical representations that they used to communicate their mathematical thinking, from their earliest marks to which they attach mathematical meanings, to their own methods to solve problems and calculations. Analysis of hundreds of children's examples enabled us to chart their developing mathematical thinking and skills as symbol users from birth to 8 years through our taxonomy (see Carruthers and Worthington 2011). We have also conducted research with teachers and practitioners, with parents and into professional development for Early Years mathematics and are currently both engaged in individual doctoral research into specific aspects of *children's mathematical graphics*.

Children's invented algorithms and notations appear to have considerable significance in supporting later understanding of mathematical notations (Carruthers and Worthington 2006, 2011; Thompson 2008). Research evidence of children of 10-11 years shows also that older primary children using their own methods and mathematical representations 'are more successful in solving new, complex mathematical problems' (Terwel et al. 2009: 25), findings that are significant for primary schools in England.

Case studies

I will now present three case studies showing how children choose to use their own graphics to communicate their mathematical thinking in play and to solve problems. The case studies show how the children's developing understanding of mathematical semiosis blends their informal 'home' cultural knowledge with that of the established cultural symbolic language of mathematics.

The case studies begin with an example from 3-year-old Shereen that may at first not seem 'mathematical'. What may appear casual or insignificant – at first intuitive, personal and informal marks and representations – has an important role to play in learning the abstract symbolic language of mathematics (Worthington 2012).

Case Study 3.1 is from a nursery in an inner city children's centre and is an example of freely chosen and spontaneous pretend play (role-play), which has the potential to provide rich contexts for semiotic communication. One of its strengths is its social nature, allowing for shared meaning making and collaborative dialogue that enables both symbolic languages (speech and mathematical) to complement and support each other (Worthington 2011).

Case study 3.1: Shereen and the café

In Shereen's family, shopping for food, preparing and sharing meals at home, in a restaurant or from a 'take-away' are especially valued cultural activities. Shereen (3 years, 5 months) draws on this cultural knowledge in her play.

At this point in her pretend play of a café with friends, Shereen asks her teacher Emma what she wants to eat, 'I'm writing chocolate bar, what you want?' Drawing some wavy lines (as writing) on her notepad, Shereen adds, 'I've got rice, chocolate, chicken?' After taking Emma's order for rice she refers to its price, 'There you go: it's two, one, two'. Later Shereen returns again to ask Emma if she wants anything else to eat and when Emma replies that she doesn't want chicken, Shereen makes some marks at the top of the paper explaining 'Chicken' and then draws a cross nearby saying, 'It says "x" – no chicken!' (Figure 3.1).

Later again in their play Shereen returns once more to Emma, who says that she would after all like some chicken, but pointing to where she'd written a cross on her notepad, Shereen explains indignantly, 'Look! No chicken!' Then pointing to a tick she'd written by her drawing of a mushroom said, 'Look! A tick, that mean we got some [mushroom]', adding 'You want ice cream? It's three, four'.

Figure 3.1 Shereen's symbols

Commentary

Shereen drew on her 'home' knowledge of taking orders in a restaurant: she was clear that each item of food had its own price and used a range of graphical representations to represent meaning. Using drawings and writing-like marks to represent these items, Shereen also explored functions of abstract symbols using a 'cross' (to signify 'No chicken!') and a 'tick' (to signify 'We got some').

Symbol use

In meaning and symbolically rich learning cultures such as this nursery's, young children often show remarkable understanding of abstract symbol use. Shereen's symbolic communication was spontaneous and it is important to emphasize that her symbols had not been directly taught, neither had an adult intervened to make suggestions about how she might represent her orders. Vygotsky (1978) emphasized that 'teaching should be organized in such a way that reading and writing are necessary for something... must be something the child needs'. Moreover, writing 'should be meaningful for children, that an intrinsic need should be aroused in them and that writing should be necessary and relevant for life' (Vygotsky 1978: 117–18). Carruthers and Worthington (2011) believe that this is equally true for mathematical representations: it is clear that Vygotsky's statement is also so for Shereen.

Communication is a significant aspect of semiotics, and Munn (1997) argues:

> the analogy with emergent writing, where children bring their own meanings to communicative mark-making, seems convincing... The depth of the analogy depends on the children's understanding of their numeric mark-making as *communicative*... If emergent number and emergent writing were truly similar, then this understanding would be present, because an understanding that symbols communicate meaning is a central element in progression.
>
> (Munn 1997: 91, emphasis added)

At home Shereen is aware of the use of symbols to communicate, and staff in Shereen's nursery are highly responsive to children's interests and exceptionally good at ensuring that the learning environment indoors and out is rich in both mathematical symbols and texts. Number lines of different lengths are displayed and, as discussions about larger numbers arise, adults make the most of such opportunities to discuss number patterns. Staff members also ensure that there are rich displays of children's own graphicacy that include both original children's examples and photographs of contexts of learning such as Shereen's.

Many of the teachers and practitioners in Shereen's nursery have developed expert knowledge of graphicacy and symbol use that translates into their practice – and modelling symbolic representations is an important part of this. This would support Munn's (1998) research evidence, which argued that 'the association between numeral use and mental activity that incorporated symbols – suggest that powerful processes are at work whereby children form cognitive models...around the notational systems that they have learnt from expert number users' (Munn 1998: 66).

Reflection

- Is the learning environment rich in meaningful mathematical print and texts?
- To what extent does display of children's symbolic representations support their understanding in your school?
- Discuss how these aspects might be developed.

If you have the opportunity, you might also wish to undertake the following activity which considers modelling mathematics in context in Nursery and in Reception classes.

- Discuss informal, daily opportunities for the teacher to model mathematics on a whiteboard through, for example, quick drawings, numerals, informal or formal symbols or informal methods for calculating. These *short* spells of modelling can be highly effective, should directly relate to the children's interests and experiences during play or everyday experiences and are best introduced spontaneously as opportunities arise.

Note: Significant changes in the children's representations and the strategies they choose to use will not be immediate and can only develop over time.

Case Study 3.2: Frances and the train

This case study shows some strategies and personal methods that children used to solve a personally meaningful problem in a Reception / Year 1 class. The children had travelled by train on a school visit and had been impressed by the size of the train, and the possible number of seats on it.

The children had gone to visit a pannier market in anticipation of planning a 'harvest market' at school. The following day they talked excitedly and

Aaron commented 'I bet there's a million seats on that train!' He wondered how they could find out the total number of seats on the train and his classmates offered various ideas, one suggesting we 'ask the train people'. Empowered by this suggestion (and with adult help) Aaron phoned the local railway station, afterwards announcing that there were '75 seats in each carriage and 7 carriages on the train'.

The children who had chosen to help Aaron solve his problem used a range of informal methods. Frances explored several strategies to help her work this out. She then decided to represent 75 seats in a carriage: checking by recounting she found that she had drawn 76 seats and crossed one out (Figure 3.2).

Figure 3.2 Frances's train carriage

Frances understood that this was a representation of only one carriage, and when invited to consider how she could help Aaron find the total number of seats on the train, her creative solution was to use the school photocopier to make an additional six copies of her drawing. When laid out end-to-end her representations of multiples of 75 on seven sheets of paper showed the sum total of '75 × 7' seats. Frances's combined strategies provided a valuable and powerful visual representation of repeated addition that children discussed for many weeks.

Commentary

Case Study 3.2 highlights children's decision-making in solving a problem using their own informal methods. Reflecting on the strategies that the children in this class used, they would seem to support Pound and Lee's (2010) observations that

> these young children demonstrate many of the strategies iden-
> tified by Polya [1957], strategies that 'successful problem solvers
> used' (Boaler 2009: 179). They worked to understand the problem
> and they made plans. Some made charts of numbers, some drew
> their plans.
>
> (Pound and Lee 2010: 35–6)

Reflection

- To what extent are children's interests and ideas used as a starting point for an investigation or problem?
- Do children use a range of ways of representing and methods by choice? What do you believe might limit or encourage diversity and symbolic thinking?

  If you have the opportunity you might wish to undertake the following activity for a Reception or Year 1 class.

- In a forthcoming lesson provide blank paper for one group of children to use to support their thinking as they explore their own methods to solve a meaningful mathematical problem. It is important to *avoid demonstrating or providing any examples* of how to work out their problem during the lesson.
- If the children have not been used to working in this way, it may be helpful to explain that you are *especially interested* in *the children's own thinking and methods*. Ask if they have any thoughts about how they might begin? Does anyone else have a *different* idea?
- Before the lesson's end discuss the different strategies each child used, listening to their various explanations and emphasizing only the positive points.
- After the lesson assess the children's various responses, again only evaluating positive points. The second part of Carruthers and Worthington's (2011: 76) taxonomy, 'calculations, children's own methods' may be of help to you.

Note: if the children have been dependent on being shown what to do, they are likely to be hesitant the first time you try this.

Concentrating on one group enables you to focus your attention on the children's thinking, strategies and representations.

Case Study 3.3: Miles and the nectarines

In this case study, Miles (7 years, 5 months) adapts an informal taught method to solve a problem. Miles's teacher posed the problem, which related to an authentic situation – a picnic the class would have on their journey to their residential trip the following day. She showed the children a pack containing three nectarines, inviting them to work out how many packs she would need to buy for everyone in the class (a total of 26 children).

Miles decided to use an empty number line, and taking a piece of A4 paper he drew a horizontal line across the sheet. Beginning on the right of his paper Miles started with jumps of '3' but soon realized that by using his paper in this position he would have insufficient space to complete his calculation. Miles adapted his jumps, twice doubling his jumps of 3 to arrive at his answer of '9 packs' and acknowledging the surplus nectarine in his answer (Figure 3.3).

Figure 3.3 Miles   calculating the number of packs of nectarines needed

Commentary

Miles's response showed his flexible thinking, enabling him to adapt this visual method for his purpose of division as repeated subtraction. His peers used a range of different strategies including writing multiples of 3 up to 27 and mentally subtracting 1; drawing repeated groups of three 'stick' people in 9 boxes (up to 27), and then crossing one person out. Ann also chose to use an empty number line, using regular jumps of 3 up to 27, and then a jump back of one to reach '26' explaining, '9 packs 1 left over'.

Originating in the Netherlands, the 'empty number line' was introduced by the National Numeracy Strategy (DfEE 1999) and continues to provide children with a flexible tool for calculating. Gravemeijer et al. (2000: 241) acknowledge children's own methods as significant in supporting 'an emergence of meaningful symbolizations that arise during collective negotiations'. The culture in the classrooms in Case Studies 3.2 and 3.3 reveals other strategies identified by Polya (1957), such as children asking themselves, 'what is involved in this problem?' Polya (1957) also taught teachers to encourage children to restate the problem in their own words, to use a drawing or diagram that might help them understand the problem. By the simple means of adapting the jumps on the empty number line he had drawn, Miles was able to readily solve his problem. Drawing on his prior knowledge of doubling numbers and the taught empty number line, Miles used his chosen visual method flexibly as a cognitive tool. At the same time the range of graphical representations the children used in response to the problem provided rich peer models and access to shared thinking and negotiated meanings though collaborative dialogue between children and teacher.

Reflection

Reflect on the role of collaborative discussion in supporting children's developing representation and strategies in mathematics, and how you might develop this with individuals and with groups.

If you have the opportunity, you might also wish to try out the following activity for a Key Stage 1 class:

- Refer to the activity on page 50. Since these children are older and more experienced it is likely that some of them will choose to use or adapt a 'taught method' such as the empty number line to help them with their *calculations* or *to solve a problem*.
- *Data handling* offers rich and meaningful contexts, enabling children to develop their understanding of a range of ways to collect, represent and analyse data in open ways.
- When they have collected their data, invite the children to discuss what they've done and to represent their findings – again in their own ways (e.g. using drawings, numerals, charts, words) – but without the teacher making any specific suggestions.

For either group activity, end the session by sharing some of the group's examples with the whole class. Invite other children (*not* those in your small group) to give positive feedback

Conclusion

These three case studies are intended to show how the approach outlined in this chapter enables children to build on their experiences of symbol use and mathematical notations, and confidently use flexible methods to communicate and calculate. Young children's symbolic understanding and methods mature and become increasingly efficient through Key Stage 1 as they integrate symbols and ways of representing from adult and peer models with their informal, personal notations, moving 'from unstructured mathematical knowledge towards mathematical understanding that is [increasingly] structured and organized using familiar and strongly formed tools' (Poland 2007: 26).

Summary

The ways in which we teach mathematics are significantly shaped by our beliefs. A widely held view is that mathematics is a 'difficult' subject (especially for young learners), and due to its abstract nature written notation is 'hard' to learn. This is often interpreted for younger children as simple tasks that are often devoid of meaningful contexts and involve only small numbers and quantities. Teachers plan activities such as copying or tracing numerals, colouring in, or rely on teacher-given models for calculations. In Key Stage 1 a common practice is for teachers to demonstrate and explain, and for children to practise. While these practices are almost always undertaken with the best of intentions on the part of the teacher, such activities and tasks result in Reception and Key Stage 1 privileging 'correctly' written numerals, horizontal calculations, correct use and positioning of signs such as '+' and '=' and neatness *above mathematical thinking and understanding*. The outcomes of such experiences are particularly evident as children move through Key Stage 1 since they have little of the *sense of ownership* referred to earlier.

The features highlighted here confirm the potential of *children's mathematical graphics* in supporting their success in Foundation Stage Profile point 8, 'use developing mathematical ideas and methods to solve problems' in the Foundation Stage, and 'using and applying number' in the National Curriculum. These key features include:

- A focus on children using and building on their informal understandings and graphical representations to support their mathematical thinking, to communicate and solve problems.
- Learning contexts that are personally meaningful and of relevance to the children.
- Immersion in rich learning cultures that promote and support children's own meanings, thinking and representations.

- Collaborative dialogue between children and teachers in which children's representations and meanings are valued and negotiated.
- Settings and classrooms where children's mathematical notations are 'meaningful for children, that an intrinsic need should be aroused in them and...[are] necessary and relevant for life' (Vygotsky 1978: 117–18).

It is hoped that by now your reading and reflection, combined with some 'possible points for action' and key features of successful learning discussed within the chapter, have helped you to appreciate how they contribute to the continuum as children move through the primary school and lead to deepening understandings of the abstract symbolic language of mathematics.

This chapter should enable you to develop your understanding of aspects of effective learning cultures and enhance children's understanding in your school. The perspective explored here rests on a belief that all children can be curious, competent and confident learners of mathematics. The aspect of mathematics explored in this chapter is one in which teachers can make a very real difference, and where there is potential for children to become expert symbol users and powerful makers of mathematical meanings.

Further reading

Carruthers, E. and Worthington, M. (2006) *Children's Mathematics: Making Marks, Making Meaning* (2nd edn). London: Sage.
This book provides a thorough introduction to the development and range of young children's mathematical representations in the birth to 8 years age group, illustrating how children make mental connections between their own early marks and mathematical symbols, and how these relate to children's own written methods for calculations.
Boaler, J. (2009) *The Elephant in the Classroom: Helping Children Learn to Love Maths*. London: Souvenir Press.
Boaler explores some of the issues and problems discussed earlier in this chapter, with particular reference to primary schools in England. She emphasizes that in her research, effective teachers 'valued all of the different ways of being mathematical and students were not simply repeating procedures.' Teachers encouraged pupils 'to communicate in different ways, to decide on the appropriateness of different methods and to adapt methods in order to solve problem' (Boaler 2009: 76–7).

The Children's Mathematics Network (http://www.childrens-mathema
tics.net/).
The Children's Mathematics Network is an international network for all
those interested in young children's mathematics and graphicacy,
with a particular focus on children's emerging and developing use
of their mathematical graphics to communicate their mathematical
thinking.

References

Bialystok, E. (1992) Symbolic representation of letters and numbers. *Cognitive Development* 7: 301–16.
Boaler, J. (2009) *The Elephant in the Classroom: Helping Children Learn to Love Maths.* London: Souvenir Press.
Brizuela, B. (2004) *Mathematical Development in Young Children: Exploring Notations.* New York: Teachers College Press.
Carruthers, E. and Worthington, M. (2005) Making sense of mathematical graphics: The development of understanding abstract symbolism. *European Early Childhood Education Research Association Journal* 13 (1): 57–79.
Carruthers, E. and Worthington, M. (2006) *Children's Mathematics: Making Marks, Making Meaning* (2nd edn). London: Sage.
Carruthers, E. and Worthington, M. (2011) *Understanding Children's Mathematical Graphics: Beginnings in Play.* Maidenhead: Open University Press.
Cobb, P., Yackel, E. and McClain, K. (eds) (2000) *Symbolizing and Communicating in Mathematics Classrooms.* London: Lawrence Erlbaum Associates.
Department for Children, Schools and Families (DCSF) (2009) *Children Thinking Mathematically.* London: DCSF.
Department for Education (DfE) (2010) *Attainment in the Foundation Stage.* London: DfE.
Department for Education (DfE) (2011) *National Curriculum: Mathematics: Ma2 Number.* Available at www.education.gov.uk/schools/teachingandlearning/curriculum/primary/b00199044/mathematics (accessed 6 December 2011).
Department for Education and Employment (DfEE) (1999) *The National Numeracy Strategy.* London: DfEE. Available at https://national strategies.standards.dcsf.gov.uk/schools/teachingandlearning/curriculum/primary/b00199044/mathematics/ks1 (accessed 27 May 2012).

Department for Education and Skills (DfES) (2007) *Practice Guidance for the Early Years Foundation Stage*. London: DfES.

diSessa, A., Hammer, D., Sherin, B. and Kolpakowski, T. (1991) Inventing graphing: Meta-representational expertise in children. *Journal of Mathematics Behaviour* 10: 117–60.

Edge Hill University (2012) *Mathematics Specialist Teachers' Programme*. Available at www.edgehill.ac.uk/education/mast/teachers (accessed 24 January 2012).

Ernest, P. (2006) A semiotic perspective of mathematical activity: The case of number. *Educational Studies in Mathematics* 61: 67–101.

Gifford, S. (1990) Young children's representations of number operations. *Mathematics Teaching* 132: 64–71.

Ginsburg, H. (1977) Learning to count: Computing with written numbers – Mistakes. In H. Ginsburg, *Children's Arithmetic: How They Learn It and How You Teach It*. New York: Van Nostrand.

Gravemeijer, K., Cobb, P., Bowers, J. and Whitenack, J. (2000) Symbolizing, modeling and instructional design. In P. Cobb, E. Yackel and K. McClain (eds) *Symbolizing and Communicating in Mathematics Classrooms*. London: Lawrence Erlbaum Associates.

Hiebert, J. (1984) Children's mathematics learning: The struggle to link form to understanding. *Elementary School Journal* 84 (5): 497–513.

Hoyles, C.P. (2010) Tackling the mathematics: Potential and challenges. Available at http://royalsociety.org/uploadedFiles/Royal_Society_Content/awards/medals-awards-prizes/kavli-education-medal/2011-01-10_Kavli-Education-ASE.pdf (accessed 4 January 2012).

Hughes, M. (1983) Teaching arithmetic to pre-school children. *Educational Review* 35 (2): 163–73.

Hughes, M. (1986) *Children and Number: Difficulties in Learning Mathematics*. Cambridge, MA: Basil Blackwell.

Kress, G. (1997) *Before Writing: Re-thinking the Paths to Literacy*. London: Routledge.

Munn, P. (1997) Writing and number. In I. Thompson (ed.) *Teaching and Learning Early Number*. Buckingham: Open University Press.

Munn, P. (1998) Number symbols and symbolic function in preschoolers. In C. Donlan (ed.) *The Development of Mathematical Skills*. Hove: Psychology Press.

Office for Standards in Education (Ofsted) (2008) *Mathematics: Understanding the Score*. Available at www.ofsted.gov.uk/node/2255 (accessed 30 January 2012).

Pape, S.J. and Tchoshanov, M.A. (2001) The role of representation(s) in developing mathematical understanding. *Theory into Practice* 40 (2): 118–25.

Poland, M. (2007) The treasures of schematising. PhD thesis, Vrije University (VU), Amsterdam.

Polya, G. (1957) *How to Solve It*. New York: Doubleday Anchor.

Pound, L. and Lee, T. (2010) *Teaching Mathematics Creatively*. London: Routledge.

Terwel, J., Van Oers, B., Van Dijk, I. and Van den Eeden, P. (2009) Are representations to be provided or generated in primary mathematics education? *Educational Research and Evaluation* 15 (1): 25–44.

Thompson, I. (2008) What do children's mathematical graphics tell us about the teaching of written calculation? In I. Thompson (ed.) *Teaching and Learning Early Number* (2nd edn). Maidenhead: Open University Press.

van Oers, B. (2000) The appropriation of mathematical symbols: A psychosemiotic approach to mathematical learning. In P. Cobb, E. Yackel and K. McClain (eds) *Symbolizing and Communicating in Mathematics Classrooms*. London: Lawrence Erlbaum Associates.

Vygotsky, L.S. (1978) *Mind in Society: The Development of Higher Psychological Processes*. Cambridge, MA: Harvard University Press.

Williams, P. (2008) *Independent Review of Mathematics Teaching in Early Years Settings and Primary Schools: Final Report*. London: DCSF. Available at http://dera.ioe.ac.uk/8365/1/Williams%20Mathematics.pdf (accessed 10 December 2011).

Worthington, M. (2011) The power of pretence: Role-play and mathematics. Paper presented at TACTYC Biennial Research Conference, 'Ready' for School?, York, 11–12 November.

Worthington, M. (2012) The power of graphicacy for the young child. In T. Papatheodorou and J. Moyles (eds) *Cross-Cultural Perspectives on Early Childhood*. London: Sage.

Worthington, M. and Carruthers, E. (2003) *Children's Mathematics: Making Marks, Making Meaning*. London: Sage.

4   ICT and mathematics

Vivien Townsend

Introduction

This chapter focuses on a particular way of supporting the learning of mathematics in primary schools – the use of information and communication technology (ICT). This is more than just a question of examining the use of subject-specific technologies such as Beebots or data handling software packages. While the chapter does look at how a subject-specific tool can be used in mathematics, it also looks at the scope for using generic tools. The peripheral benefits of ICT use will also be examined; namely the increase in the quantity and quality of pupil talk, and how setting online homework can improve parental involvement in their child's learning of mathematics.

Chapter aims

The purpose of this chapter is to inform and, I hope, improve, your understanding of how ICT can enhance the teaching of mathematics by:

- Describing the context and background to the use of ICT in schools generally in order to identify some generic key issues
- Relating these broad issues to the use of ICT in mathematics specifically
- Sharing some case studies and examples related to these points
- Inviting you to reflect on how ICT is, and how it could be, used in your school.

This chapter begins by exploring the context and background to the use of ICT in schools generally and then focuses on three key issues which relate to mathematics classrooms.

The mathematics curriculum and children's learning

There is, at present, something of a dilemma in the use of ICT in mathematics teaching in primary schools. For many of the current generation of primary school children, born since the year 2000, technology is central to their everyday lives (Green and Hannon 2007; Oblinger 2008; Abbot et al. 2009). Such is their familiarity with ICT that these children have been termed 'digital natives' or 'cyberkids' and, thanks to their use of the internet, the generation to which these children belong has been described as the net generation, or 'n-gen' (Downes 2005; Green and Hannon 2007: 16; Byron 2008). However, while the majority of the current generation of primary school children seem to be very familiar with the use of ICT, it is important to acknowledge that this is not true of all pupils. There is still a significant minority of youngsters who do not have regular access to digital technologies outside of school. In 2010, the e-Learning Foundation charity estimated that 2 million school children do not have access to the internet at home, 1 million of whom do not have access to a computer at all (BBC 2010).

Our context, therefore, is one where many (but not all) children are comfortable and familiar with the use of ICT. Alongside this, it is reported that in schools, levels of ICT hardware provision have increased (Williams 2008), and there is an ever-increasing range of online resources available to support the teaching of mathematics.

In addition to the ready availability of hardware and software there are also compelling reasons why ICT might be used for teaching mathematics. Alongside pupil familiarity with technologies, ICT is believed to make specific contributions to pupil learning, in part because the use of ICT can be highly motivational for learners (Somekh et al. 2002; O'Hara 2008). These 'affordances' are discussed later in the chapter but on the basis of these benefits, both statutory and non-statutory guidance in the UK promotes the use of ICT in schools. The current National Curriculum (DfEE 1999) recommends that teachers plan for pupils to experience tasks in mathematics using appropriate pieces of software and hardware (British Educational Communications and Technology Agency (Becta) 2003), and more recently, the Primary National Strategies Renewed Frameworks (DfES 2006), from which many primary teachers take their objectives, include specific reference to pupil use of ICT across the Handling Data and Understanding Shape strands.

However, despite all of these compelling reasons for using ICT, it has been reported by Ofsted (2008) and the National Centre for Excellence in the Teaching of Mathematics (NCETM 2010) that the actual use of technologies in mathematics by learners has declined. The next section will look at some key issues in the use of ICT in mathematics teaching and explore some possible reasons why this decline might have occurred.

Conceptual and theoretical perspectives

Identifying key issues

It does seem surprising that the level of ICT use has declined over recent years and the intention of this section is to provide a little more detail on the contribution that ICT can make to the teaching of mathematics. This is done through exploring key issues which could help teachers to think about how ICT could be integrated into their mathematics teaching.

Kadijevich (2012) identifies three key factors in the underuse of ICT in the mathematics classroom:

- *Technological* considerations
- *Mathematical* considerations
- *Pedagogical* considerations.

Let us discuss each in turn.

Technological considerations

> ICT is not a panacea, but neither should it be treated as a pariah.
>
> (O'Hara 2008: 38)

One possible reason why ICT use in classrooms may be lower than expected is that some teachers simply lack confidence in using ICT (Ainley et al. 2010), in part perhaps because of a lack of familiarity with ICT (Green and Hannon 2007). While many pupils boldly and intuitively get to know new software and hardware, and discover and explore features without the use of a manual, adults can be fearful of breaking something and cautious of clicking if the consequences of their click are unknown (Green and Hannon 2007). It is this difference in attitude to ICT that can make teachers wary of introducing new technologies with which they may quickly become less proficient than most of their pupils (Lerman 2004; Green and Hannon 2007; NCETM 2010).

However, if teachers only 'stick with what they know', and never introduce new tools, then there is a chance that they and their children may be missing out on some beneficial pieces of software and hardware. If teachers are brave and try something new, they will need to have gained enough confidence in using the tool to enable them to anticipate and deal with technical problems and user errors that might be encountered in lessons. It seems however that many teachers do not use new tools frequently enough in their mathematics classrooms for either they or their pupils to reach this level of fluency and confidence (Wright 2010).

Without time or support to discover what a tool can do and gain familiarity, the use of new technologies can be limited to like-for-like replacements of old technologies. For example a common use of interactive whiteboards is simply as a digital blackboard (Smith et al. 2005; Prue 2011), with the full digital interactive potential unexploited. As teachers gain familiarity with a tool, and perhaps with support from others, the affordances (i.e. what becomes possible when ICT is used) of the technology start to become evident, which can then provide the basis for informed judgements to be made about the possible benefits of its use (Webb and Cox 2004; NCETM 2010; Clark-Wilson 2011).

Being given time to explore any new and 'exciting' tools normalizes them for pupils and ensures more focused mathematical application later (O'Hara 2008; Abbot et al. 2009; Bradford and Davidson 2011). This results in pupils being well placed to use everyday ICT to achieve mathematics objectives (Becta 2003).

Affordances can be thought of as being of benefit to both teachers and pupils, and indeed to others, as will be demonstrated later in this chapter. For example, online tests that automatically enter results into a digital mark book may be of particular interest to a teacher as this affordance lightens a teacher's workload. In contrast, pupils may receive benefits from receiving instant feedback or may simply be motivated by using a particular 'fun' tool. Whatever the ICT, its successful use is, 'dependent on the practitioner understanding the benefits which ICT tools bring to the learning experience' (Abbot et al. 2009: 18).

Mathematical considerations

While confidence and familiarity with the technology in question is crucial, sound mathematical subject knowledge is similarly significant if the technology is to be most appropriately integrated into teaching. Ofsted (2008: 22) have reported that 'weaknesses in subject knowledge and pedagogy often have a limiting effect ... this represents the biggest challenge in raising the quality of teaching, and thereby standards'.

In light of this, understanding the affordances provided by technology and being critical of the use of any resources – technological or otherwise – seem important considerations in any decision to incorporate technology into mathematics teaching. ICT should not be used thoughtlessly and Becta (2003) suggests that time in lessons should be balanced between using and not using technology according to the needs of the learner and the suitability of the technology in supporting the learning objectives. For example, looking at images of three-dimensional shapes on an interactive whiteboard is no substitute for handling them.

In Ofsted's (2011) report on good practice in primary mathematics classrooms, the authors illustrated how by using a calculator (a very common ICT tool), pupils were able to 'think clearly about the strategies that they are using to solve the problem without getting bogged down in the mechanics of the actual calculation itself' (Ofsted 2011: 29). This affordance – that ICT can perform some menial aspects of mathematics to free the user up to do different, often higher level, mathematics such as noticing patterns or hypothesizing – will be illustrated through the third case study. Understanding such affordances allows activities to be better matched to learning objectives. For example, if the objective is to interpret data, pupils might be best using a piece of graphing software to quickly create a bar chart so they can move on to the analysis rather than laboriously drawing a bar chart by hand and running out of time for discussing what it shows.

If ICT is used in mathematics lessons, it is also important that it does not dominate and that the mathematical learning is at the forefront of the lesson. Jones (2008) reported that in lessons observed for his project, the plenaries of mathematics lessons in which ICT was used sadly tended to focus on the ICT and not the mathematical thinking that the class had been engaged in.

This leads us to think about what we do with ICT and how we do it in order to maximize the benefits of working with technology.

Pedagogical considerations

It is not ICT per se but the pedagogically-guided student activity, for which ICT is used, that makes the difference.

(Thorvaldsen et al. 2011: 12)

A number of authors have identified that the pedagogy in classrooms may well need to change in order to realize the benefits of working with ICT (Somekh et al. 2007; NCETM 2010; Wright 2010). Simply turning an existing paper worksheet into a digital document for pupils to complete at a computer is not taking full advantage of what ICT has to offer. And while drill and practice tools giving instant feedback have their place (and are both widely available and used), it is authentic, investigative opportunities for pupils to use their ICT skills to explore aspects of mathematics which are most likely to provide a flavour of what it is to be working and behaving as a 'real' mathematician (Ofsted 2008; Joint Mathematical Council of the UK (JMC) 2011).

For example, when pupils are investigating patterns using computer software, the instant feedback provided supports them to explore conjectures and engage in higher levels of mathematical thinking (Clements 2000; Wright 2010). Ofsted (2008), however, reported that when children had been given opportunities to work in groups, using ICT to work on some interesting mathematics (an online puzzle, for example, often at the end of a term), the pupils did not see this as being 'real maths' and were oblivious to the skills they were honing (Ofsted 2008). This would suggest that the opportunity to engage in higher level mathematical thinking must be supported and developed by an appropriate pedagogy.

Becta's Deep Learning project found that 'collaboration and team working are thought to support the learning experience' (Abbot et al. 2009: 11) and that ICT tools can provide the stimulus around which such work can take place. Case Study 4.1 in particular shows how, through group work, pupils engaged in extensive mathematics and were also 'negotiating and learning the complexities of social interactions with their peers' (McDonald and Howell 2011: 6–7).

This constructivist view sees learning as a 'building activity in which individuals build on an understanding of events, concepts and processes, based on their personal experiences and often supported and developed by, amongst other things, activity and interaction with others' (Pritchard 2007: 2). This is in contrast with behaviourist approaches. McWilliam (2008) suggests that in order for ICT to have most impact in classrooms, the role of the teacher needs to fundamentally change from being behaviourist – where the teacher is what she calls a 'sage on the stage' – to becoming a 'meddler in the middle' (McWilliam 2008: 263) to provoke and facilitate children's interactions and activities.

Jarrett (1998) argues that, in general, teachers who use technology have: raised expectations of pupils; a more student-centred approach to teaching; and a greater willingness to experiment. The Becta report into deep learning also highlights that 'practitioners who are using ICT are reporting that students are learning more effectively and have improved retention, improved outcomes and improved satisfaction' (Abbot et al. 2009: 17). However, there is much work still to do in most classrooms as there is 'a gap between the potential benefits of ICT for deep learning and the actual way that ICT is being used' (Abbot et al. 2009: 17).

Case studies

The three issues discussed above and their significance in positively influencing the successful and suitable use of technologies will be seen in practice in the three case studies that follow. Each case study is based on the use of commonly available software or hardware and therefore easily replicable in other settings. Commentaries and reflection points will help you relate the issues to your own practice as a teacher.

As adults and teachers, we are probably familiar with and regularly use a wide range of software (programs) and hardware (equipment). Before continuing, reflect on the following questions.

Reflection

- What software and hardware do you use regularly outside of school?
- What do you use in school at least once each half-term?
- How confident are you with these technologies?

If ICT tools are familiar, then both the teacher and pupils should be able to focus on their mathematics and not be distracted by the complexities of the technology they are using (Becta 2003). The first case study reports on the experiences of a Year 6 (aged 10–11) teacher using digital cameras as part of a mathematical scavenger hunt.

Case Study 4.1: Digital cameras

I wanted to make more of the outdoors in maths lessons and had tried a variety of things with my class but by far the most successful activity was the scavenger hunt. Each mixed-ability group of four was given a digital camera and a list of mathematical concepts. They were instructed to find evidence for, or examples of, the concepts, and photograph what they had seen.

Immediately, the children started talking among themselves and asking each other what the vocabulary meant. I'd never seen children engage with vocabulary like that! This was a real surprise. The question on ratio got them talking the most. I'd asked them to find an example of a ratio of 4:1. There was a big debate in different groups and children were really engaging with the mathematics by asking each other questions like, 'What does that mean?'

and 'What could that look like?' If a child wasn't sure what the vocabulary meant, another child explained it. There was a really collaborative feel to the lesson.

I gave the groups 15 minutes to gather and edit their images and when they returned I quickly loaded the images on to the computer so that we could discuss them as a class. One group brought back a picture of some ornamental brickwork (Figure 4.1). The children debated which images were best examples of the mathematical concepts. Using the interactive whiteboard, we were able to annotate the pictures and children noticed not only the intended mathematics but additional concepts too! (See www.ncetm.org.uk/resources/30914 for more on this work.)

Figure 4.1 Ratio

Commentary

The pupils collaborated in groups with the ICT as the recording tool. Their conversations were focused on the mathematics and discussions supported the children in developing a greater understanding of the mathematical concepts as they initially talked about which photographs to take, reviewed their images, decided which to keep, and finally debated the merits of pictures from other groups. O'Hara (2008) has seen children in the Early Years behave similarly, concluding that it is the instant feedback provided by the camera which makes the discussions, and hence the learning, so rich.

The social affordances of working with ICT are well documented. 'ICT seems to provide a focal point which encourages interaction between pupils, as well as between pupils and the technology itself' (Becta 2003: 3;

see also Hudson 1997). Where disagreements do happen, pupils re-solve these, using the ICT to prove a point (Clements 2000). However, while technology may provide a purpose for the group, it does not guar-antee successful relations, and squabbles over who uses the camera (or mouse or microphone) may well still happen (O'Hara 2008).

The teacher in this case study is confident with using digital cameras, uploading images to a computer, and displaying them on an interactive whiteboard for whole-class annotation. The photographs could just have easily been loaded on to a shared space for the class to access in a computer suite. Pupils could then have added their images to word processing, desktop publishing or presentational software and annotated them in the same way to demonstrate their own understanding of the mathematics in the pictures. It would be expected that annotations would cover the specific mathematics from the lesson (in this case, ratio), but that pupils would also describe any patterns, symmetries and other mathematics that they had observed. The skills of annotating a document are generic and therefore, while the teacher might need to remind some pupils what to do, the technology should not get in the way of the mathematics for most (Jones 2008).

Reflection

- Scavenger hunts can, of course, be carried out without the use of ICT. What does using ICT bring to the activity?
- What skills do a teacher and children need to be able to replicate this?
- Choose a specific aspect of mathematics and consider some generic software that could be used to enhance teaching and learning.

Using ICT to link home and school

Case Study 4.1 looked at the contribution that existing non-subject-specific technology can make to the teaching of mathematics. The use of the digital cameras also extended learning beyond the classroom by allowing pupils to explore and take images of their surroundings. Case Study 4.2 continues the theme of extending learning beyond the class-room, but this time through exploring the potential of ICT to enable links between home and school to be enhanced (Prue 2011). The *Independent*

Review of Mathematics Teaching in Early Years Settings and Primary Schools (Williams 2008) highlighted some important issues associated with parents supporting their children's mathematics learning at home and recommended that sharing the methods of teaching used in classrooms with parents is particularly useful. Before reading on, consider the following question.

Reflection

How do you encourage parents at your school to become involved in their children's learning of mathematics?

Becta (2008) reported that parents often become more closely involved with their child's education when learning technologies are used in the home and this has been found to enhance a child's engagement and achievement. Case Study 4.2 details how one school is setting online homework for pupils and consequently forging closer links with parents.

Case Study 4.2: Linking home and school

In our school we already had really good relationships with our parents and a high proportion of our Key Stage 2 students (aged 7–11) were good at returning paper homework. But as we have begun to use ICT elsewhere for teaching and administration, we began to consider whether it could be used for homework as well. The secondary school which most of our students will move on to bought into a homework subscription site and we'd heard good things so we found out more and eventually purchased it for our school.

The site comes with a huge bank of resources and teachers can just click to allocate differentiated tasks to pupils. When students are working on tasks, they get feedback on their performance so they can redo questions if they wish, and when they are finished, their marks get automatically entered into the online mark book. We showed the children how to use the site in school and held a meeting to show parents. One thing that we have had to do is to make the school's ICT suite available during the school day for any pupils who don't have access to the internet at home, so they can do their homework in the same way as everyone else.

Alongside tasks, there are short 'lessons' that children can watch to remind them of the mathematics involved. We don't teach from these in class so we do have to ensure that they follow the same methods as us. Parents have commented to us that they find these lessons really helpful because so often the strategies we teach are different from those they learned when they were at school.

We've also noticed that parents are having more focused conversations with us about mathematics. We have a hunch that this is because the software provides them with some of the skills and also the language to use. The tasks are levelled so conversations at parents' evenings about levels and targets have also become more meaningful. The site has a comment facility and parents are talking with their children about how they would 'rate' tasks in terms of enjoyment and difficulty. Really getting them involved!

Commentary

In this example, the Key Stage 2 teachers have become familiar with the technology and recognize its affordances. For the teachers, these are the ease with which work can be allocated and marks collated and analysed. For the pupils, the affordances are that they get to work on computers (which they like) and can get instant feedback to let them know their progress. There are also affordances for parents; the online lessons gave them access to materials and provided them with a means to be able to better support their child. Furthermore the comment tool allows them to provide feedback to the teacher.

It should be noted, however, that even though this particular school is in quite an affluent area, they still had pupils without internet access at home. So, while this use of ICT had a number of benefits, it was not without its limitations.

This approach of using 'digital worksheets' follows a behaviourist rather than constructivist pedagogy (Pritchard 2007) with the teacher (or computer) as the holder of knowledge and the judge of the 'right' answers. Although there are affordances as described above, the benefits for learning are limited because the inflexible system does not stimulate pupils' opportunities for interactions with others. However, given that 'worksheets' are a popular choice for homework tasks, the ICT in this case appears to enhance the provision.

Although the online tool used by this school is a commercial product, many school learning platforms or websites could be used to facilitate similar ways of working.

Reflection

- What are the issues around the setting of online homework?
- What do you think would be the benefits and limitations to moving towards a homework system like this?

Using mathematical tools

Case Study 4.3 explores the potential for using mathematics-specific software in the primary classroom. While this category could include use of data handling packages and both physical and on-screen direction and movement tools, the case study will focus on a free online tool (GeoGebra™) that joins geometry, algebra, tables, graphing, statistics and calculus. It is described as a 'dynamic' tool because, for example, users can create shapes on the screen, adjust aspects of them and instantly see and interpret the changes on the screen. In Case Study 4.3, a subject leader describes how she used the software across different year groups.

Case Study 4.3: Using dynamic geometry software

I was both the mathematics and ICT subject leader in our school so I quickly recognized the value of the dynamic geometry software and began using it with my classes. I always began by allowing the children to play with it, to work out what it would do, before setting them any focused mathematical tasks. I showed it to other colleagues who were excited by it initially but I'm not sure that they ever used it much. I don't think they put in the time to really become confident with it and then didn't use it regularly so forgot about it.

Key Stage 1 children (aged 5–7) were excited by creating their own shapes and moving the corners to alter them. Sometimes we did this at computers but most often we used an interactive whiteboard and it was a whole class or guided group activity. There was always lots of discussion, especially when I asked them tricky questions like 'is it always, sometimes or never true that a triangle has three sides' and we would use the ICT in our answers.

With Key Stage 2 classes (aged 7–11), the pupils used the software in pairs in the computer suite. One of the real advantages of using ICT is that it boosts the confidence of those children who perhaps normally work slowly or have motor problems so they work messily with paper and pencil or practical equipment.

When we were learning about coordinates, we used the on-screen tools to plot and join points rather than drawing out axes and doing the whole thing by hand. Every child produced something attractive and felt a real sense of achievement. In another lesson, I wanted the children to discover that the angles of a triangle always sum to 180°. Rather than drawing lots of triangles on paper and using protractors to measure (which is slow and will have mixed levels of accuracy), we used the online tools. This meant that as children created and altered their triangles, they could opt to have the angle displayed at each corner as shown in Figure 4.2. They could then focus on summing the angles and noticing the mathematics.

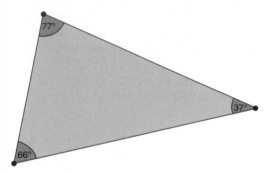

Figure 4.2 Angles

They were concentrating on what was important for that lesson and doing lots of talking about it. It's a different way of teaching.

Commentary

This is an example of what Ofsted (2011) commended as being the use of ICT to enable pupils to 'think clearly about the strategies that they are using to solve the problem without getting bogged down in the mechanics' (Ofsted 2011: 29). By allowing the pupils to explore the software first and discover what it could do, the teacher was supporting what Green and Hannon (2007) describe as peer-to-peer learning, a more constructivist approach than that explored in Case Study 4.2. This approach reflects how many young people learn to use new technologies outside of school; by talking and sharing with friends and peers, rather than asking an adult or using a manual (Green and Hannon 2007). And, as with Case Study 4.1, when pupils work with this software in pairs or small groups, it acts as a stimulus for quality mathematical talk (Becta 2003: 3).

Part of what makes this lesson a success is the teacher's willingness to try new tools, which comes from her general confidence with technology. She has taken time to become familiar with the technology in order to discover its affordances (Webb and Cox 2004; NCETM 2010) and has then also allowed her pupils time to explore the features of the ICT so that the novelty of a new tool does not detract from the mathematics (O'Hara 2008; Abbot et al. 2009).

Reflection

- How do you or might you use ICT in your mathematics teaching so that it encourages children to 'think clearly about the strategies that they are using to solve the problem without getting bogged down in the mechanics' (Ofsted 2011: 9)?
- How might this change the way they talk to each other about their learning?

Summary

This chapter has examined the use of ICT in mathematics lessons. The technological, mathematical and pedagogical reasons to include ICT have been discussed, as have some reasons for its decline as reported by NCETM (2010).

Jones (2008) claims that, especially when using ICT, it is the teacher's ability to question and facilitate discussions between pupils which best promote the deep learning of mathematics. However, 'in order to have effective teacher led questioning and discussion, teachers must fully understand the concepts being learned as well as the intricacies of how children learn and develop deep understanding of such concepts' (Jones 2008: 6). So while knowledge of technology is important, it is knowledge of mathematics and pedagogy which are paramount. As Abbot et al. (2009: 19) suggest, 'there is nothing inherent in technology that automatically guarantees learning'.

Further reading

Green, H. and Hannon, C. (2007) *Their Space*. London: Demos.
This report by Demos into how young people use technology is particularly interesting in its illustration of the gap between teacher and pupil use of technology.

Becta (2003) *What the Research Says about Using ICT in Maths*. Available from www.education.gov.uk/publications/eOrderingDownload/ 15014MIG2799.pdf. (accessed 10 January 2012).
This short report brings together some of the key literature in this area and raises some important questions for schools about their use of ICT in mathematics.

References

Abbot, I., Reynolds, L., Johnston-Wilder, S. and Townsend, A. (2009) *Literature Review: Deep Learning with Technology in 14- to 19-Year-Old Learners*. Available at www.e-learningcentre.co.uk/Resource/CMS/ Assets/5c10130e-6a9f-102c-a0be-003005bbceb4/form_uploads/14_19 _deep_learning_literature_review.pdf (accessed 10 January 2012).

Ainley, J., Eveleigh, F., Freeman, C. and O'Malley, K. (2010) *ICT in the Teaching of Science and Mathematics in Year 8 in Australia: Report from the IEA Second International Technology in Education Study (SITES) Survey*. Available at http://research.acer.edu.au/acer_monographs/6 (accessed 1 February 2012).

BBC (2010) A million UK children 'lack access to computers'. BBC News, 28 December. Available at www.bbc.co.uk/news/education-12075057 (accessed 2 March 2012).

Bradford, M. and Davidson, T. (2011) Using ICT to support learning mathematics in the primary classroom. In A. Oldknow and C. Knights (eds) *Mathematics Education with Digital Technology*. London: Continuum.

British Educational Communications and Technology Agency (Becta) (2003) What the research says about using ICT in maths. Available at www.education.gov.uk/publications/eOrderingDownload/15014MIG 2799.pdf (accessed 10 January 2012).

British Educational Communications and Technology Agency (Becta) (2008) Harnessing technology: Next generation learning. Available at http://webarchive.nationalarchives.gov.uk/20101102103654/ publications.becta.org.uk/display.cfm?resID=37348&page=1835 (accessed 10 January 2012).

Byron, T. (2008) *The Byron Review*. Nottingham: DCSF.

Clark-Wilson, A. (2011) Supporting teachers in introducing new technologies. In A. Oldknow and C. Knights (eds) *Mathematics Education with Digital Technology*. London: Continuum.

Clements, D.H. (2000) From exercises and tasks to problems and projects: Unique contributions of computers to innovative mathematics education. *Journal of Mathematical Behaviour* 19 (1): 9–47.

Department for Education and Employment (DfEE) (1999) *The National Curriculum*. London: DfEE.

Department for Education and Skills (DfES) (2006) *Primary Framework for Literacy and Mathematics*. Nottingham: DfES.

Downes, S. (2005) E-Learning 2.0. *eLearn Magazine* 2005: 10.

Green, H. and Hannon, C. (2007) *Their Space*. London: Demos.

Hudson, B. (1997) Group work with multimedia. *MicroMath* 13 (2): 267–90.

Jarrett, D. (1998) *Integrating Technology into Middle School Mathematics: It's Just Good Teaching*. Northwest Regional Educational Laboratory. Available at www.nwrel.org/msec/book6.pdf (accessed 10 January 2012).

Joint Mathematical Council of the UK (JMC) (2011) *Digital Technologies and Mathematics Education*. Available at http://cme.open.ac.uk/cme/JMC/Digital%20Technologies%20files/JMC_Digital_Technologies_Report_2011.pdf (accessed 10 December 2011).

Jones, T. (2008) Multimodalities in primary school mathematics with ICT. Paper presented at the British Educational Research Conference, Edinburgh, 3 September

Kadijevich, D.M. (2012) TPCK framework: Assessing teachers' knowledge and designing courses for their professional development. *British Journal of Educational Technology* 43 (1): E28–E30.

Lerman, S. (2004) Researching numeracy teaching and learning with ICT: Facing the problems of innovation. In I. Putt, R. Faragher and M. McLean (eds) *Mathematics Education for the Third Millennium: Towards 2010*. Proceedings of the 27th Annual Conference of the Mathematics Education Research Group of Australasia (MERGA-27), Townsville, QLD, Vol. 2, pp. 619–22. Sydney: MERGA.

McDonald, S. and Howell, J. (2011) Watching, creating and achieving: Creative technologies as a conduit for learning in the Early Years. *British Journal of Educational Technology*. Available at http://onlinelibrary.wiley.com/doi/10.1111/j.1467-8535.2011.01231.x/abstract (accessed 12 March 2012).

McWilliam, E. (2008) Unlearning how to teach. *Innovations in Education and Teaching International* 45 (3): 236–69.

National Centre for Excellence in Teaching Mathematics (NCETM) (2010) *Mathematics and Digital Technologies: New Beginnings*. Available at www.ncetm.org.uk/public/files/3399763/NCETMDigitTechReport2010.pdf (accessed 10 December 2011).

Oblinger, D.G. (2008) Growing up with Google: What it means for education. *Emerging Technologies for Learning* 3: 11–29.

Office for Standards in Education (Ofsted) (2008) *Mathematics: Understanding the Score*. Available at www.ofsted.gov.uk/node/2255 (accessed 10 December 2011).

Office for Standards in Education (Ofsted) (2011) *Good Practice in Primary Mathematics: Evidence from 20 Successful Schools.* London: The Stationery Office. Available at www.ofsted.gov.uk/resources/good-practice-primary-mathematics-evidence-20-successful-schools (accessed 10 December 2011).

O'Hara, M. (2008) Young children, learning and ICT: A case study in the UK maintained sector. *Technology, Pedagogy and Education* 17 (1): 29–40.

Pritchard, A. (2007) *Effective Teaching with Internet Technologies.* London: Sage.

Prue, R. (2011) Home and school: Bridging the gap. In A. Oldknow and C. Knights (eds) *Mathematics Education with Digital Technology.* London: Continuum.

Smith, H.J., Higgins, S., Wall, K. and Miller, J. (2005) Interactive whiteboards: Boon or bandwagon? A critical review of the literature. *Journal of Computer Assisted Learning* 21 (2): 91–101.

Somekh, B., Lewin, C., Mavers, D., Fisher, T., Harrison, C., Haw, K., Lunzer, E., McFarlane, A. and Scrimshaw, P. (2002) *ImpaCT2: Pupils' and Teachers' Perceptions of ICT in the Home, School and Community.* Available at www.becta.org.uk/research/impact2 (accessed 23 September 2009).

Somekh, B., Underwood, J., Convery, A., Dillon, G., Jarvis, J., Lewin, C., Mavers, D., Saxon, D., Sing, S., Steadman, S., Twining, P. and Woodrow, D. (2007) *Evaluation of the ICT Test Bed Evaluation: Final Report June 2007.* Available at http://dera.ioe.ac.uk/1584/1/becta_2006 _icttestbed_annualreport_report.pdf (accessed 29 May 2012).

Thorvaldsen, S., Vavik, L. and Salomon, S. (2011) The use of ICT tools in mathematics: A case-control study of best practice in 9th grade classrooms. *Scandinavian Journal of Educational Research* 56 (2): 213–28.

Webb, M. and Cox, M. (2004) A review of pedagogy related to information communications technology. *Technology, Pedagogy and Education* 13 (3): 235–86.

Williams, P. (2008) *Independent Review of Mathematics Teaching in Early Years Settings and Primary Schools: Final Report.* London: DCSF. Available at http://dera.ioe.ac.uk/8365/1/Williams%20Mathematics.pdf (accessed 10 December 2011).

Wright, D. (2010) Orchestrating the instruments: Integrating ICT into the secondary mathematics classroom through handheld technology networks. *Technology, Pedagogy and Education* 19 (2): 277–84.

5   Playing with pedagogy

The role of games in the teaching and learning of mathematics

Steve Sherer

Introduction

While many teachers claim to use games within mathematics lessons, their use is more often peripheral to the main business of teaching and learning. Offered as prompts, starters, time fillers and rewards, they may have little relation to the curriculum, either in content or pedagogical focus. Key reports on mathematics teaching from Cockcroft (1982) through to the *Excellence and Enjoyment* Report (DfES 2003) and the Williams Report (2008) identify the need to improve children's understanding of and attitudes to mathematics. In this chapter I will explore the use of mathematical games as a pedagogical approach which can support children's learning as well as help develop their interest and enjoyment of the subject.

Chapter aims

This chapter examines ways in which the use of games can be included within mathematics teaching as a pedagogical approach, exploring the ways in which they support the development of mathematical skills, knowledge and understanding, in addition to their potential for promoting interest in and positive attitudes towards mathematics. It will also consider:

- The nature of mathematical 'games' and 'activities'
- The ways in which a mathematical game can be adapted to meet a range of needs.

While several types of games and their uses in particular areas of mathematics will be discussed, a more in-depth case study of one game, based on the TV show *Play Your Cards Right*, will illustrate how a single game can be adapted for use in a wide range of situations.

The mathematics curriculum and children's learning

Mathematics has long been seen as 'hard' and predominantly only for 'clever' people. Cockcroft (1982: para. 228) reported that it is 'a difficult subject both to teach and to learn' and Dowker (2004:4) found that 'many children have difficulties with mathematics'. For many adults, memories of complex procedures and wrong answers have contributed to what Haylock (2010: 4) identifies as 'anxiety about mathematics and feelings of inadequacy in this subject'. In his research with trainee teachers, arguably in a position to be less intimidated by either schooling or mathematics, Haylock (2010) found they described their memories of mathematics in terms of fear, terror and horror. It is clearly a major problem, and one which can be transmitted from one generation to the next.

Such is the disengagement with mathematics that, as Cannon and Ginsburg (2008) identify, 81 per cent of parents prefer to teach their child language rather than mathematics, because they feel less skilled at mathematics than language. This is important because, as Blevins-Knabe and Musun-Miller (1996: 40) found, in families who engaged in more numerical activities, the children were described as 'doing more with numbers'. It might be inferred that these children will then also develop a better disposition towards mathematics. In a country that, as Williams (2008: 3) noted, 'is still one of the few advanced nations where it is socially acceptable – fashionable even – to profess an inability to cope with the subject', this is crucial in attempts to raise standards.

The matter of mathematics anxiety is an important one. The 'feeling of tension and anxiety that interferes with the manipulation of numbers and the solving of mathematical problems in a wide variety of ordinary life and academic situations' (Richardson and Suinn 1972: 551, cited by Ashcraft and Moore 2009: 197) is a limiting one. Ashcraft and Moore (2009) found that college students on mathematics, science and engineering courses tended to express low levels of mathematics anxiety, but for those on humanities and non-mathematics related disciplines, levels were higher. However, what caused them the greatest concern was their finding that the students expressing the highest levels of anxiety were those training to become teachers in elementary schools. It is likely, indeed probable, that some of your colleagues (perhaps yourself?) will have some degree of mathematics anxiety.

Reflection

Consider your own attitudes towards mathematics.

- What are they, and how do you think they were formed?
- How might they inform your teaching of mathematics?

In a culture where mathematics is perceived to be 'hard' and only for 'clever' people, and mathematical incompetence socially acceptable, we need to consider how we, as teachers and educators, can address this. How can, for example, a pedagogy of games (within a broader tool-set) take us some way towards addressing this? Can it be justified in terms that relate to children's understanding of and achievement in mathematics? Pressures on schools to produce acceptable test results can leave teachers wary of such approaches, despite the DfES (2003) strategy document *Excellence and Enjoyment: A Strategy for Primary Schools* urging them to adopt more individualized and creative approaches to curriculum delivery. Charles Clarke, the then Secretary of State for Education, strongly believed that 'what makes good primary education great is the fusion of excellence and enjoyment' (DfES 2003: 3). His view that 'children learn better when they are excited and engaged' is a sentiment that few would disagree with. Teachers still report however that the use of games (and other more creative pedagogies) tends to happen mainly with younger children, falling out of favour as assessment stakes become higher.

However, embedded within the National Curriculum documentation (DfEE 1999) is a requirement that children develop communication skills, mathematical language and collaborative problem solving. The use of games and other less 'traditional' (for want of a better word) pedagogies would appear to be well suited to supporting the development of these skills.

The examples used in this chapter demonstrate the opportunity for in-depth discussion and reasoning that is possible throughout school. It is also worth noting, that while games may be regarded by some as a recreational activity more suited to younger or less able pupils, rather than a valid pedagogy for all pupils, it is older and more able students who engage in deeper levels of discussion and reasoning, and thus, support each other in their co-construction of knowledge.

Conceptual and theoretical perspectives: playing with mathematics

In an attempt to move away from the practice of rote learning in mathematics, Skemp (1976) drew a distinction between 'instrumental' and 'relational' understanding. Even though the former may have resulted in achieving correct answers, he did not consider it demonstrated understanding, describing it merely as following rules, without knowing reasons. Children who demonstrated relational understanding, on the other hand, knew both what they were doing and why they were doing it. Instrumental understanding is often linked to a didactic pedagogy, involving a teacher telling and a pupil 'knowing'. However, although Skemp (1976) acknowledged that within a certain context, a case may exist for instrumental learning to provide short-term gains, in the longer term, no such case can be made. If we are to help children develop such relational mathematical understanding we need to provide experiences where children can be 'co-constructors' of knowledge. Bragg (2007) used a constructivist paradigm to examine how mathematical games could be used to build on students' cognitive structures by generating a cognitive disequilibrium within their existing conceptual structures, which required them to accommodate new conceptual understandings before potentially achieving cognitive equilibrium.

Despite key differences in their philosophy of learning, both Vygotsky (1978) and Piaget (1971) saw children as active constructors of knowledge. Vygotsky's concept of the Zone of Proximal Development (ZPD) is defined as

> the distance between the actual developmental level as determined by independent problem solving and the level of potential development as determined through problem solving under adult guidance, or in collaboration with more capable peers.
>
> (Vygotsky 1978: 86)

Mathematical games can provide a wealth of opportunities for children to construct and apply their knowledge and if appropriately managed by teachers, can ensure that the gap between actual and potential development can be addressed.

Mathematical games

What is a mathematical game? Gough (2001a) considered that it needed to include a certain degree of mathematical thinking. It should be played by two or more people (as opposed to a 'puzzle' which was a solitary activity), taking turns and having some degree of choice in what to do in order to win. While there was a certain degree of chance involved, dependent for example on the roll of dice, it was important that within a true 'game' there were alternative choices of how to play; one player's moves may influence the moves of an opponent and success was therefore not wholly reliant upon chance. This explains why Gough (2001a) classes 'Snakes and Ladders' (where the outcomes rely entirely on the luck of die-rolling) as a 'game-like activity' rather than a game, describing it as 'merely a luck-race from start to finish'. In his view 'its sole redeeming educational feature is that it helps very young children learn how to handle the mechanics and manners of game playing' (Gough 2001a: 18). He does, however, class the die and board game Ludo as a mathematical game because there is an element of player choice based on informed and strategic decision.

Davies (1995) noted how children were motivated when playing mathematical games, seeing them as an enjoyable activity rather than a mechanistic paper exercise. This would suggest a positive impact on children's attitudes to mathematics, and if managed appropriately by a teacher, then the potential to capture and build on increased motivation allows the introduction of increasingly deep thinking and conceptual engagement. It is crucial however that teachers fully understand the need to plan these experiences as effectively as they plan other more 'standard' approaches. As Swann and Marshall (2009: 5) note, where games had been systematically taught and used as an integral part of a mathematics programme, they did improve mathematical skills and problem solving, but when they were 'not considered to be serious pedagogical tools the results would be patchy at best'.

Types of mathematical games

The format-based typology of mathematical games produced by Way (1999) includes Race, Board, Numerical Strategy, Card, Arithmetical, Matching and Mystery Games. Each category is explained in terms of the specific mathematical learning its games aim to develop. In some cases, the games are simplified versions of existing games (such as Mini Draughts), and designed with reduced complexity to ensure that the concept can be easily explored and developed without children feeling overwhelmed by the larger scale or complexity of the full version.

Probability, for example, can be explored when playing versions of roulette or Yahtzee; card games like Snap! or Happy Families can be used to address topics from simple number bonds to ten or equivalent areas of shapes; calculations carried out when playing darts or hoopla encourage mental arithmetic and Connect 4 can be used to encourage children to use and explain strategy and logical thinking. Siegler (2009) discusses how the use of a linear board game with 4 and 5 year olds (where they used a spinner to move along a horizontally arranged board numbered 1–10) for just four 15–20 minute sessions over a two- week period helped them improve their number line estimates and, he suggested, their understanding of numerical magnitudes.

> ### Reflection
>
> Consider a range of mathematical games that you know of. In the light of your own practice, consider their appropriateness, and in particular, how they might be adapted to meet specific learning outcomes

Play Your Cards Right – a study of a mathematical game

In this section, I will discuss how a single game, Play Your Cards Right, can, as Davies (1995) suggests, be adapted to meet a variety of teaching and learning needs in mathematics across a range of ages, and stages of learning. I have chosen this game in particular because of its versatility and its capacity to motivate and engage children, encouraging them to articulate and logically justify their reasoned choices.

Play Your Cards Right is a television game show (based on an American programme, *Card Sharks*) which has been running since 1980. The basic premise is that contestants have a line of five playing cards from a standard 52-card deck which they turn over one at a time, after predicting or guessing whether the new card will be higher or lower in face value than the previous one. If the guess is successful, the contestants move on to the next card; if unsuccessful, then they return to the beginning of the line and new cards are dealt. The aim of the game is to get to the end of the line (where high value prizes are the reward) through making successful decisions.

At the outset of the game, when the first card is revealed, contestants have an option of whether or not to keep the card and play the game, or pass it over to the opposing contestants. The decision is one of probability. For example, if the first card is an ace (equivalent to 1), the probability that the next card is higher is 48/51 (or approximately 0.94). As there are only three aces remaining in the deck, the probability of one of these being turned over next (and equivalent cards also cause the contestant to lose) is 3/51. Thus, they would want to keep an ace and play. Likewise, a Jack would be a good starter card, as the probability of the next card being lower (i.e. having a value from an ace to a 10) is 40/51. If, however, the card following is higher (a King or Queen) or of the same value (i.e. a Jack from another suit) then the contestant loses. The probability of this happening would be 11/51.

The closer the starter card is to the middle of the suit (i.e. a 7) then the more difficult it becomes when attempting to predict whether the second card will be higher (24/51) or lower (24/51) than the 7, and thus much more difficult deciding how, or even whether, to proceed. However, contestants can consider previous cards that have been turned over to help inform their decision-making. For example, following three 'low' cards (e.g. a 4, 5 and 2), then turning over a 7 as the fourth card, there would be a slightly greater probability of the fifth card being higher, as 24 of the 48 unused cards would be higher than the 7 (24/48) and only 21 would be lower than 7 (21/48) with three other 7s also remaining unused (3/48).

This game therefore exhibits many of the traits of a mathematical game as identified by Gough (1999) as it involves an element of competition within a set of rules, between pairs of players who must make informed choices in order to win.

Once children are familiar with the basic rules and conventions of the TV game, the format can be adapted to meet a range of needs. It is important to note here that it will not be only the teacher who can make suggestions as to how the game can be adapted; once the pupils become familiar with the format, they will start to make their own suggestions – something that teachers can encourage. When children can introduce their own rules or adaptations to familiar and established games and activities, they tend to have more 'ownership' and thus exhibit a much higher degree of engagement than they do for non-customized games. In the Numbers Count early intervention programme, pupils and teachers together devise mathematical games based upon a theme which reflects the children's interests. These games are used in school to address individual needs identified as part of the Diagnostic Assessment and then sent home to help parents/carers in supporting their child's learning. Sheldon and Epstein (2005) suggest that strategies such as these encourage parental involvement in their children's mathematics learning, improving not only children's skills, but also attitudes to mathematics.

Case studies

I will now discuss the way in which (like many other games) *Play Your Cards Right* can be adapted for use with a range of ages and abilities through the presentation of two case studies.

Case Study 5.1: Starter for ten – a sense of number

This case study comes from my own classroom research with primary school children in Year 1.

As a prerequisite to the game, I ensured that the children were all secure in their understanding of the numbers from 0 to 10, and could understand a simple number line. Using a randomly shuffled pack of number cards, we drew one card at a time, discussing its approximate location on a number line. We then watched a short YouTube clip of the TV show to help demonstrate the rules, aims and entertaining aspects of the game. Then, I explained how we were going to play a version using just a single set of oversized number cards from 0 to 10. The mathematical objectives for the lesson were to

- compare and order numbers, using the related vocabulary
- use knowledge of place value to position these numbers on a number line
- describe ways of solving problems, explaining choices and decisions orally.

Children were paired, with a free choice of partner. The starter card drawn was a 3 and was placed on an empty number line that was used as a visual image to scaffold the game. The 3 was then the focus of the initial discussion, as I asked whether or not it was a good card for us to start with, or whether we should consider exchanging it for a better card.

Reflection

Before continuing with this story, let us pause for a while and reflect on what is happening.

- At this stage in the game, what do you think you could reasonably expect the children to be talking about?
- What would indicate that they have some understanding of the numbers being used in the game?
- What kinds of things would you look for that may indicate problems?
- How would you deal with differences of opinion between partners?

Most of the children were happy to accept the 3 as a starter. However, Joseph, a confident individual who I considered to have quite a good sense of number, disagreed with the majority. The discussion went as follows:

Me: shall we keep this '3' as our starter card?

Class: (chorus) Yes!

Joseph: I don't think we should keep it. We need a very high or a very low card to make it easier to guess 'higher' or 'lower'.

Me: Do we agree with Joseph?

Discussion with partners followed.

Rachel: (high maths ability) It would be too risky; we might get a card right in the middle. Then, it would be even harder to guess 'higher' or 'lower'.

On a majority show of hands, the 3 was retained, and placed at the appropriate point on the number line.

Me: So, will the second card be 'higher' or 'lower' than 3?

Class: (unanimously) Higher!

As a class group, we discussed the probability of this higher outcome by saying that there were seven possible chances of a higher card, compared with only three possible chances of a lower one.

Me: (turns second card) 4!

Joseph: Only just higher!

Me: Yes, next to the 3 (placed on number line). So what do we think about the third card?

Class: (following more discussion and pointing at the number line) Higher!

Me: 6 (placed on number line). Now what about the fourth card?

Rachel: (counting on her fingers to help explain her choice of 'lower') There are six chances of lower than 6 (0, 1, 2, 3, 4 and 5) but only four chances of higher (7, 8, 9 and 10) so there are more chances of the fourth card being 'lower'.

Joseph: No! The 3 and 4 are already used, so that means there are only four lower and four higher.

Although Joseph continued to say that because it was 'four each' they could not guess 'higher' or 'lower', the majority elected to stick with Rachel and her 'lower' guess. Joseph chose 'higher'. Their excited response at seeing an 8 turned over gave some indication of their level of engagement and motivation. With the majority of the class now 'out' of the game, yet still engaged in discussing options with their partners, from the few who remained, all but one elected to guess 'lower' for the final card, because, as Ranjit said, 'there are lots more lower than higher'. Without much effort, Joseph persuaded his partner that they should choose 'higher' simply 'because we wanted to'. The final card proved to be a 10.

Commentary

The decision to present a very simplified version of the television game in that there was only one card of each value (rather than four, as in a deck of playing cards) was particularly important in this case. The complexity of the full-size game is difficult for children to understand, and the 'chance' element can appear more significant than the 'skill' element when the decision-making process seems so opaque to them. Thus, scaling down this game allowed the introduction of an accessible demonstration of probability. In saying that 'There are six chances of lower than 6, but only four chances of higher', Rachel clearly demonstrates her developing understanding of probability, using the word 'chance' to articulate it.

A specific purpose of this game was to consolidate children's understanding of the number line, and develop the language and concept of ordinality. Listening to the children's justifications of their choices provided clear evidence of their understanding of both. The children were able to identify, for example, that if 7 and 9 are already located on the number line and 8 is drawn from the deck, then its place is in between them. Stressing the need for children to see numbers as relational and ordinal as well as quantifcatory, Haylock and Cockburn (2008: 37) suggest that 'We cannot stress too strongly that numbers are not just ways of representing sets of things.' The use of ordinal vocabulary relating to the 'first', 'second' or third' card for example when drawing the cards provided another opportunity to consolidate this concept in a meaningful situation.

The decision in this case to allow the children to work with a partner of choice helped produce freer and fuller discussion about the choices they were making. This, coupled with effective teacher interjection of open ended, or scaffolding questions meant that the development of the intended mathematical learning objective was focused and maximized. Furthermore, timely requests to the children to explain their thinking when they made a choice aided both their thinking and their communication skills.

Reflection

- What do you think you can learn from children playing this version of the game?
- How could you assess their learning?

Case Study 5.2: Same but different – fractions, decimals and percentages

This case study relates to the way in which the game was used with six higher ability Year 6 pupils, where the lesson objectives were to

- recognize the equivalence between fractions, decimals and percentages
- explain reasoning and conclusions.

Here, the game included a range of self-made cards, depicting fractions, numbers to three decimal places and percentages, and comprising different representations of equivalent values, from the lowest (zero) to the highest (1 'whole' or 100 per cent), with cards such as 50 per cent, 0.5 and 7/14. The fact that children had to transfer from one representation to another, explain equivalence and then justify a 'higher' or 'lower' decision, gave rise to a very high standard of discussion and illustrates how the game can be made even more challenging. We begin the story with a child choosing a starter card marked 0.65.

Teacher: Do you want to keep the starter card of 0.65?
Chris: No, because it is only just higher than half. I'll change it.
Teacher: OK . . . change it for . . . '40 per cent'. How do you feel about that?
Jon: 40 per cent is only 10 per cent off 50 per cent which is half way . . . the 0.65 card is the same as 65 per cent, which is 15 per cent more than 50 per cent which is half. So we are now worse off!

Jon explained to Chris that they now had less than a 60 per cent chance of a 'higher' card, compared to their original position of less than a 65 per cent chance of a 'lower' card. Logically, they guessed that the next card would be 'higher'.

Teacher: 9/20.
Chris: Um. 9/20. This will be close. It's just less than half. 10/20 would be half . . . 0.5 . . .

A prompt was needed to move the discussion on.

Teacher: Could 9/20 be simplified further?
Jon: 9/20 would be the same as 4 and a half out of ten, and we need higher than 40 per cent . . . 4 and a half out of 10 is greater than 4 out of 10 . . . which is 40 per cent, so it is 'higher'!

Commentary

The journey to the answer here was aided considerably by the initial comments from Chris and the teacher prompts, identifying again the importance of discussion as a tool for learning. Chris moves seamlessly between decimals and fractions as he explains his reasoning, something which is again seen in Jon's words. Opportunities to rehearse explanatory dialogue help prepare pupils for National Curriculum tests (commonly known as Standard Assessment Tests, or SATs), as increasingly, pupils are being asked to justify and explain their answers.

More importantly, however, discussions of this type, particularly when made public and shared through the playing of a game, help all children in developing their understanding. This connectionist approach, in this case, the making of connections between decimals, fractions and percentages and essentially seeing them all as the same concept, is something which Askew et al. (1997) noted as key in helping children make progress. Bottle (2005: 60–1) further adds that 'making connections does not usually happen by accident' and that 'it is incumbent on teachers to plan to highlight these connections'. The more informal pedagogy of the game, and the built-in need for explanatory dialogue, provide just the opportunity for such connectionist planning. Throughout the game, all the children were engaged in similar discussions, even when it was not their turn to play. The element of competition in the game meant that they felt the need to fully understand each decision as it was being made, in order to aid their own fluency in decision-making when their turn came along.

Listening to the discussions also provides an important opportunity for the teacher to assess the children's conceptual understanding. Jon and Chris, for example, clearly demonstrated understanding of the equivalences between decimal, fraction and percentage notations.

Choosing an appropriate game

The examples featured in the two case studies are based on an existing, albeit customized game. The ways in which it has been adapted for particular age groups and purposes echoes Way's (1999) identification that the complexity of some everyday games can be such that the mathematics is less easily accessed and explored than it might be. The element of chance in the game, which means that although well-informed decision-making is a crucial skill, also means there is the possibility that a weaker player can do well – a key factor in motivating all children (Alridge and Badham 1993).

The importance of matching the design of the game to the pedagogical intent is emphasized by authors such as Alridge and Badham (1993) and Way (1999), with Way further suggesting that the best means of ensuring that this happens may be to design the game yourself. She suggests a series of key evaluative questions such as reviewing the degree of match to the mathematics objective, the suitability of the ability and age range, the degree to which 'chance' is a feature, and the extent to which repeated playing might improve player skill as crucial at this stage. In Chapter 8 of this book, Lynne McClure further suggests not only that teachers can design their own games, but also that for pupils, 'making up a good game is actually quite a sophisticated piece of thinking, involving analysis and synthesis, and then evaluation – those higher order skills of Bloom'. In this way the use of games can provide much needed enrichment activities for able pupils.

A brief word about electronic games

Choosing to focus this chapter on non-ICT-based games was not for any ideological reason. Rather, it was in order to reflect both the pedagogical and motivational potential of games that can be played with low cost, often home-made, resources. Indeed, in my work with children, part of the planning for games has involved them designing and making the cards for this, and other similar games.

For readers with a particular interest in electronic games, it is worth noting that in their comprehensive study on the uses of computer gaming in the teaching of mathematics, Mor et al. (2006) found that many of the underlying principles outlined in this chapter also pertain for electronic games. For example, the importance of children actively thinking about and discussing the mathematics embedded in the computer games, together with teacher attitudes, supporting activities and collaboration, are crucial so that mathematical learning can take place.

Summary

This chapter has outlined the nature of mathematical games and explored how a single game, when closely matched to specific learning objectives, can be adapted to meet the learning needs of pupils of all ages and abilities. Using a range of carefully posed questions and comments, teachers can facilitate discussion where pupils explain and justify reasoning to each other. Within a context of socially constructed learning, children learn with and from their peers, in challenging, yet non-threatening situations, which engage and motivate. When planned with specific outcomes in mind, and introduced to the children within the context of their normal learning, games can have a significant and positive impact on children's concept development, reasoning, mathematical vocabulary and attitudes to mathematics.

Further reading

Gough, J. (2001b) Playing mathematical games: Make a game or adapt a game. *Australian Primary Mathematics Classroom* 7 (1): 14–17.
John Gough has written extensively on the uses of games within mathematics over recent decades, much of it in Australian journals. These articles are very readable and draw many links with more academic studies on the uses of games in mathematics education, which in turn can be followed up to give a more in-depth understanding of the concepts covered. This article discusses how games can be adapted, and includes a design brief to make a game for a competition that he ran.
Way, J. (1999) *Learning Maths through Games Series*. Avaiable at http://nrich.maths.org/2489/index (accessed 23 May 2012).
In this series of four short articles, Jenni Way provides a concise yet informative review of the literature on learning mathematics through games, together with suggestions on how a wide range of games can be used and evaluated within the mathematics classroom. Many of these games can be adapted for use with children of different ages and abilities.

References

Aldridge, S. and Badham, V. (1993) Beyond just a game. Pamphlet Number 21. Primary Mathematics Association.
Ashcraft, M.H. and Moore, A.M. (2009) Mathematics anxiety and the affective drop in performance. *Journal of Psychoeducational Assessment* 27: 197–205.
Askew, M., Brown, M., Rhodes, V., Wiliam, D. and Johnson, D. (1997) *Effective Teachers of Numeracy: Report of a Study Carried Out for the Teacher Training Agency*. London: Kings College, University of London.
Blevins-Knabe, B. and Musun-Miller, L. (1996) Number use at home by children and their parents and its relationship to early mathematical performance. *Early Development and Parenting* 5: 35–45.
Bottle, G. (2005) *Primary Mathematics Team*. London: Continuum.

Bragg, L. (2007) Students' conflicting attitudes towards games as a vehicle for learning mathematics: A methodological dilemma. *Mathematics Education Research Journal* 19 (1): 29–44.

Cannon, J. and Ginsburg, H.P. (2008) 'Doing the math': Maternal beliefs about early mathematics versus language learning. *Early Education and Development* 19 (2): 238–60.

Cockcroft, W.H. (1982) *Mathematics Counts: Report of the Committee of Inquiry into the Teaching of Mathematics in Schools* (Cockcroft Report). London: HMSO. Available at www.educationengland.org.uk/documents/cockcroft (accessed 31 January 2012).

Davies, B. (1995) The role of games in mathematics. *Square One* 5 (2).

Department for Education and Employment (DfEE) (1999) *The National Curriculum*. London: DfEE.

Department for Education and Skills (DfES) (2003) *Excellence and Enjoyment: A Strategy for Primary Schools*. London: HMSO.

Dowker, A. (2004) *What Works for Children with Mathematical Difficulties?* DfES Research Report 554. Available at www.education.gov.uk/publications/eOrderingDownload/RR554.pdf (accessed 28 May 2012).

Gough, J. (1999) Playing mathematical games: When is a game not a game? *Australian Primary Mathematics Classroom* 4 (2): 12–17.

Gough, J. (2001a) Playing mathematical games: Get to know your local games shop. *Australian Primary Mathematics Classroom* 6 (1): 15–19.

Gough, J. (2001b) Playing mathematical games: Make a game or adapt a game. *Australian Primary Mathematics Classroom* 7 (1): 14–17.

Haylock, D. (2010) *Mathematics Explained for Primary Teachers* (4th edn). London: Sage.

Haylock, D. and Cockburn, A. (2008) *Understanding Mathematics for Young Children*. London: Sage.

Mor, Y., Winters, N., Cerulli, M. and Bjork, S. (2006) Learning patterns for the design and deployment of mathematical games. Available at http://eprints.ioe.ac.uk/4223/1/LP-LitReview-v2.pdf (accessed 2 April 2012).

Piaget, J. (1971) *Science of Education and the Psychology of the Child*. London: Longman.

Richardson, F.C. and Suinn, R.M. (1972) The Mathematics Anxiety Rating Scale. *Journal of Counselling Psychology* 19: 551–4.

Sheldon, B.S. and Epstein, J.L. (2005) Involvement counts: Family and community partnerships and mathematics achievement. *Journal of Educational Research* 98 (4): 196–206.

Siegler, R.S. (2009) Improving the numerical understanding of children from low-income families. *Child Development Perspectives* 3 (2): 118–24.

Skemp, R.R. (1976) Relational and instrumental understanding. *Mathematics Teaching* 77: 20–6.

Swann, P. and Marshall, L. (2009) Mathematical games as a pedagogical tool. Paper presented to Third International Conference on Science and Mathematics Education (CoSMEd), Penang, Malaysia, 10–12 November.

Vygotsky, L.S. (1978) *Mind in Society: The Development of Higher Psychological Processes*. Cambridge, MA: Harvard University Press.

Way, J. (1999) Learning Maths Through Games Series. Available at http://nrich.maths.org/2489/index (accessed 2 April 2012).

Williams, P. (2008) *Independent Review of Mathematics Teaching in Early Years Settings and Primary Schools: Final Report*. London: DCSF. Available at http://dera.ioe.ac.uk/8365/1/Williams%20Mathematics.pdf (accessed 10 December 2011).

6 Thinking beyond the classroom

Making mathematics real and purposeful

Victoria Grinyer and Sue Bailey

Introduction

> *Learning outside the classroom is about raising achievement through an organized, powerful approach to learning in which direct experience is of prime importance. This is not only about what we learn but importantly how and where we learn.*
>
> (DfES 2006a: 3)

This chapter will explore the reasons why 'thinking beyond the classroom' is important in children's mathematical learning. It will identify how real and purposeful experiences (drawing on the work of van Oers (2009) and Sparrow (2008)) can provide a tool for supporting children's mathematical understanding both inside the classroom environment and beyond. Different ways of integrating other areas of the curriculum will also be discussed.

Chapter aims

The chapter will use case studies from two primary schools in order to develop and discuss key points about children's learning beyond the classroom, illustrating ways in which real and purposeful activities have been integrated into the teaching and learning of mathematics. Reflection points will enable you to consider these in relation to your own classroom and school environment.

By the end of this chapter you should have:

- Explored how 'thinking beyond the classroom' can enhance the teaching and learning of mathematics

- Considered ways of integrating real and purposeful mathematical experiences inside and outside the classroom and across the curriculum
- Become aware of the benefits of this approach to the teaching and learning of mathematics.

The mathematics curriculum and children's learning

The Plowden Report of 1967 'At the heart of the educational process lies the child' identified the importance of identifying, building on and strengthening children's intrinsic interest in learning, and through that lead them to learn for themselves (Central Advisory Council for Education 1967; Gillard 2004). Individual learning, flexibility in the curriculum, the importance of play and the use of the environment and learning by discovery are also key features of the report as we discuss later.

In 1982, the Cockroft Report identified mathematics as a powerful means of communication and a key factor in the development of logical thinking, accuracy and spatial awareness. It stresses the appreciation and enjoyment of mathematics as a subject in its own right:

> The primary mathematics curriculum should enrich children's aesthetic and linguistic experience, provide them with the means of exploring their environment and develop their powers of logical thought, in addition to equipping them with the numerical skills which will be a powerful tool for later work and study.
>
> (Cockcroft 1982: 84)

The Cockcroft (1982) report reiterates the importance of a 'broadly based curriculum' enabling 'the ability to apply mathematics' to be developed and that the 'emphasis on arithmetical skills does not of itself lead to ability to make use of these skills in practical situations'.

The National Curriculum (DfEE and QCA 1999) established statutory programmes of study for children of compulsory school age. The emphasis in the Key Stage 1 mathematics programme was to develop a knowledge and understanding of mathematics through practical activity, exploration and discussion ensuring that appropriate connections were made between the sections on 'number' and 'shape, space and measures'. At Key Stage 2 these connections were extended to 'handling data' and pupils were encouraged to explore features of shape and space, develop measuring skills in a range of contexts, discussing and presenting their methods and reasoning using a range of mathematical language, diagrams and charts.

Interestingly, there was no separate section of the programme of study that corresponds to the first attainment target, using and applying

mathematics and teaching requirements relating to this attainment target are subsumed within the other curriculum areas. Subsequent curriculum initiatives such as the National Numeracy Strategy (DfEE 1999),
which introduced a structured daily mathematics lesson for all primary
school pupils, and the Renewed Primary Framework for Mathematics
(DfES 2006b) sought to address concerns about achievement and progress
in mathematics. While the Numeracy Strategy focused on developing key
'numeracy skills', the Renewed Framework provided a more developed
set of guidance materials in relation to 'using and applying mathematics',
and also suggests ways in which opportunities for mathematics across
the curriculum may be identified. Similarly, the Statutory Framework for
the Early Years Foundation Stage (DCSF 2008) identified the importance
of providing children with a broad range of contexts in which they can
explore, enjoy, learn, practise and talk about their developing understanding, and suggested that it should be achieved through planned, purposeful
play with a balance of adult-led and child-initiated activities.

Reflection

Consider the ways in which the National Numeracy Strategy, the Renewed
Framework for Mathematics and the Statutory Framework for the Early Years
Foundation Stage impacted on your ability and disposition to 'Think beyond
the classroom for mathematics: making mathematics real and purposeful'?
As curriculum requirements change, consider whether and how they will
continue to impact on and inform your understanding of young children's
mathematical development.

More than arithmetic

Nunes et al. (2009: 1) support the view that mathematics is broader than
arithmetic skills. One of the key findings of a research project looking
at the development of competence in different aspects of mathematics is
that 'Mathematical reasoning, even more so than children's knowledge of
arithmetic, is important for children's later achievement in mathematics.'
At the time of writing, both the Early Years Foundation Stage framework
and National Curriculum are under review. The report of the Expert Panel
for the National Curriculum Review (DfE 2011) recommends that schools
should be given greater freedom over the curriculum and that the National
Curriculum should set out only essential knowledge, leaving schools more
freedom to design a curriculum that best suits their needs and those of

their pupils through a process of local or school-level decision-making. The report also recommends that schools should decide *how* to teach this most effectively to ensure that the curriculum is motivating and meaningful to pupils. The proposed Local Curriculum (DfE 2011: 59) highlights the need for 'motivating and meaningful' provision which provides scope for 'the development of particular interests and curricular innovation for schools'. This level of flexibility could potentially allow for the development of mathematical reasoning, as well as arithmetic skills. Further, such flexibility would allow schools to build on existing strengths, and make cross-curricular links in a more developed and meaningful way than they may have previously done.

Reflection

Considering the particular interests and curricular innovations in your school, what do you think an appropriate Local Curriculum might look like? How might it encourage the development of mathematical reasoning?

Conceptual and theoretical perspectives: thinking beyond the classroom

> Children do not learn by first mastering the skills ... They learn in meaningful contexts ... by trial and error and furthermore this learning should be enjoyable and rewarding.
>
> (Donaldson 1987, cited in Dixon 2005: 30)

This chapter is based around our beliefs that children learn mathematics more effectively if it makes sense to them. We believe that the teaching of mathematics should be carefully and creatively planned, within and beyond the classroom in order to engage and inspire all children. When discussing mathematics 'beyond the classroom' we mean this in its widest sense, in order to make mathematics personal and meaningful to each individual child in a range of situations. We discuss the ways in which this can be achieved through what we have called 'real and purposeful mathematical experiences' across the curriculum.

ngful mathematics

(2011) suggests that children are more likely to understand, re-
apply their learning to different situations if their mathematics

experiences are meaningful to them. Barnes suggests that in this respect, a meaningful experience is both cognitive and affective in nature, defining it as 'an encounter that emotionally triggers and drives a child or children to want to understand and know more' (Barnes 2011: 9). He further identifies the emotional response as important in promoting deep learning which is transferable to other contexts. Likewise, Skinner et al. (2008) propose that a positive emotional response drives children's effort and involvement in learning whereas negative responses result in disaffection, reducing their effort and persistence.

Learning experiences which provoke a negative response, for example anxiety, particularly in relation to mathematics, can adversely impact upon cognitive skills such as working memory (Ashcraft et al., 1998, cited in Chinn 2009). This is particularly important, as working memory has been found to be a predictor of mathematical achievement (Keeler and Swanson 2001, cited in Chinn 2009). Barnes (2012: 238) argues that offering powerful and 'emotionally relevant' experiences as part of lessons provide the best chance of including all pupils in 'meaningful' learning.

How can we, as teachers, address these matters? How can we know about pupils' current interests and prior knowledge and understanding? This, as both Fisher (2008) and Barnes (2011) point out, can be especially challenging in a culture which emphasizes rigid measures of achievement and progress. Additionally, what may seem meaningful to the teacher in terms of their pupils' learning could well have little relevance or interest to the children.

Traditionally, teachers have tried to make mathematics meaningful to children through topic work. Based on the concept that children do not naturally compartmentalize their learning into specific subject areas (Fisher 2008), 'topic webs' were an attempt to develop cross-curricular learning. However, Fisher believes that because topics are often planned by whole staff teams together, 'the links that are made between areas of learning are not seen by the children but engineered by adults' (Fisher 2008: 53). Linklater (2006) proposes that we often don't listen to what children say about themselves and their lives and advocates the importance of working with children. Similarly, Barnes has argued that 'topic webs' were bland and suggests 'we should consult the children about what they want to learn about' (Barnes 2011: 200) in order to create meaningful contexts for children.

Donaldson (2007) proposes that children should experience mathematics in real life contexts but should also be provided with opportunities to undertake investigations of mathematics, emphasizing that mathematics is valuable in itself. Dunne (2010), however, insists that placing an emphasis on using real-life contexts and situations makes mathematics more difficult for children. He suggests that 'Real life was not designed for learning maths' and argues that because the language of mathematics is so precise it should be taught in a way that preserves its straightforwardness and simplicity (Dunne 2010: 1).

This view is not uncontested, with Edgington (2002) and Fisher (2008) suggesting that experiences not embedded in familiar contexts, or related to current need, can seem pointless to children. Mitchell (1999) insists that if the content of mathematics is irrelevant to children, this will negatively impact on their learning and understanding, recommending that children should be 'empowered' to understand the relevance of mathematics in their lives. This seems to bring us to the importance of having 'conversations' (in the broadest sense of the word) with the children, their parents and other important adults, as well as making careful observations of the children (Fisher 2008). Peters and Kelly (2011), discussing just what conversations might be approached and how they could be structured, propose the 'Mosaic approach' which draws from a range of methods such as observations, interviews with important adults and children to draw together pieces of information to create a complete picture of children's perspectives (Peters and Kelly 2011).

In summary, it can be seen that the factors involved in developing real and purposeful mathematical experiences include:

- consideration of the child's emotional response to mathematical activities and situations
- conscious efforts from teachers to provide learning experiences that generate a positive emotional engagement
- identification of what is 'meaningful' from the child's perspective through taking the time to find out
- carefully planned mathematical contexts, building on children's current interest and prior knowledge.

Case studies

Three case studies, each from a different curriculum stage, are used to illustrate key ways in which meaningful and purposeful mathematical experiences may be provided for children.

Case Study 6.1 explores how the potential of role play developed through consulting children about their own learning can create meaningful contexts for mathematical learning. It is presented in three parts interspersed with commentary.

Case Study 6.1: Role play and mathematical learning

Part 1

Yasmin worked in a school that had specifically created role-play rooms for each year group in Key Stage 1 with the purpose of providing opportunities to develop problem-solving skills and mathematical language. The role-play rooms were an integral part of the planning and colleagues often worked together to think about appropriate role-play situations as well the learning opportunities that could be created, in consultation with the children. Previous role-play scenarios included a launderette, a post office and a florist.

Yasmin consulted the children about their ideas for what the role-play room could be made into in the following half term. The children had suggested either a bank or hairdresser's salon. Within the planning meeting a discussion developed about which scenario would lend itself better to handling money and the teaching staff agreed to build on the children's idea of a bank.

Commentary

It was important for Yasmin to take time to consult with the children about what they would like for their role play. Samuelsson and Johansson (2009) suggest that since Piaget (1976) first introduced the research world to the notion of actually listening to children, there is more encouragement for children to express their own views and experiences of their world. Indeed, Fisher (2008) stresses the importance of allowing children to initiate their own learning and insists that adults must listen, facilitate and support children's learning responding appropriately to whatever children initiate. Similarly, Tzuo (2007) discusses Dewey's (1998) ideas that teachers and children should decide together what experiences are meaningful to children's current learning needs and future development and learning.

In this study it is interesting to note that while the children were involved in deciding upon a mathematical context, the educators eventually made the final decision (on the basis of opportunity for learning), in line with Fisher's (2008) reminder that quality of learning should be central when adults and children negotiate contexts for learning.

The children's excited discussion about the role play would seem to align with Martlew et al. (2011) who suggest that increased child engagement comes from being actively involved, having autonomy and the opportunity for choice within learning activities.

Part 2

In order for the idea of a bank to be successful, Yasmin knew that time would need to be spent on setting the scene for the children, ensuring that those children who didn't have much experience of banks could understand the main purpose of them. It was decided that a few children from the year group would visit a nearby bank and then share the experience with the other children on their return.

Yasmin recorded the children on their trip to the bank and permission was sought to record inside the building, so that the main purposes of a bank could be shared with the whole year group. The children engaged thoroughly with the idea of creating a bank and a rich discussion about the purposes of a bank developed from watching the recording.

Commentary

Making sure that the context for the mathematics learning is real for the children is key at this stage. The discussion that followed the video viewing was an important part of ensuring that children both understood and were interested in the bank role play. Van Oers (2009) suggests that meaningful mathematical learning should be embedded in cultural practices that make sense to those involved, emphasizing that mathematical learning can take place in real or simulated situations as well as in school environments. Furthermore, Sparrow (2008: 4) states that for some children 'the mathematics of the classroom has no obvious connection to the mathematics of their world' and that real mathematics engages them by connecting with their interests of the moment. This, along with purposeful activities will 'bring together mathematical skills and knowledge that they have' (Sparrow 2008: 8).

Part 3

As a result of the trip, the children became very keen to be involved in setting up their own bank. The experience of using money in this way had a significant impact on the children's understanding. The children were keener to use money because this learning had derived from their own interest and was set in a context they had some prior experience of.

For example, when observing Phillip at the cash desk during their role play, Azra, a 'customer' at the bank, asked if she could have change for one pound. Phillip successfully counted it out in ten pence pieces. At this point, Yasmin joined in and asked the children if they could think of other ways of changing one pound. They had a discussion about how this could be done and created different piles of coins totalling one pound.

Also, when giving receipts to customers, Yasmin was able to intervene when observing Zahra, a more able child, writing receipts for a given amount. A discussion entailed around the importance of writing amounts in different ways, for example 276p and £2.76.

Commentary

Providing this particular meaningful context within the role play situation enabled the children to practise and develop their mathematical skills further. Yasmin's timely and appropriate interventions helped the children consolidate their learning. Donaldson (2012) suggests that role play also provides teachers with opportunities to effectively address children's misconceptions by intervening or joining in.

Yasmin's story effectively demonstrated the potential for ensuring curriculum coverage, while still being flexible enough to develop real and meaningful context-based experiences. Craft (2000: 118) describes this as anticipation and imagination 'backed up by strong organization and judgement'.

Reflection

Dunne (2010) suggests that real-life experiences make learning in mathematics more difficult. Consider this in relation to Yasmin's story, and then in relation to your own practice. Do you think that you have to agree with one or other perspective, or is it possible to agree to some extent with each?

Mathematics across the curriculum

Lewis (1994: 80) suggests that 'there are some strong overlaps sometimes between mathematics and other curriculum areas'. Greenwood (2007: 380) discusses how 'cross-curricular' is assumed to mean an approach which attempts to bring together 'aspects from different subject areas which contribute in a meaningful and appropriate way to the unit's whole' and he asserts that links should focus on content, skills and concepts.

Recognizing, developing and planning around skills and concepts rather than subject content can help build more positive attitudes to mathematics in children, taking them beyond the 'separate subjects in the timetable' (Fox and Surtees 2010: 68). They point out that while children are working in this more holistic way, teachers can assess their 'true understanding' of mathematics as children are able to consolidate and develop their skills and understanding. Furthermore, they emphasize that mathematics taught in a discrete lesson can be revisited in new and interesting ways.

Turner and McCullough (2004) suggest that if children are made aware of the diverse uses of mathematics, they may accept mathematics more easily than if it is only taught discretely. Subjects such as geography, science, social education and sport can provide a rich source of stimulus and motivation for pupils to improve their mathematics skills. Although research informs us that subject progression is more likely to be ensured by limiting the subjects involved in cross-curricular work to two or three (Roth 2000, cited in Barnes 2011; Jacobs 2004; Barnes and Shirley 2007) when planning mathematics with links to one or two other subjects, learning is often enhanced in both subjects.

Greenwood (2007) discusses how children view the world in a holistic way and infers that separating subjects into compartments may prevent important links between subjects being explored (Morrison and Ridley 1988; Cohen et al. 2004; Barnes 2007, cited in Greenwood 2007). Furthermore, links between curriculum subjects have been closely linked to stimulating creative thinking (Ofsted 2002, 2010; Roberts 2006, cited in Barnes 2012). Making explicit links with mathematics and other curriculum subjects can increase children's ability and willingness to use mathematics that they already know.

Case Study 6.2 highlights how children can draw upon other subjects, in this case geography, to improve their mathematics skills, and also their understanding of another curriculum subject. Again, commentary and reflection points are interspersed.

Case Study 6.2: Sandra teaches measure

Sandra is an experienced Year 5 teacher who had noticed that when teaching measures to her class, the children found it very hard to visualize distances. She discussed this with other members of the team and found it was a common observation. In order to find ways of helping children make real sense of distance, they decided to address it through their current work on geography, where they had been discussing the Amazon River, and had found it almost meaningless when they heard its length was approximately 6500 km. Realizing that they actually had little concept of what a single kilometre looked like, Sandra decided to take them outside to measure the length of the school field. They worked out that nine lengths of the field was equivalent to one kilometre, and from that, started to speculate how many lengths would be equivalent to the length of the Amazon. They also, however, began to relate it to distances between familiar places, wondering how many lengths of the field would be equivalent to the distance travelled on a visit to the seaside.

Sandra was pleased with their progress and the way in which they extended their own understanding into other contexts, but still felt some surprise when the following term, as they began their science work on the solar system, the children remembered using the school field measurements to help them visualize very large distances, and asked to measure the scale of the solar system on the playground. They marked out distances with one centimetre representing one million miles and this experience, as well as giving them an understanding of scale, helped them to estimate and measure longer distances and the distance between planets.

Commentary

Sandra's story highlights how linking mathematics to other curriculum subjects, such as geography and science, can enhance learning in both subjects. Barnes (2012) describes such experiences as 'multidisciplinary cross-curricular learning' where parity of importance is given to two subjects and learning is extended through the use of a single stimulus or experience. The teacher had carefully considered the specific learning objectives in *both* mathematics and geography in planning the first experience. Barnes (2012) explains how subject progression can be difficult to achieve in cross-curricular learning and insists that detailed planning towards specific objectives in both subject areas is of central importance to the success of cross-curricular learning. Importantly, Barnes (2012) stresses that teachers need to engage in appropriate professional development to support the planning of powerful and meaningful cross-curricular experiences for children.

Reflection

- How far do you currently plan links between mathematics and other curriculum subjects?
- How easy do you find spotting links?

- How far do you agree that teachers need to engage in 'appropriate professional development' to plan good cross-curricular learning experiences?
- What might such professional development look like?

Motivation to learn

> Children, like adults, lack concentration when they are required to do something that they find meaningless and irrelevant. All too often this can happen when activities that practitioners plan do not take account of children's own experiences and interests.
>
> (Fisher 2008: 78)

The importance of motivation in learning has been articulated by many writers.

Aunola et al. (2006), for example, points out that children's interest and motivation in a particular subject plays a pivotal role in their performance, particularly in mathematics. The two previous case studies also highlight the importance of providing personally meaningful experiences for children.

Case Study 6.3 highlights how making mathematics learning personally meaningful through the use of real life situations and information can increase children's enjoyment, engagement and *motivation* to learn.

Case Study 6.3: Fantasy stock market

Sally was in her seventh year of teaching at a primary school and she had recently gained her status as the Mathematics Specialist Teacher (*having followed a recognized master's level award bearing programme of study in England*). She was asked to plan and deliver several mathematics sessions that would provide the pupils with 'enrichment and enjoyment'. The class teacher wanted the children to develop their skills of using and applying calculation, including using decimals and a calculator.

Sally began the sessions with exploring the *Financial Times* and she set the children the task of spending a fantasy £100 on shares. Having explained in a simple manner to the children the way in which share-dealing worked, she gave them free choice in the spending of their £100. The children selected which shares to buy based on their own interests and understanding of the stock market. Sally explained to them that they would return to the index in six weeks to see who had made the most money.

The children worked from photocopied pages of the *Financial Times* and discussions followed in relation to the possible strategies that could be used, such as placing all your money on one stock, buying the cheapest or buying what you know. Sally noticed how all the children in class remained focused and she noticed that there was a high level of engagement in each ability group.

Commentary

The real life information from the *Financial Times* clearly has caught the children's attention, and they are highly engaged with the process of spending a fantasy £100 on things that are *meaningful to them*. It would appear that most of the children were motivated by the element of competition, and the (imaginary) monetary reward, which seems to confirm Aunola et al.'s (2006) suggestion that children will not fully engage if they do not value the activity *even if they believe they have the ability to deal with the task*. In Case Study 6.3, even those children in lower ability groups, who may have felt insecure about their mathematics skills, were engaged with the task because they saw personal value in it.

While it is important that children are motivated by activities, it is also important to remember that the activities in themselves have mathematical value. In this case, the skills used were: using all four operations to solve money or 'real life' word problems, choosing appropriate operations and calculation methods, using inverse operation and rounding up or down depending on the context. The children were required to use decimal notation for tenths and hundredths and were expected to know what each digit represents. They also developed their calculator skills in processing the necessary calculations of total spend and balance, and prediction of gain at the end of the six-week period.

Case Study 6.3 highlights how real life information can be used to create meaningful mathematical activities that engage and inspire pupils. The teacher purposefully created the activity with 'enrichment and enjoyment' as a key focus. Aunola et al. (2006) infer that teachers have a pivotal role in increasing motivation in mathematical learning and have observed that 'mathematical related task motivation increases in those classrooms where teachers emphasize motivation or self concept development as their most important pedagogical tool' (Aunola et al. 2006: 21). Barnes (2012: 250) builds on this by cautioning us that enjoyment should not be the only aim of education, although it can help 'build motivations towards new and deep learning', reminding us that teachers should aim for excellence in learning as well.

Reflection

Consider possible strategies and activities that you could draw from to increase children's motivation in mathematical learning. How can you ensure that these activities would also produce excellence in mathematics?

Summary

Most children benefit greatly if they are taught by educators who think deeply and creatively about how mathematics is presented and taught. Providing children with mathematical activities that are meaningful to them and that evoke a positive emotional response helps to inspire and motivate them, assists them in remaining focused and ensures they enjoy their learning.

Prescriptive curricular requirements can suggest a compartmentalized approach to both teaching and learning, but as our case studies show, effective planning can help reduce compartmentalization, and provide opportunities for what we have called 'real and purposeful' mathematics experiences for children. Taking mathematics teaching beyond the traditional mathematics classroom does not have to dilute the effective teaching (and learning) of mathematical concepts and skills. Indeed, as a range of research, and our own case studies show, it is likely to enhance both skills and concept development.

Further reading

Fox, S. and Surtees, L. (2010) *Mathematics Across the Curriculum: Problem-Solving, Reasoning and Numeracy in Primary Schools*. London: Continuum.

This book is focused on teaching mathematical concepts through different subjects. The discussion will allow you to explore the reasoning and research which underpins problem-solving and investigation techniques, while the case studies will allow you to consider ways of integrating working in this way into your own classroom practice.

Skinner, C. (2005) *Maths Outdoors*. London: Beam Education.

This very practical book gives ideas of how a numeracy-rich outdoor mathematics environment can be created for young children. It gives ideas for resources, activities to support and assess mathematical development, outdoor maths games and maths trails, problem solving in the outdoor environment and using maths in context.

References

Aunola, K., Leskinen, E. and Nurmi, J. (2006) Developmental dynamics between mathematical performance, task motivation, and teachers' goals during the transition to primary school. *British Journal of Educational Psychology* 76 (1): 21–40.

Barnes, J. (2011) *Cross Curricular Learning 3–14* (2nd edn). London: Sage.

Barnes, J. (2012) An introduction to cross curricular learning. In P. Driscoll, A. Lambirth and J. Roden (eds) *The Primary Curriculum: A Creative Approach*. London: Sage.

Barnes, J. and Shirley, I. (2007) Strangely familiar: Cross curricular and creative thinking in teacher education. *Improving Schools* 10 (2): 289–306.

Central Advisory Council for Education (1967) *Children and their Primary Schools* (Plowden Report). London: HMSO.

Chinn, S. (2009) Mathematics anxiety in secondary students in England. *Dyslexia* 15 (1): 61–8.

Cockcroft, W.H. (1982) *Mathematics Counts: Report of the Committee of Inquiry into the Teaching of Mathematics in Schools* (Cockcroft Report). London: HMSO. Available at www.educationengland.org.uk/documents/cockcroft/ (accessed 31 January 2012).

Cohen, L., Manion, L. and Morrison, K. (2004) *A Guide to Teaching Practice* (5th edn). London: Routledge.

Craft, A. (2000) *Creativity across the Primary Curriculum: Framing and Developing Practice*. London: Routledge.

Department for Children, Schools and Families (DCSF) (2008) *Statutory Framework for the Early Years Foundation Stage*. Nottingham: DCSF.

Department for Education (DfE) (2011) *The Framework for the National Curriculum: A Report by the Expert Panel for the National Curriculum Review*. London: DfE. Available at www.education.gov.uk/publications/standard/publicationDetail/Page1/DFE-00135-2011 (accessed 30 January 2012).

Department for Education and Employment (DfEE) (1999) *The National Numeracy Strategy*. London: DfEE.

Department for Education and Employment (DfEE) and Qualifications and Curriculum Authority (QCA) (1999) *The National Curriculum Handbook for Primary Teachers in England*. London: DfEE and QCA. Available at www.education.gov.uk/schools/teachingandlearning/curriculum/primary/b00199044/mathematics/ks1 (accessed 30 May 2012).

Department for Education and Skills (DfES) (2006a) *Learning Outside the Classroom Manifesto*. Nottingham: DfES.

Department for Education and Skills (DfES) (2006b) *Primary Framework for Literacy and Mathematics*. Nottingham: DfES.

Dewey, J. (1998) *Experience and Education: The 60th Anniversary Edition.* West Lafayette, IN: Kappa Delta Pi.

Dixon, P. (2005) *Let Me Be: A Book for Parents, Teachers and all those Concerned about Early Years Education.* Winchester: Peche Luna.

Donaldson, D. (2007) Inner city spaces. In R. Austin (ed.) *Letting the Outside In: Developing Teaching and Learning Beyond the Early Years Classroom.* Stoke-on-Trent: Trentham Books.

Donaldson, G. (2012) An introduction to mathematics. In P. Driscoll, A. Lambirth and J. Roden (eds) *The Primary Curriculum: A Creative Approach.* London: Sage.

Driscoll, P., Lambirth, A. and Roden, J. (eds) (2012) *The Primary Curriculum: A Creative Approach.* London: Sage.

Dunne, R. (2010) Interview. In H. Ward, Must trig harder: How can we make maths count in primaries? *TES Newspaper*, 26 March. Available at www.tes.co.uk/article.aspx?storycode=6039830 (accessed 28 May 2012).

Edgington, M. (2002) High levels of achievement for young children. In J. Fisher (ed.) *The Foundations of Learning.* Buckingham: Open University Press.

Fisher, J. (2008) *Starting from the Child.* Maidenhead: Open University Press.

Fox, S. and Surtees, L. (2010) *Mathematics across the Curriculum: Problem-Solving, Reasoning and Numeracy in Primary Schools.* London: Continuum.

Gillard, D. (2004) 'The Plowden Report': Encyclopaedia of Informal Education. Available at www.infed.org/schooling/plowden_report.htm (accessed 31 January 2012).

Greenwood, R. (2007) Geography teaching in Northern Ireland primary schools: A survey of content and cross-curricularity. *International Research in Geographical and Environment Education* 16 (4): 380–98.

Jacobs, H. (2004) *Interdisciplinary Curriculum, Design and Implementation.* Heatherton, VIC: Hawker Brownlow Education.

Lewis, A. (1994) *Discovering Mathematics with 4 to 7 Year Olds.* London: Hodder & Stoughton.

Linklater, H. (2006) Listening to learn: Children playing and talking about the Reception year of Early Years education in the UK. *Early Years* 26 (1): 63–78.

Martlew, T., Stephen, C. and Ellis, J. (2011) Play in the primary school classroom? The experience of teachers supporting children's learning through a new pedagogy. *Early Years* 31 (1): 71–83.

Mitchell, T. (1999) Changing student attitudes towards mathematics. *Primary Educator* 5 (4): 2–7.

Morrison, K. and Ridley, K. (1988) *Curriculum Planning and the Primary School*. London: Paul Chapman.

Nunes, T., Byrant, P., Sylva, K. and Barros, R. (2009) *Development of Maths Capabilities and Confidence in Primary School*. DCSF Research Report 118. London: DCSF.

Office for Standards in Education (Ofsted) (2002) *The Curriculum in Successful Primary Schools*. London: Ofsted.

Office for Standards in Education (Ofsted) (2010) *Learning Creative Approaches that Raise Standards*. Nottingham: Ofsted.

Peters, S. and Kelly, J. (2011) Exploring children's perspectives: Multiple ways of seeing and knowing the child. *Waikato Journal of Education* 16 (3): 19–30.

Piaget, J. (1976 [1929]) *The Child's Conception of the World*. Savage, MD: Littlefield Adams.

Samuelsson, I.P. and Johansson, E. (2009) Why do children involve teachers in their play and learning? *European Early Childhood Education Research Journal* 17 (1): 77–94.

Skinner, E., Furrer, C., Marchand, G. and Kindermann, T. (2008) Engagement and disaffection in the classroom: Part of a larger motivational dynamic? *Journal of Educational Psychology* 10 (4): 765–81.

Sparrow, L. (2008) Real and relevant mathematics: Is it realistic in the classroom? *Australian Primary Mathematics Classroom* 13 (2): 4–8.

Turner, S. and McCullough, J. (2004) *Making Connections in Primary Mathematics*. London: David Fulton.

Tzuo, P.W. (2007) The tension between teacher control and children's freedom in a child-centered classroom: Resolving the practical dilemma through a closer look at the related theories. *Early Childhood Education Journal* 35 (1): 33–39.

van Oers, B. (2009) Emergent mathematical thinking in the context of play. *Educational Studies in Mathematics* 74 (1): 23–37.

7 Learning difficulties in mathematics

Carol Rushworth-Little

Introduction

> Dyscalculia is a problematic area for educators, not only because evidence is complex and contested, but also because it comes from scientific disciplines like neuro-psychology, with different theoretical perspectives and research methodologies. Some of these have implicit assumptions which conflict with current theories of mathematics learning.
>
> (Gifford 2006: 36)

Many children have difficulties with some or many aspects of arithmetic, failing to make the expected progress in mathematics. A significant number of pupils have severe and specific difficulties which are sometimes described as dyscalculia. This chapter explores existing research and literature about dyscalculia and mathematical learning difficulties and raises awareness of the difficulties experienced by certain pupils that can impact upon their mathematical learning and development.

Chapter aims

This chapter discusses possible indicators and learning behaviours of pupils which, excluding language difficulties, are associated with a learning difficulty in mathematics. These are discussed through a case study which compares the observed learning behaviours and characteristics exhibited by pupils who have been identified as having a mathematical learning difficulty, to those characteristics identified by teachers. The aims of this chapter are to:

- Increase knowledge of current research around dyscalculia and mathematical learning difficulties

- Develop a wider understanding of factors that can affect mathematical learning
- Encourage teachers of mathematics to track back and delve deeper into the underlying issues that may be presenting stumbling blocks in learners' mathematical development.

The mathematics curriculum and children's learning

Within the *Independent Review of Mathematics Teaching in Early Years Settings and Primary Schools* (Williams 2008) is a section on under-attainment in mathematics in primary schools in England identifying that, despite the introduction of the National Numeracy Strategy (NNS) in 1999, around 6 per cent of pupils each year fail to achieve a National Curriculum level 3 in mathematics by the time they leave the primary sector.

It is not a specifically English phenomenon; individual differences in arithmetic among pupils of the same age are also very great in most other countries (Dowker 2004).

The term 'mathematics' encompasses a wide range of interconnected skills and knowledge that, at primary school level, include number, using and applying, organizing and using data, and shape, space and measure.

While it is recognized that pupils can experience difficulties in learning in any (or all) of these mathematical strands, the term 'mathematical learning difficulty' is commonly used to describe those pupils who have significant difficulty with number.

In recent years, the term 'dyscalculia' has been introduced to describe the inability to acquire arithmetic skills and understand simple number concepts. There is ongoing debate surrounding the dyscalculia label, with dispute and lack of consensus between academics and researchers not only on cause and identification of dyscalculia but also on definition. While the discussion more comfortably resides with the academics, it is important for the educator, while focusing on supporting the struggling learner, and coping with parental pressure for diagnosis, to have an insight into current, research-informed perspectives.

Conceptual and theoretical perspectives: dyscalculia

Defining dyscalculia or mathematical learning difficulty

The term developmental dyscalculia was introduced by psychologist Ladislav Kosc in 1974. Subsequent studies have used different terms to describe what would appear to be the same difficulties (Geary and Hoard 2001) including 'mathematical disability', 'arithmetic learning disability', 'number fact disorder' and 'psychological difficulties in mathematics'. There is ongoing debate as to what dyscalculia is and whether or when the term should be used. Some regard it as a brain-based disorder, involving abnormal function of those areas which are known to be involved in number and arithmetic. Others regard it in functional terms involving specific and severe mathematical difficulties without reference to a cause. In 2001 the DfES published a definition that involved identifying characteristics that describe the learning difficulty:

> a condition that affects the ability to acquire arithmetical skills. Dyscalculic learners may have difficulty understanding simple number concepts, lack an intuitive grasp of numbers and have problems learning number facts and procedures. Even if they produce a correct answer or use a correct method, they may do so mechanically and without confidence.
>
> (DfES 2001: 2)

This has become an accepted definition of dyscalculia within the UK although some consider that its manifestation is simply the lower end of the continuum of ability or achievement in mathematics (Dowker 2009).

Prevalence of dyscalculia

As there is no universally agreed definition of dyscalculia, there is a range of figures given for the prevalence of dyscalculia or specific mathematics learning difficulties. However, a large number of studies put the figure at about 6 per cent. Some quick arithmetic will identify that this is equivalent to 1 or 2 children in an average class of 30 pupils. Clearly this has major implications for every class teacher.

Reflection

Consider the fact that in an average class of 30 children it is likely that 2 pupils will have significant difficulty in understanding simple number concepts, will lack an intuitive grasp of numbers and will experience problems learning number facts and procedures.

What indicators might help you, as a teacher, to identify those pupils?

Identifying a dyscalculic pupil

The British Dyslexia Association (BDA) identifies behavioural commonalities or characteristics that can increase our understanding of the learning difficulties experienced by dyslexic pupils. It would be helpful if such a list of indicators existed for dyscalculia. Despite the lack of agreement surrounding this mathematical learning difficulty, Ronit Bird, a teacher of dyscalculic pupils, included the following list of indicators in her 'Dyscalculia Toolkit' published in 2007 (reproduced here with permission from Sage Publications).

Indicators for dyscalculia are:

- An inability to subitize (see without counting) even very small quantities
- An inability to estimate whether a numerical answer is reasonable
- Weaknesses in both long-term and short-term memory
- An inability to count backwards reliably
- A weakness in visual and spatial orientation
- Directional left/right confusion
- Slow processing speeds when engaged in mathematics activities
- Trouble with sequencing
- A tendency not to notice patterns
- A problem with all aspects of money
- A marked delay in learning to read a clock to tell the time
- An inability to manage time in their daily lives.

(Bird 2007)

A number of these characteristics could also describe a dyslexic pupil who has difficulty in acquiring mathematics skills and research suggests that there is an overlap or co-occurrence of dyscalculia with other learning difficulties, including dyslexia, dyspraxia and attention deficit hyperactivity disorder (ADHD) (Geary 2004).

It would be unwise to unquestioningly accept Bird's (2007) indicators of dyscalculia without exploring other perspectives. Consequently, the remainder of this chapter is divided into two sections; the first section looks at each of Bird's descriptors, identifies research that relates to it, and considers its impact on mathematical learning and development. The second section uses a case study to explore which characteristics were most commonly observed in pupils with a mathematical learning difficulty and compares these results with the indicators of dyscalculia that were most commonly identified by teachers.

What we know about indicators of dyscalculia or a mathematical learning difficulty

In this section, Bird's (2007) indicators of dyscalculia are examined in turn and discussed with reference to current research and theory.

An inability to subitize even very small quantities

Subitizing refers to the ability to look at a random cluster of objects or dots and know how many are there, without counting. Most adults can subitize between five and seven items.

A study that involved matching displays of dots found that dyscalculic children needed to count the number of dots whereas non-dyscalculic children could recognize the threeness of three without counting (Koonz and Berch 1996). It is believed that this fundamental capacity, recognizing small numerosities without counting (subitizing), could be tied to a child's understanding of number. Butterworth's (1999) work similarly shows that dyscalculic pupils lack the ability to subitize and he refers to this as part of 'the missing starter kit'.

Reflection

As teachers we need to be aware that, while the majority of pupils can 'see' that there are more dots on the right than there are on the left, some pupils will have to count how many dots are on each side of the diagram and then use their knowledge of number to identify the larger quantity. Consequently, the time required to complete what we consider to be a relatively simple task is greatly increased.

An inability to estimate whether a numerical answer is reasonable

Some pupils lack skills in estimation due to lack of experience in doing so in both the social and educational context. It is suggested that embedding 'real life' contexts into the teaching of mathematical concepts supports those pupils who do not make the intrinsic link between what happens in a mathematics lesson to the everyday arithmetic problems encountered in the world outside.

Weaknesses in both long-term and short-term memory

In identifying the impact of memory weakness upon mathematical learning, it is helpful to use a simplistic dual-store memory model (Atkinson and Shiffrin 1968).

In this model, long-term memory is recognized as a limitless storing of associations among items, while short-term memory is seen as a temporary storage system that holds items for around 20–30 seconds.

Weak long-term semantic memory

To be successful in basic mathematics pupils are required to remember a huge variety of facts and concepts. It is necessary to recall:

- written symbols, e.g. $+$, $-$, $\times$, $\div$, $=$ and the processes that they represent
- a large number of basic number facts such as $3 + 7 = 10$, $10 \times 6 = 60$, double 8 is 16.

Good long-term memory is also required for recall and application of procedural rules.

Geary (2004) found that many children with mathematics learning difficulties (MLD) had difficulties in retrieving basic arithmetic facts from long-term memory and this tended not to improve over time.

Reflection

Teachers frequently describe a pupil as having mathematical difficulties because 'he can't remember his times tables' or 'she doesn't even know the number bonds of 10'. When we test or assess a pupil in mathematics, does the test reflect their overall arithmetic ability or is it weighted in favour of the ability to quickly retrieve number facts from memory?

Weak short-term memory

Short-term memory can be regarded as the system for temporarily storing and managing information required to carry out complex cognitive tasks such as learning, reasoning and comprehension. Short-term memory can receive information from both visual and auditory input.

The most universally accepted model of *working memory* is that proposed by Baddeley (1986). Working memory is comprised of one supervising system, the central executive and two modality-specific storage systems, the phonological loop (auditory short-term memory) and the

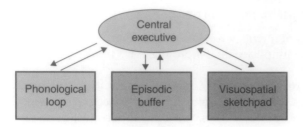

Figure 7.1 A simplified model of working memory

visuospatial sketchpad (visual short-term memory). The phonological loop is specialized for the storage and rehearsal of speech-based verbal information (Baddeley 1992), whereas the sketchpad is specialized for holding visual and spatial material (Logie 1986). See Figure 7.1.

It has been shown that working memory deficits in both the phonological and visuospatial domains contribute to mathematics difficulties (Wilson and Swanson 2001).

In a typical test of auditory memory span, an examiner reads a list of random digits aloud at the rate of one digit per second. At the end of a sequence, the person being tested is asked to recall the items in order. It is suggested that the number of items or digits that a child is able to hold in short-term memory aligns to their age in years up to the age of 7: an average 2-year-old will be able to retain two digits, an average 5-year-old five digits and so on. This appears to reach a ceiling at 7 years of age, with the average retention of digits for adults currently placed at seven.

The case study section of this chapter found that the majority of pupils identified as having a mathematical learning difficulty were unable to hold more than four digits in short-term auditory memory.

An element of *working memory* is the phonological loop where words are temporarily held while they are part of a process, such as adding numbers.

Reflection

Consider the difficulties experienced by pupils who are unable to hold more than four digits in short-term memory when they are participating in a fast paced oral and mental session that requires them to add two 2-digit numbers, such as 'What is the sum of 28 and 36?'

Working memory will be overloaded with the retention and recall of the digits and consequently the process of adding those numbers becomes impossible.

- How might the pupils respond?
- What can teachers do to support pupils with weak short-term memory skills?

Poor working memory in the visuospatial domain may result in an unreliable visuospatial sketchpad which will affect mathematical working not due to lack of understanding but because of mistakes when copying or transferring data.

Recent studies in Finland (Kyttälä et al. 2010) identified that children with mathematical difficulties performed less well than age-related peers in all areas of working memory but *specifically* the visuospatial working memory.

An inability to count backwards reliably – sequencing

Although Bird (2007) suggests that an inability to count backwards reliably is an indicator of dyscalculia, this is not a widely acknowledged characteristic. Chinn and Ashcroft (2007) note that it is not uncommon to identify children who find counting backwards difficult; however, their findings link this difficulty to the dyslexic learner, which resonates with Butterworth and Yeo's (2004) findings of co-occurrence.

Directional left/right confusion

Directional confusion is a recognized characteristic of dyslexia and/or dyspraxia. The lack of directional consistency in mathematics can be the cause of major difficulty and confusion for a number of learners.

Consider the written sequence of the number 14, where the order, when the number is spoken, would seem to imply 4 followed by 10 but in fact means one ten followed by four units and is represented in that order, 14. Thus we write the number in the reverse *direction* to that in which it is said. (We say four ten but write ten four.) However, when the pupil moves beyond 'teen' numbers that rule changes; forty-two, representing four tens followed by two units, is represented as 42. (We say four tens and two and write it in the same order.) This time the direction is not reversed.

There is also a lack of consistency in the direction in which procedures are performed.

Consider the following two calculations and the confusion that could be experienced due to the directional inconsistency of written procedures. Let us explore two examples. First, the calculation $252 + 12$.

Procedure: align the numbers so that the first is *above* the second. Carry out the column addition procedure working *from the right to the left* and write the answer *underneath* the calculation.

$$
\begin{array}{r}
2\,5\,2 \\
+1\,2 \\
\hline
2\,6\,4
\end{array}
$$

Next, the calculation $252 \div 12$.

Procedure: align the numbers so that the first comes before the second on the same line. Carry out the division procedure working *from left to right* and write the answer *above* the calculation:

$$
\frac{2\,1}{12\,|\,2\;5^{1}2}
$$

This lack of consistency in direction of basic procedures can be the source of considerable confusion for pupils with directional difficulties.

Slow processing speed when engaged in mathematics activities

Chinn's (1995) study compared the average time to stop work on 21 basic numeracy questions for a mainstream school population and a specialist dyslexia school population, and found that, on average, dyslexic learners took 50 per cent longer to stop attempting the task. The major focus of Chinn's (1995) work has been upon the mathematics difficulties experienced by dyslexic pupils; although Butterworth and Yeo (2004) propose that dyscalculia is best understood in terms of a specific numerical processing deficit, they allow that dyscalculic pupils may have problems with the speed at which they process numbers.

Trouble with sequencing

Sequencing difficulties have long been identified as characteristics of the dyslexic learner (Williams 2008).

Sharma (2003) believes that one of the manifestations of dyscalculia can be difficulty in following sequential directions and sequencing – including reading numbers out of sequence, substitutions, reversals, omissions and doing operations backwards.

Sequencing difficulties will affect a pupil's ability to recognize patterns in common number sequences such as odd and even numbers.

A tendency not to notice patterns

Pattern is at the heart of mathematical learning and understanding, with the ability to 'see' a pattern leading onto the more advanced concept of generalization. As many mathematical concepts are usually more easily understood if they can be associated with a visual image, impairment in the visuospatial sketchpad could result in the inability to notice visual sequences in number. Hannell (2005) suggests that pupils with dyscalculia may not use visual images effectively and may find reasoning that depends upon spatial reasoning difficult to understand. Similar, measurement, shape and space have a direct link to visuospatial abilities; weaknesses in this area could result in the inability to see patterns not only in number but also in shape.

Reflection

There are a number of reasons why a pupil may have difficulties with certain areas of mathematics. As teachers we see the 'result' of that difficulty (e.g. an inability to recognize pattern within the five times table) but when we are trying to unpick the 'cause' of the problem would we necessarily link it to an inability to 'see' patterns generally? How might we test that ability?

Difficulties experienced with understanding money and time

Bird's (2007) final three indicators can be regarded as presentational effects of dyscalculia rather than an underlying difficulty. Difficulties in handling and using money have been highlighted by a number of researchers who have worked with dyscalculic individuals. Sharma (1990) identifies difficulties found in handling a bank account, giving and receiving change and tipping. These findings are supported by Butterworth and Yeo (2004), who state that dyscalculics find it difficult to work with money and often find that shopping is a humiliating experience. They also comment on the difficulties presented by everyday planning, as those with dyscalculia struggle to learn to tell the time.

Emotional response to mathematics

One aspect of dyscalculia upon which all researchers seem to agree is the negative emotional impact that it has on those who live with the learning difficulty.

Butterworth and Yeo (2004) identify that most dyscalculic pupils do not enjoy number work, feel discouraged in mathematics lessons and as a consequence many develop avoidance strategies. They believe that the lack of understanding of peers, parents and teachers can lead to mathematics anxiety, which further undermines their ability in making sense of numbers. Chinn and Ashcroft (2007) affirm this and suggest that it is the 'uniquely judgemental nature of mathematics, often exacerbated by those who design teaching programmes and those who actually teach mathematics that makes mathematics a topic that creates negative attributional style in so many students (and thus in adults)' (Chinn and Ashcroft 2007: 33).

Indicators of dyscalculia or a mathematical learning difficulty – report from a case study

This section looks at research conducted in 2009 and 2010. The aim of the study was to identify pupil indicators or learning behaviours associated with a specific mathematical learning difficulty or dyscalculia and to compare these observed characteristics with those identified by teachers. These characteristics were aligned to Bird's (2007) indicators of dyscalculia.

Context

The study focused upon 44 pupils identified as having specific learning difficulties linked to mathematics, and a group of 36 teachers and teaching assistants. Pupils with global learning difficulties were not included within the study. The group of 24 females and 20 males were aged between 7 and 16 years of age (31 primary school pupils and 13 secondary school pupils). I carried out the observed element of the research – assessing and recording mathematical understanding and difficulties through means of a diagnostic assessment test in a one-to-one situation. Throughout the assessment pupils were encouraged to explain their methods and reasoning both verbally and through written methods and jottings.

The group of teachers and teaching assistants (hitherto called 'teachers') was comprised of 4 teachers from the primary phase and 12 from the secondary phase of education. These teachers were asked to identify a typical profile of a pupil who they perceived as having a specific learning difficulty in mathematics and then to answer 11 questions with that pupil in mind. The questions were drawn from Bird's indicators of dyscalculia but with the omission of 'ability to manage time in daily life' as it was felt that teachers would not be able to comment with certainty upon this.

Results – an overview

The results of significant behavioural characteristics identified by observation of pupils are shown in Table 7.1 as are those regarded as significant

Table 7.1 Most common behavioural characteristics identified through observation

Behavioural characteristics	Observed	Identified by teaching staff
Pupil does not have a good short-term memory	84 per cent	31 per cent
Pupil is unable to identify number sequences	61 per cent	36 per cent
Pupil has slow processing speeds when engaged in maths activities	57 per cent	69 per cent
Pupil never notices pattern in number and shape	55 per cent	31 per cent
Pupil does not have the ability to make a reasonable estimate	52 per cent	61 per cent

by teachers. The purpose of this is to identify how closely the two sets of data align.

The highlighted characteristics are those that were identified as significant (greater than 50 per cent) both in observation of pupils and as recognized by teachers.

The significant behavioural characteristics identified by my observation of, and guided discussion with pupils, are identified in Table 7.1 in order of frequency of observed occurrence

The significant learning behaviours identified by teaching staff are listed in Table 7.2 in order of frequency.

Table 7.2 Most common behavioural characteristics identified by teaching staff

Behavioural characteristics	Observed	Identified by teaching staff
Pupil has slow processing speeds when engaged in maths activities	57 per cent	69 per cent
Pupil lacks the ability to estimate whether a numerical answer is reasonable	52 per cent	61 per cent
Pupil lacks the ability to count backwards reliably	30 per cent	53 per cent

Reflection

Take a moment to look again at the results in Table 7.1 and Table 7.2 and consider the correlation between characteristics that were identified as most common by teachers and the incidences of those observed. How does this relate to your perception and understanding of pupils with mathematical difficulties?

Results in greater detail

The results of the study highlighted seven significant features.

Weak short-term memory

Weak short-term memory skills was the most frequently observed characteristic of pupils but was identified as a problem by only 31 per cent of teaching staff. About 84 per cent of pupils, when tested on auditory recall of digits, achieved below age appropriate recall, yet only 31 per cent of the teachers perceived weak short-term memory as a characteristic of such pupils. In particular, there is a distinct lack of correlation between staff perception and pupil demonstration in this area for pupils of secondary school age; 12 out of 13 of these pupils had weak short-term memory but only 4 out of 12 of secondary phase teaching staff identified this as a characteristic.

Emma, aged 16, articulated the difficulty and frustration that she felt when asked to recall a five-digit sequence.

'When I see a maths problem written down that's not so bad but mental maths is a problem. When you gave me those numbers, just now, I could see them all in my head for a split second, then they all just sort of merged together and I couldn't remember any of them.'

It would appear that there is a lack of awareness of both the existence and impact of weak short-term memory upon arithmetic or mathematical competency in many teachers.

Difficulties in spotting patterns in number and shape

A significant number (55 per cent) of the pupils exhibited difficulties in spotting patterns in both number and shape. However, only 31 per cent of teachers identified this as an indicator of dyscalculia.

> Joe, aged 8, has difficulty in spotting patterns in numbers. His teacher expressed concern that he could not see the pattern in the five times table.
>
> 'We've laid out number cards with multiples of 5 on them up to 50 and then got Joe to make each of the numbers using base 10 equipment so that he can see an image of the 10s and 5s that make up the pattern but he just doesn't seem to get it.'

I tested Joe to see if the inability to 'see' a pattern was linked specifically to number, or also to shape, by placing a repeated pattern of coloured pegs in a line and asking Joe to continue the pattern. He was able to continue a repeated pattern of red, yellow, red, yellow pegs but consistently failed to repeat patterns of three colours. The relatively small percentage of teachers identifying pattern spotting difficulties as a characteristic of dyscalculia could possibly be attributed to the limiting nature of the DfES (2001) definition of dyscalculia focusing specifically on number difficulties and not linking these to difficulties in spatial sense. Thus, a pupil who has difficulty in noticing patterns within shape could be displaying dyscalculic characteristics.

Reflection

Spotting pattern in both number and shape underpins the development and understanding of many mathematical concepts. Has the focus on identification of dyscalculia as being linked solely to number difficulties contributed to a lack of recognition of underlying visuospatial difficulties?

Inability to identify number sequences

61 per cent of pupils exhibited difficulty in identifying simple number sequences. Despite the fact that only 1 of the 12 secondary school teachers perceived that pupils had difficulty identifying number sequences, in actuality, 7 of the 13 secondary aged pupils could not identify odd and even numbers to 20.

Jenny, aged 13, said:

'I learned this in First School. If you pair your fingers then you get the even numbers – it doesn't really work after 10.'

Jenny can recite her two times table to 20 but makes no connection between this and pairing her fingers.

Chinn and Ashcroft (2007) claim that dyslexic pupils are unable to automatize many mathematical number sequences. Thus it would seem likely that if a pupil has a specific learning difficulty that impacts upon mathematical ability, be it dyslexia or dyscalculia, then an ability to recognize number sequences is certainly an identifiable characteristic.

Slow processing speeds when engaged in mathematics activities

Pupil reponse time when attempting ability-appropriate mathematical progress tests were noted. Results showed that 57 per cent of pupils required at least 50 per cent extra time to complete the assessment paper. Staff perception of slow processing speeds in mathematics was high: 75 per cent of primary level teachers and 58 per cent of secondary phase teachers (69 per cent overall) identified slow processing skills in mathematics as an indicator of a specific learning difficulty in this area. It is possible that the National Strategies, with their focus on pacey oral and mental sessions within the mathematics lesson, have heightened teacher awareness of speed of response. This lack of speed in number processing can present difficulties for teachers struggling to adhere to both the attainment and inclusion agendas within education. I once observed the 'oral and mental starter' session of a lower Key Stage 2 mathematics lesson. The focus of the observation was 'including pupils with a Special Educational Need (SEN) within the daily mathematics lesson'. The session had been well planned and the teacher had included questions differentiated by number size, to maximize the participation of the less able. I had the opportunity to focus upon Victoria's responses. Victoria had slow processing speeds in number; however, she had learned the method of calculation and was keen to put up her hand to give the answer. Her solution to the problem was correct; unfortunately the answer that she gave was the correct answer to a problem set two minutes earlier. In this fast paced environment Victoria's success was perceived as failure.

Reflection

- Are you aware of any pupils who have slow processing speeds with number within your class?
- What strategies could you employ to ensure that they have enough time to answer a question correctly?

Inability to estimate

One of the most frequently commented upon characteristics of a pupil with mathematical difficulties was a lack of 'feel' for the size of number.

One primary school teacher described the difficulties of Charlotte, aged 8, as follows:

'It's as though Charlotte is just a random number generator, you know. I ask, 'What number is 1 more than 5?' and she says, '3? No 8. I don't know, 20?' It's as though she's just guessing or using some words that she's heard before.'

Alice, aged 10, also exhibited a lack of understanding of the size of numbers. She was asked to solve the mathematical problem 35 + 27 and to explain her methods

Alice: You write down 35 and then put 27 underneath and then you just add them, so 5 add 7 (*counts on fingers*) is 12. Write it down. Then 3 + 2 is 5.

$$
\begin{array}{r}
3\,5 \\
2\,7+ \\
\hline
5\,12
\end{array}
$$

> **Tester:** So you've got the answer five hundred and twelve. Do you need to check? Does it seem right that thirty-five add twenty-seven is five *hundred* and twelve?
>
> **Alice:** Yes, that's right, that's how we do it.

There may be a number of reasons why Charlotte and Alice, in common with many pupils, respond with unreasonable answers. One of these may be an inability to estimate. The inability to provide a reasonable estimate was perceived as a characteristic of dyscalculia by 61 per cent of teaching staff in the study, whereas results of pupil observation identified 52 per cent of pupils overall having difficulty with estimation. An interesting result of this study was the strong gender bias in the results. There were more than twice as many female pupils unable to estimate than males with 71 per cent of female pupils unable to estimate compared with 35 per cent of male pupils. The results also indicated a perseverance of this difficulty for females across the age ranges, while this was not reflected in the boys' results.

Inability to count backwards reliably

Across the primary and secondary age range, 53 per cent of all teachers recognized that dyscalculic pupils had difficulty in counting backwards. This varied from 63 per cent in the primary phase of education to 33 per cent in the secondary school phase. These teacher perceptions aligned to observed pupil characteristics, where 64 per cent of pupils in the 7.1–8.0 age range were unable to count backwards reliably, whereas only 1 out of 13 pupils (8 per cent) had the same difficulty at secondary school level. This may suggest the possibility of developmental delay rather than a lifelong disability. However, it is also possible that older pupils have had the opportunity to experience a range of learning experiences that have helped in the development of this skill.

Negative emotional response to mathematics

A significant percentage of pupils had a negative emotional response to mathematics; a characteristic that was identified and recognized by teachers.

Discussion around mathematical difficulties with David, a 12-year-old, elicited the following:

David:	One of the reasons that I find this stuff difficult is because of all the supply teachers last year. I got hot-seated a lot so I missed most of the stuff that got taught.
Interviewer:	What's hot-seating all about? I don't think I've come across that.
David:	It's like when you mess about and act up, you get hot-seated and you have to go and work outside the year head's office and they don't set you the work from class. They just give you easy stuff to shut you up – so I didn't learn anything last year.
Interviewer:	Did you get hot-seated a lot the year before?
David:	Not really. I just didn't understand a lot of what was going on.

David's avoidance strategy was to present behavioural difficulties that would have him removed from a situation where there was the potential for his peers to recognize his mathematical difficulties. He believed that recognition for being the 'bad boy' was preferable to being identified as 'stupid'.

Amy, aged 9, had her own avoidance strategies.

Interviewer:	If you had to give a mark out of 10 for independent work in numeracy, that's working just on your own, what would you give that?
Amy:	Probably 3.
Interviewer:	What about working with a partner?
Amy:	Could I choose the partner? (interviewer nods) Well if I could work with Jason he's really good so probably 10.
Interviewer:	What about working in a group?
Amy:	I think not so good, as they wouldn't always listen to what I said, so probably 5.

Amy is not alone in choosing to work with a partner who she identifies as more intelligent, believing that her lack of understanding will be masked. It is interesting to note that she has self-identified her role within a group and believes that her ideas or mathematical suggestions would not be well received.

Reflection

Response to mathematics anxiety or a negative attitude towards mathematics can manifest itself in many ways, often with attempts to mask the emotion. David misbehaves so that he will be removed from the situation, Anna enjoys working with a mathematically stronger partner so that her difficulties are hidden. Can you identify other responses or strategies used by struggling pupils?

Summary

In conclusion, it is suggested that Bird's (2007) list of 'indicators of dyscalculia' should not be regarded as a 'tick list' for the identification, or labelling, of pupils, but more as a starting point in introducing teachers to factors that can present stumbling blocks in mathematical learning and development. Discussion of them in relation to current research helps teachers develop deeper understanding of mathematical difficulties.

The case study highlighted specific areas of shortfall in teacher understanding of difficulties experienced by dyscalculic pupils. Specifically there is a need for teachers to develop a greater understanding of the role that short-term and working memory plays in the ability to store and manipulate numbers mentally. They should also be encouraged to recognize the qualitative nature of dyscalculia that involves difficulty in spatial and visualization sense.

Despite the fact that this chapter has focused on establishing commonalities in the characteristics of a dyscalculic learner, it is important to recognize that no two children with arithmetic difficulties are the same. We need to find out the specific strengths and weaknesses of an individual pupil to enable us to provide appropriate support and to guide our teaching strategies.

The focus of this chapter has been to highlight the underlying difficulties that can affect mathematical progress and to prompt self-reflection on how pedagogy can be modified or improved to support pupils with mathematical difficulties. The Williams Report (2008) recognized that early intervention is a key feature in supporting the mathematical development of under-attaining pupils. It is also widely recognized that a one-to-one remedial intervention, formulated in response to a diagnostic assessment of an individual's strengths and weaknesses, is the most effective way to support those with mathematical learning difficulties. Consequently, there has been no recommendation of any one intervention programme. However, those who wish to familiarize themselves with the effectiveness of intervention schemes may wish to read Dowker's (2009) comprehensive research on this matter.

Further reading

Bird, R. (2007) *Dyscalculia Toolkit* London: Sage.
This is a practitioner's guide to supporting pupils who have a specific learning difficulty in mathematics; it contains a number of teaching strategies and games.
Chinn, S. and Ashcroft, R. (2007) *Mathematics for Dyslexics Including Dyscalculia* (3rd edn). Chichester: Wiley.
A number of the indicators of dyscalculia explored in this chapter have reflected those mathematics difficulties experienced by dyslexic learners. This book provides a background understanding of why dyslexic pupils may have difficulties in mathematics and provides structured ideas for addressing the individual needs of the learner.

References

Atkinson, R.C. and Shiffrin, R.M. (1968) Human memory: A proposal system and its control processes. In K.W. Spence and J.T. Spence (eds) *The Psychology of Learning and Motivation* (Vol. 8). London: Academic Press.
Baddeley, A.D. (1986) *Working Memory*. Oxford: Oxford University Press.
Baddeley, A.D. (1992) Working memory. *Science* 255: 556–9.
Bird, R. (2007) *Dyscalculia Toolkit*. London: Sage.
Butterworth, B. (1999) *The Mathematical Brain*. London: Macmillan.
Butterworth, B. and Yeo, D. (2004) *Dyscalculia Guidance*. London. David Fulton.
Chinn, S. (1995) A pilot study to compare aspects of arithmetic skill. *Dyslexia Review* 4: 4–7.
Chinn, S. and Ashcroft, R. (2007) *Mathematics for Dyslexics Including Dyscalculia* (3rd edn). Chichester: Wiley.
Department for Education and Skills (DfES) (2001) *The Daily Mathematics Lesson: Guidance to Support Pupils with Dyslexia and Dyscalculia*. DfES 0512/2001. London: DfES.

Dowker, A. (2004) *What Works for Children with Mathematical Difficulties.* DfES Research Report RR 554. London: DfES.

Dowker, A. (2009) *What Works for Children with Mathematical Difficulties: The Effectiveness of Intervention Schemes.* DCSF 00086-20096KT-EN. Available at www.nationalnumeracy.org.uk/resources/22/index.html (accessed 26 May 2012).

Geary, D.C. (2004) Mathematics and learning disabilities. *Journal of Learning Disabilities* 37 (1): 4–15.

Geary, D.C. and Hoard, M.K. (2001) Numerical and arithmetical deficits in learning-disabled children: Relation to dyscalculia and dyslexia. *Aphasiology* 15 (7): 635–47.

Gifford, S. (2006) Dyscalculia: Myths and models. *Research in Mathematics Education* 8 (1): 35–51.

Hannell, G. (2005) *Dyscalculia: Action Plans for Successful Learning in Mathematics.* London: David Fulton.

Koontz, K.L. and Berch, D.B. (1996) Identifying simple numerical stimuli: Processing inefficiencies exhibited by arithmetic learning disabled children. *Mathematical Cognition* 2: 1–23.

Kosk, L. (1974) Developmental dyscalculia. *Journal of Learning Disabilities* 7: 159–62.

Kyttälä, M., Aunio, P. and Hautmäki, J. (2010) Working memory resources in young children with mathematical difficulties. *Scandinavian Journal of Psychology* 51: 1–15.

Logie, R.H. (1986) Visuo-spatial processing in working memory. *Quarterly Journal of Experimental Psychology* 38A: 229–47.

Sharma, M. (1990) Dyslexia, dyscalculia and some remedial perspectives for mathematics learning problems. *Mathematics Notebook* 8 (7–10).

Sharma, M. (2003) Skillswise expert column: Dyscalculia. Available at www.bbc.co.uk/skillswise/tutors/expertcolumn/dyscalculia (accessed 16 April 2010).

Williams, P. (2008) *Independent Review of Mathematics Teaching in Early Years Settings and Primary Schools: Final Report.* London: DCSF. Available at http://dera.ioe.ac.uk/8365/1/Williams%20Mathematics .pdf (accessed 10 December 2011).

Wilson, K.M. and Swanson, H.L.(2001) Are mathematics difficulties due to a domain-general or domain-specific working memory deficit. *Journal of Learning Disabilities* 34: 237–48.

8 Highly able children in ordinary classrooms

Lynne McClure

Introduction

Every so often we meet a child whose mathematical behaviour seems significantly more advanced than that of those we usually teach. Depending on whether or not we are confident in our own mathematics, these children can present a major challenge or threat. Whichever, we probably remember them long after they've left our care. In this chapter, we'll look at what we mean by 'advanced ability' in mathematics, how we can tell which children exhibit 'gifted' behaviour and what we might and should do to meet their classroom needs.

Chapter aims

The aims of this chapter are to:

- Examine the characteristics of 'gifted' behaviour and ways to identify them
- Provide examples of this behaviour in the ordinary classroom
- Present possible strategies for enabling, supporting and promoting mathematical thinking both within and outside the school environment
- Indicate where you might find support and resources for the children in your own class.

The mathematics curriculum and children's learning

A word about language

The UK literature on this topic uses a variety of vocabulary: gifted, talented, precocious, promising, exceptionally able, etc., and these labels are usually attached to individual children. In the official literature, gifted and talented children are

> 'those with an ability to develop to a level significantly ahead of their year group (or with the potential to develop those abilities)'. In particular 'gifted' learners are those who have abilities in one or more academic subjects, like maths and English, while 'talented' learners are those who have practical skills in areas like sport, music, design or creative and performing arts.
>
> (Directgov 2012)

Now this rather supposes a model where each person's mathematical ability is fixed, that is, we each possess our own particular information-processing or problem-solving capacity that remains fairly stable throughout our lives and is associated with traditional intelligence or IQ tests (Niesser et al. 1996). There is, however, an alternative view to this: that intelligence is malleable and can be improved or altered by attitudes, behaviour and contexts.

What you believe affects what you do. Dweck (2006) and others found that students who believed that intelligence is malleable (a 'growth mindset') actually learned better than students who believed that intelligence is fixed and unchangeable (a 'fixed mindset'). Students who learned to rely on their ability, whether labelled high or low, reacted differently from those who believed that with effort they could improve what they could do. So let us start by distinguishing between *identifying* aspects of high ability in your pupils, and using that information to *label* the children in your class. The former allows us to make a tailored appropriate response to each pupil, while the latter can lead to a 'one size fits all' approach that may not be suitable for any single individual who has been so labelled. Although the title of this chapter includes the phrase 'highly able children', I'm not advocating that they are a static group. Some will find difficult mathematics easy, others will struggle. The important thing is that if we focus on what they do and the effort they put in, rather than labelling them, we can help them all to become better mathematicians, and what they can do may surprise us if they are given the chance.

Why this is important

> high attaining pupils require greater challenge in lessons: many primary teachers need stronger subject knowledge to do this well...It is of vital importance for pupils of all abilities to shift teaching and learning in mathematics away from a narrow emphasis on disparate skills towards a focus on pupils' mathematical understanding.
>
> (Ofsted 2008)

There are three main reasons for considering why we should pay particular attention to children who exhibit sophisticated mathematical behaviour:

- *Equal opportunities:* all children have the right to achieve as highly as possible. Children who find difficult mathematics easy need to be challenged to work hard to achieve even more, and they need teacher support to do this. 'Able' children are just as entitled to teacher time as those who struggle.
- *Institutional standards:* if we keep our eye on what we know is sophisticated mathematical behaviour, we find ourselves looking for it in *all* our children. In this current climate of questing for ever higher targets, teachers who develop a deeper understanding of what it is to think like a mathematician, and encourage it in all their pupils, raise the standards of the whole class (Her Majesty's Inspectorate (HMI) 1992: viii).
- *National need:* many children who find mathematics easy also find it boring (Nardi and Steward 2003) which means they are unlikely to choose to study it at a higher level. We desperately need top class mathematicians (National Numeracy 2012) for our future prosperity, and the responsibility for inculcating the enthusiasm for that begins in the primary school.

Conceptual and theoretical perspectives: what do we mean by 'highly able' behaviour in mathematics?

Reflection

You might like to think for a moment about a child you are teaching, or have taught recently, whom you would consider to be highly able in mathematics. What is it that they do, or say, that leads you to believe they are better at mathematics than the other children in your class?

Did you use any of the following criteria?

- They always achieve high scores on assessments.
- They appear to learn mathematical content easily and are very accurate in their work.
- They can solve more complicated problems than other children.
- They know far more about a mathematical topic than the other children in the class even before you've introduced it.

Definitions of ability are tied up with our ways of identification and there are probably as many different definitions of high ability in mathematics as there are researchers. The four criteria above all refer to *achieving* an end product – the solution of a particular problem or a high score on a test. You may have found them useful, but most theorists in this area prefer instead to consider the *way* in which such children solve problems; and what kinds of behaviour they exhibit.

Straker (1983) looked at the mathematical behaviour of very young children. In particular she noted the tendency to impose order or pattern, to systemize. For example she describes small children who sort their toys according to unexpected criteria, who seek to impose some pattern or symmetry on the arrangement and who enjoy explaining and justifying their decisions. Straker (1983) suggests that children who exhibit these sorts of early behaviours later develop sophisticated mathematical thinking.

Krutetskii is one of the best known researchers in this field. He wanted to identify aspects of mathematical ability 'in which differences between pupils capable of learning mathematics, and pupils less capable, would be the most striking' (Krutetskii 1976: 84). He began his studies by observing and questioning young secondary aged pupils while they were solving problems. The characteristics he identified are included in Table 8.1.

Krutetskii (1976) distinguished between what he saw as the three stages of problem solving: interpreting, processing and retaining information. He concluded that more able pupils often ended up with a more elegant way of working than others, and this was because they could think flexibly about problems, drawing on their understanding and previous experience of appropriate approaches. How did they do this? Krutetskii (1976) suggested that these pupils saw problems in a different way: he called it 'a mathematical cast of mind' through which they saw the structure of a problem as a logical series of steps or perhaps an image to be manipulated. And because they remembered generalized approaches and chains of reasoning rather than, or as well as, detailed factual knowledge, they were in a good position to apply these in a variety of situations. It is interesting that Krutetskii was not really interested in how well these pupils could remember facts and did not recognize that as indicative of high ability.

Krutetskii (1976) then explored whether able children younger than these had the same characteristic ways of working. He found that children as young as 8 were beginning to work in these ways and that between 8 and 10 there was a noticeable development, especially in generalizing. At this sort of age, able children's mathematics is characterized by moving from describing objects to noticing the relationships between them, and from noticing specific cases towards noticing a general rule. However, Krutetskii did not find much evidence of children at this age remembering generalized approaches or chains of reasoning, or independently using more elegant or shorter ways of working, or working flexibly. Krutetskii (1976: 339) said that young children 'remember the general and the particular, the relevant and the irrelevant, the necessary and the unnecessary', and with maturity this is refined.

Table 8.1 Variation in outcomes from assessments

	High test scores	Lower test scores
Highly able	Usual	Reinterpret the question to fit their own interest. Answers do not fit marking rubric Work exceptionally quickly but not carefully Reading difficulty Uninterested Purposeful failure in order not to appear exceptional; perhaps an effect of peer pressure
Not highly able	Achieved with practice and if test emphasizes procedures and factual recall	Usual

Source: Adapted from Krutetskii (1976)

Other influential researchers in this field who are concerned with high ability generally (rather than specifically in mathematics) include Bloom (1985). Through studying very successful adults, he suggested a three stage development of high ability. In the first 'playful' stage, the individual finds the area of study fascinating and becomes immersed in it. The second 'mastery' phase is characterized by a more ordered exploration in which the individual seeks to make sense of the domain, to clarify the rules. And in the third 'creative' or 'personal style' phase, the individual uses their knowledge of the rules to create something new or different. Gardiner (2002) found that in primary school, most able children are in the first two phases and are unlikely to produce anything unique until they are older.

How can we identify mathematical behaviour?

Summative assessment, i.e. mathematics tests

In the previous section we considered what children say or do that leads us to believe they are able in mathematics. One of the criteria I offered was achieving high scores on assessments. Since formal testing is very common (partly because it is perceived as one of the easier forms of identification), it is worth exploring it first.

The correlation between ability and achievement is, usually, pretty high but we do need to look at those situations when it is not. Children who appear to learn mathematical content easily and are very accurate in their work usually do well in test situations especially where the questions are of a predictable form and can be practised. But do these children exhibit the characteristics identified by researchers such as Krutetskii? Examination of recent Key Stage 2 National Curriculum questions indicates that only occasionally (but more in recent years than previously) are there opportunities to show, for example, chains of reasoning or the use of different strategies to solve a problem. Mostly, the questions are about remembering factual information and applying it (Figures 8.1 and 8.2). So high scores on tests can be achieved by children who are careful and consistent and who have good memories for facts and procedures.

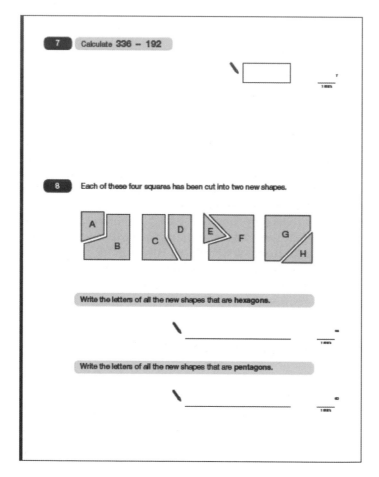

Figure 8.1 Memory of factual information

The opposite is also occasionally true – highly able children sometimes do not do well in tests for a variety of reasons, including misinterpreting the question to make it more challenging!

Formative assessment, i.e. observation, conversation, annotation

Formative assessment is intended to inform future actions and provide detailed information about what a child can and cannot do. Of course that information can be obtained from a test, but tests do not reveal the

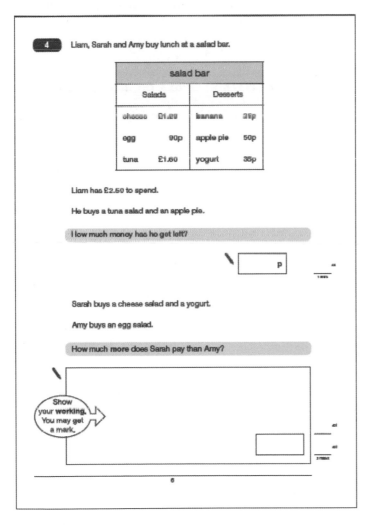

Figure 8.2 Using chains of reasoning

richness of a child's ways of working and why they choose certain strategies. The usefulness of formative assessment may, however, be limited by the sort of activity the child is invited to do. If it is a consolidation worksheet, an observant teacher might discover where a child makes mistakes, or how quickly and carefully they work, but it will not tell much about those chains of reasoning, or thinking flexibly, or the other Krutetskii hallmarks of high ability.

Let us go back to that list of characteristics. We could further refine the sort of task we offer, or the context in which we offer it, by choosing those that specifically target the sort of behaviour we're looking for (Table 8.2).

Most of these characteristics can *only* be identified through problem-solving or investigative activities, and therefore an effective way of identifying high ability is to observe children during lots of opportunities to solve problems and do investigations.

Polya (1990) is known for his seminal work on mathematical problem solving. Figure 8.3 is an adaptation of Polya's problem-solving cycle with Krutetskii's hallmark characteristics inserted. This emphasizes even further how children's work in problem solving and investigation is an essential component in the identification of ability.

Ideally these sorts of activities should be accessible to all children in the class, so that they have opportunities to use more and more sophisticated thinking and perhaps surprise you. At the NRICH project in Cambridge, these are known as 'low threshold high ceiling' activities; we will return to these in the next section to learn more about what useful tools they are in the teacher's toolbox.

In this section, we have explored strategies to identify the mathematical behaviour of highly able pupils. There are of course also batteries of general tests for cognitive ability and non-verbal reasoning, and while a discussion of their relative merits is beyond the scope of this chapter, it is worth finding out more about them (see for example www.psychometric-success.com/faq/faq-cognitive-ability-test.htm).

Models of classroom provision to support mathematical behaviour

Identification in itself is only useful if some appropriate action follows. What strategies might we use to meet the needs of pupils who would benefit from greater challenge? Freeman (1998) identifies two different models – the 'diagnose and treat' model and the 'sports' model – underpinned by opposing philosophies.

In the 'diagnose and treat' model, a definition for high ability is adopted, children who fulfil that definition are identified and labelled as

Table 8.2 Opportunities for identifying mathematical behaviour

Definition or characteristic of mathematical behaviour	Opportunities for encouraging, supporting, identifying
*A liking for numbers	Informal exposure to numbers of different types, including very large, fractions, negative numbers and zero
*Pattern-making revealing balance or symmetry	Free play with groups of regular and irregular objects
*Precision in setting out toys, e.g. teddies in order or size, cars according to colour	
*Using sophisticated criteria for sorting	Free play with objects that could be grouped in lots of different ways, containers for sorting
*Enthusiasm for mathematics	Sharing their personal mathematics
*Using connectives such as 'if', 'because' to question and reason	Judicious questioning: Why did you? How did you know?
*Describing, explaining and justifying their method (chains of reasoning)	Opportunities to refine and rehearse their explanations
**Can understand the 'big picture' of the problem and the necessary processes	Offered problems for which the route is unclear, multistep problems without signposts
**Recognize problems which have similar problem-solving approaches	Offered problems which have the same underlying structure, opportunities to talk about their methods of working
**Have a variety of different methods for solving problems and switch between them	Offered problems for which the route is unclear, multistep problems without signposts
**Work backwards and forwards to solve problems	Offered problems for which the route is unclear, multistep problems without signposts
**Reason logically and link arguments together in chains	Offered problems for which the route is unclear, multistep problems without signposts
**Leave out steps and abbreviate their recording	Given choice of recording media and format
** Use mathematical symbols as part of the thinking process	Encouraged to use their own recording and be introduced to accepted symbolic forms when appropriate

Table 8.2 (*Continued*)

Definition or characteristic of mathematical behaviour	Opportunities for encouraging, supporting, identifying
**Can draw out a generalization, pattern or rule, from several examples **Remember generalizations rather than specific examples	Investigations which have an underlying generalization which is not evident at the start Opportunities to work in depth on longer examples as well as consolidation through shorter examples

Sources: *Straker (1983), **Krutetskii (1976). Adapted from Eyre and McClure (2001: 68)

Represent

Identify the big picture in a problem

Choose a suitable representation

Simplify it using symbols, diagrams, models

Choose an appropriate strategy

Communicate and reflect

Communicate and discuss

Make connections with previous problem and solutions

Consider the elegance and efficiency of the solution

Analyse

Use appropriate procedures

Use appropriate reasoning

Make connections with other problems

Visualize, work systematically, identify patterns and relationships

Explore and conjecture

Interpret and evaluate

Form chains of reasoning and convincing arguments

Find patterns and exceptions

Figure 8.3 Problem solving Cycle 9 (adapted from Piggott (2010) Rich Tasks and Contexts, available at http://nrich.maths.org/5662)

'gifted', 'highly able', 'bright', etc., and are then given a specially devised programme of study. The underlying philosophy here is Dweck's (2004) 'fixed mindset' described at the beginning of this chapter. Schools and teachers who hold this philosophy tend to practise an exclusive model of provision. What might this look like?

Acceleration

The most prevalent 'diagnose and treat' strategy is acceleration. Children who are accelerated in mathematics do the same work as every other child but do it more quickly and therefore meet it earlier. Typically they work with the materials, books and resources usually offered to older children. They may be doing this independently, working alone or in a small group within their usual class. Many older pupils report that they remember primary school as a time where they taught themselves mathematics (with the teacher suggesting they ask for help if they get stuck) but otherwise they plough through the exercises with little intervention. Sometimes such children will be moved into the next class to work with older pupils – this solves the immediate problem for their own teacher. However, if this is a policy in the school, these children are unlikely to be working with the most able as they too will have moved to the next class, and so they will be working with children in the middle of the older ability range.

However, the main problem with acceleration is that it sets up future problems. Gardiner (2002) suggests there are three conditions that should be in place before acceleration is even discussed:

- Children should have absolute mastery of their age-appropriate curriculum.
- Children should be emotionally mature enough to cope with advanced ideas
- A long-term plan for the child's mathematical education should be in place, i.e. they are not accelerated to an abrupt stop.

The problem of maintaining continuity and progression is solvable perhaps within a single institution but can have really damaging effects if primary and secondary schools do not communicate about individual children. There is a whole discussion to be had here about the acceleration of Year 6 children in order to take level 6 tests (recently reintroduced as a result of the Bew (2011) inquiry into Key Stage 2 assessment) and how primary and secondary schools will use the results to respond to individual students' needs.

In Freeman's (1998) alternative 'sports model', teachers offer children activities that require more and more sophisticated thinking – a bit like raising the bar in a high jump. This is indicative of Dweck's (2006) 'growth

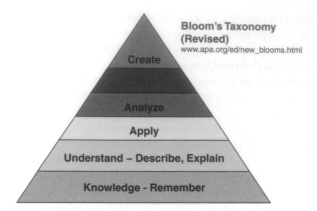

Figure 8.4 Bloom's taxonomy of thinking (Based on an APA adaptation of Anderson and Krathwold (2001)

mindset': we can know what children can do only if we offer them opportunities to show us. This philosophy usually leads to an inclusive curriculum model. In classroom terms what does this mean?

Deepening understanding

Bloom's (1956) taxonomy (Figure 8.4) is often used by teachers as a planning tool. We can also link Bloom's taxonomy back to the problem-solving cycle, and the characteristics of highly mathematical behaviour. By starting with an activity and then extending it to include the higher orders of thinking of analysis, evaluation and synthesis (or creation) teachers are able to offer more sophisticated versions of tasks to children who need more challenge. The interesting thing here is that in order to do this we rarely need to teach children additional content, which means that most children in the class can begin the task but some (perhaps not previously identified) will engage with it at a much higher level – hence an inclusive strategy. This is the origin of the term 'low threshold high ceiling'.

At the NRICH project in Cambridge, we specialize in devising rich tasks, many of which are low threshold high ceiling. We'll explore one of these, 'Magic Vs', in detail later. Low threshold high ceiling tasks:

- are accessible to a wide range of learners
- offer different levels of challenge for all learners
- allow for different methods and different responses (different starting points, different middles and different ends)
- engage the learner in the mathematics either because the starting point is intriguing or the mathematics that emerges is intriguing

- offer opportunities to identify elegant or efficient solutions
- allow learners to pose their own problems
- have the potential to broaden students' skills and/or deepen and broaden mathematical content knowledge
- encourage creativity and imaginative application of knowledge
- have the potential for revealing patterns or lead to generalizations or unexpected results
- have the potential to reveal underlying principles or make connections between areas of mathematics
- encourage collaboration and discussion
- encourage learners to develop confidence and independence as well as to become critical thinkers.

(Adapted from Piggott 2010)

Enriching the curriculum

The word 'enrichment' is used in different ways in the literature. Here I am using it to mean the additional mathematics that children are offered that is outside the core curriculum. This may be through linking mathematics with another subject, such as looking at the history of a particular piece of mathematics, considering the symmetry in the art of the Aztecs or looking for number patterns in musical composition, or alternatively finding out about some mathematics which is of interest but not central to the curriculum, for example the mathematics of codes and ciphers. It would be lovely to think that all children would have the opportunity to study these aspects of mathematics but we know that the curriculum is already too full for most children. Realistically, then, enrichment is usually an exclusive if worthy model.

Reality in the classroom

Of the three models above, we're going to focus here on deepening understanding. By now it should be evident that helping them to think mathematically is important for all children and is a way of increasing challenge. It is of course also central to the current curriculum but is an aspect of mathematics that many teachers find the most difficult. What exactly does 'thinking mathematically' mean?

Cuoco et al. (1997) talk about mathematical 'habits of mind'. They say that children should learn to be 'pattern sniffers, experimenters, tinkerers, visualizers, conjecturers, guessers' and to that we could add 'systematic workers' and 'provers'. Let us explore what this looks like in the classroom.

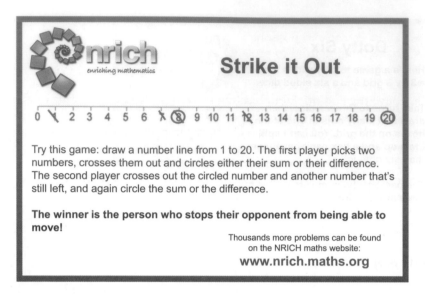

Figure 8.5 Strike it Out

Choosing tasks carefully

Closed procedural tasks rarely allow children to think mathematically. Low threshold high ceiling (LTHC) tasks as described above are those that allow children to move up through Bloom's hierarchy.

Some of these offer consolidation of basic skills or knowledge – which all children need – and combine this with opportunities to develop a strategy or proof, both of which involve working systematically and developing chains of reasoning. For example Strike it Out (Figure 8.5) consolidates addition and subtraction to 20. For many children this will be sufficiently engaging, but those who need more challenge can work towards the longest possible chain of calculations and then be asked whether it is possible to cross all the numbers out – and justify their answer.

Similarly Dotty Six (Figure 8.6) consolidates number bonds to 6, and allows children to develop a winning strategy. With this activity children can also choose to change the rules in some way to make their own game. Making up a good game is actually quite a sophisticated piece of thinking, involving analysis and synthesis, and then evaluation – those higher order skills of Bloom.

Giving children choices in what they do in mathematics is another way of supporting children's mathematical behaviour. Joseph Renzulli is known for his work on the Schoolwide Enrichment Model (Renzulli and Reis 1976), in which he suggests that for children to achieve highly, they

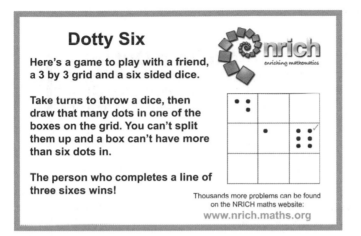

Figure 8.6 Dotty Six

need to be of above average ability, be creative, and be committed to what they want to do, that is, work hard. Renzulli's curriculum model (Renzulli and Reis 1976), used in many North American schools, offers children choices about what they want to study so that they are more likely to be engaged with it.

Longer tasks can be a suitable vehicle for children to gain some independence in mathematics. Most activities in school are started and completed within a short time, but real mathematicians often spend long periods working on one idea or problem. Combining an element of choice with a longer 'simmering' activity can often be very motivating. Dotty Six (Figure 8.6) is a good example of an activity that the children could take home to work on, or pursue in their free time within the school day.

Children who enjoy mathematics do sometimes feel a little left out in the classroom, especially if the ethos is not one of excellence, or if they are significantly more able than anyone else in the class. Part of the role of being a classroom teacher also involves being a 'champion' for children with minority interests or abilities and communicating with them about, for example, mathematics in the news, competitions, and appropriate activities or visits outside school.

Ways of working in the classroom

Facilitating purposeful talk

Any task is only as good as the way it is presented and the context in which it is undertaken. Vygotskian social constructivism suggests that meaning is constructed through interaction with people and through purposeful talk.

> What the research shows consistently is that if you face children with intellectual challenges and then help them talk through the problems towards a solution, then you almost literally stretch their minds. They become cleverer, not only in the particular topic, but across the curriculum.
>
> (Adey 2001)

Recognizing and modelling mathematical processes
In conversations with all children it is important to use mathematical vocabulary to describe not only the content, but also the processes being used (e.g. Cuoco's habits of mind) and to use this terminology when modelling behaviour.

Opportunities to explore
The most usual way of introducing new mathematical content in primary classrooms is through a teacher demonstration, followed by some examples that the children then work through. Ruthven (1989) offers a different structure in which children are given opportunities to explore a new situation – a bit like Bloom's playful phase. This is followed by a teacher-led discussion during which the learning that has taken place is formalized (codified) through sharing and questioning. Then the children work through some examples to consolidate their learning. This cycle of exploration–codification–consolidation requires deep teacher knowledge and a positive and safe classroom climate so that children can take risks in the way they work. It is suitable for all children but especially engaging for those who find mathematics easy.

Asking good questions
Watson and Mason (2004) suggest ideas for opening up questions in order to promote mathematical thinking. Closed questions can confirm what children do or do not know, while open questions help to understand how they think.

Magic Vs

Let us now explore some of the ways in which a classroom activity, Magic Vs, can provide means of supporting gifted and talented learners. A description of the task is punctuated with opportunities for reflection.

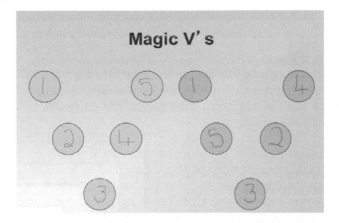

Figure 8.7 Magic Vs

Commentaries are drawn from experience of using this approach in a number of primary classrooms.

Magic Vs (nrich.maths.org/6274) is a typical LTHC task that can be used with children from age 5 upwards. The task begins with identifying what a magic V is, by comparing two Vs (Figure 8.7). The children are asked what is the same and what is different.

Reflection

Do this yourself: identify five similarities and five differences. How is this introduction inclusive?

Commentary

There would be very few children who couldn't identify something the same and different. Some will be simple, others more sophisticated. By listening to others' ideas they develop their own.

The teacher then focuses on the 'magic' V and ensures that everyone is clear about the definition of 'magic', that the two 'arms' add to the same total. Each pair of children are given 15 linking cubes and asked to make towers to show the numbers 1–5. Can they place them to make a different magic V?

Reflection

Do this yourself – if you don't have linked cubes, use other resources. Why have towers been chosen as a preferred resource?

Commentary

The choice of towers rather than random arrays carefully scaffolds children into thinking about the two sides of the V having the same total height. That simplifies to knowing that the two left-hand circles and two right-hand circles must have the same cumulative height, because the apex tower is common to both. The structure would be less clear with random collections and at this stage the activity is intended to be as inclusive as possible. Working in pairs promotes purposeful talk.

The teacher asks pairs if they have found a magic V. Can they find another with a different number at the bottom? How many do they think there are? How do they know they've found them all?

Reflection

How are these questions structured? What sort of responses would you expect? What other questions might you ask?

Commentary

The questions are structured to support increasingly high levels of thinking. Being able to find one magic V requires elementary counting and equivalence. Being able to find another pushes the children's idea of same and different, because many children will rearrange the towers on the arms without changing the bottom number. An idea of how many possible ones there are introduces the idea of working systematically, which is built on in the next question. Answering this requires significantly more sophisticated thinking. If you have done the activity yourself, you will realize that it is only possible to make a magic V with one of the 1, 3 or 5 towers at the apex. Knowing whether all have been found depends on being able to analyse why this is so and developing a convincing chain of reasoning.

The teacher allows the class to continue working until the majority have realized that 1, 3 and 5 have to be at the bottom, then brings the class together. How many magic Vs did we find altogether? Selected children come and record them on the board, with the teacher seeking agreement that each is different from the previous ones. The teacher facilitates a discussion about what constitutes same and different, and that only 1, 3 and 5 can be at the bottom. She asks whether anyone had 2 or 4 and whether it is possible, asking then why not.

Reflection

What is the teacher's role here? What would you do next?

Commentary

The teacher is formalizing the learning that has taken place. Those who are sure of their argument are asked to frame their explanation for others. By the end of this section of the lesson, all the children know that because the towers add up to an odd number there has to be an odd number at the bottom, leaving an even number to be divided between the two arms of the V. Some will have generalized this and others will need consolidation.

Pairs then return to work and given a choice of possible next tasks:

1. Swap towers for number cards and record how many different magic Vs they can make.
2. Predict then confirm, using towers (or number cards) 2, 3, 4, 5 and 6 to make as many different magic Vs as possible.
3. Predict then confirm, using towers (or number cards) 3, 4, 5, 6 and 7 to make as many different magic Vs as possible.
4. Predict then confirm, using towers (or number cards) 1, 2, 3, 4, 5, 6 and 7 to make as many different magic Vs as possible.
5. Be able to make a rule about what number will be at the bottom of any magic V.
6. Make up your own set of numbers for magic Vs.

Reflection

What is the teacher's role here? What sort of responses would identify what types of mathematical thinking?

Commentary

The tasks are designed to scaffold children's thinking. Each requires some additional sophistication. Giving choice allows children to opt in where they feel confident. The teacher's role is to provoke children to explain their thinking by asking questions that will draw them further up the thinking hierarchy.

1. Move from drawing as representation to using symbols, still counting and confirming: consolidation, symbolic representation.
2. Understand that an odd number goes at the bottom for 1–5 but may not know why, trial and improvement to find that an even number is at the bottom this time, try to explain this: consolidation, conjecturing, reasoning.
3. Make a reasoned prediction based on partial explanation, e.g. middle number of set is odd, therefore bottom number must be odd, or making pairs to same total by matching smallest to largest, leaving middle number as bottom: consolidation, conjecturing, reasoning.
4. Make a reasoned prediction based on full explanation: reasoning, conjecturing, generalizing.
5. Can say what numbers should go at the bottom for any consecutive set of numbers, by deciding whether total is odd or even or alternative explanation: reasoning, generalizing, analysing, justifying.
6. Choose a very large set of consecutive numbers, predict correct using argument similar to 5, or choose non-consecutive numbers, e.g. even numbers and predict characteristic of bottom number, or perhaps choose set of very large numbers and generalize without doing arithmetic: analysing, synthesizing, evaluating.

The teacher draws the activity to a close indicating the 'messy maths wall' where findings can be displayed.

Reflection

How might the teacher evaluate this lesson? What is the purpose of the display?

Commentary

The evaluation should be against the objectives of the lesson, which may be about children's increasing confidence working with even and odd numbers, and/or about the processes of generalizing, working systematically and justifying. It could include assessing children's explanatory language. It is a suitable activity to both identify able learners and challenge them, in all primary ages. Some 5 and 6 year olds are capable of very sophisticated thinking, although their recording and justifications may not be so clear.

The display will be added to over the next week, making this a simmering activity. Some children will be very engaged in it and want to continue exploring in their own time. At suitable junctures the teacher will comment on new additions and offer additional prompts so that the children realize that some mathematical problems can be extended to last a long time.

Summary

In this chapter we have examined what is meant by high ability in mathematics. We have considered ways of identifying the behaviour that mathematicians value and how we may be surprised by children if we offer them rich tasks to display their thinking. We have looked at the sort of tasks we might offer and the ways of working that run in parallel with them. As teachers we have a responsibility to all the children in our class and providing appropriately for the most able is important for the children themselves, for us as teachers, and for all our futures

Further reading

McClure, L. (2011) *Low Threshold High Ceiling Tasks in Ordinary Classrooms*. Available at http://nrich.maths.org/7701 (accessed 30 January 2012). This article picks out some favourite LTHC tasks which are suitable for teachers and pupils new to the idea.

Kennard, R. (2001) *Teaching Mathematically Able Children*. London: NACE/Fulton.
A summary of the research and implications for teaching across the age range. The following are also useful titles:
McClure, L. and Piggott, J. (2007) *Meeting the Needs of your Most Able Pupils: Mathematics*. Abingdon: Routledge.
Mason, J., Burton, L. and Stacey, K. (1985) *Thinking Mathematically*. London: Addison-Wesley.
Mislevy, R.J. (2012) *What You Test is What You Get*. College Park, MD: College of Education, University of Maryland. Available at www.education.umd.edu/news/news2008/news0803QATest.html (accessed 30 May 2012).

Useful websites

(All accessed 30 May 2012)
Government Information on Gifted and Talented Children: www.direct.gov.uk/en/Parents
National Association for Gifted Children: www.nagcbritain.org.uk
National Numeracy: www.nationalnumeracy.org.uk
NRICH: www.nrich.maths.org.uk

References

Adey, P. (2001) In need of second thoughts. *The Times*, 2 March.
Anderson, L.W. and Krathwold, D.R. (eds) (2001) *A Taxonomy for Learning, Teaching, and Assessing: A Revision of Bloom's Taxonomy of Educational Objectives*. New York: Longman.
Bew, P. (2011) *Independent Review of KS2 Testing*. Available at www.education.gov.uk (accessed 30 January 2012).
Bloom, B.S. (ed.) (1956) *Taxonomy of Educational Objectives*. New York: McKay.
Bloom, B.S. (ed.) (1985) *Developing Talent in Young People*. New York: Basic Books.
Cuoco, A., Goldenberg, E.P. and Mark, J. (1997) Habits of mind: An organizing principle for mathematics curriculum. *Journal of Mathematical Behavior* 15 (4): 375–402.
Directgov (2012) *Supporting Gifted and Talented Children*. Available at www.direct.gov.uk/en/parents/schoolslearninganddevelopment/examstestsandthecurriculum/dg_10037625 (accessed 30 May 2012).

Dweck, C. (2004) *How Can Teachers Develop Students' Motivation – and Success?* Available at www.educationworld.com/a_issues/chat/chat010.shtml (accessed 30 January 2012).

Dweck, C. (2006) *Mindset: The New Psychology of Success.* New York: Random House.

Eyre, D. and McClure, M. (eds) (2001) *Curriculum Provision for the Gifted and Talented in the Primary School.* London: NACE/Fulton.

Freeman, J. (1998) *Educating the Very Able: Current International Research.* London: HMSO.

Gardiner, A. (2002) If you want to build higher, you'd better first dig deeper. *Primary Mathematics* 6 (2). Leicester: Mathematical Association.

Her Majesty's Inspectorate (HMI) (1992) *The Education of Very Able Children in Maintained Schools.* London: HMSO.

Krutetskii, V.A. (1976) *The Psychology of Mathematical Abilities in Schoolchildren.* Chicago, IL: University of Chicago Press.

Nardi, E. and Steward, S. (2003) *Is Mathematics T.I.R.E.D? A Profile of Quiet Disaffection in the Secondary Mathematics Classroom.* Available at www.tandfonline.com/doi/abs/10.1080/01411920301852 (accessed 30 January 2012).

National Numeracy (2012) *National Numeracy: For Everyone, for Life.* Available at www.nationalnumeracy.org.uk/home/index.html (accessed 30 May 2012).

Neisser, U., Boodoo, G., Boucard, T.J., Boykin, A.W. et al. (1996) Intelligence: Knowns and unknowns. *American Psychologist* 51 (2): 77–101.

Office for Standards in Education (Ofsted) (2008) *Mathematics: Understanding the Score.* Available at www.ofsted.gov.uk/node/2255 (accessed 30 January 2012).

Piggott, J. (2010) *Rich Tasks and Contexts.* Available at http://nrich.maths.org/5662 (accessed 30 January 2012).

Polya, G. (1990) *How to Solve It.* London: Penguin.

Renzulli, J. and Reis, S.M. (1976) *The Schoolwide Enrichment Model: Executive Summary.* Available at www.gifted.uconn.edu/sem/semexec.html (accessed 30 January 2012).

Ruthven, K. (1989) An exploratory approach to advanced mathematics. *Educational Studies in Mathematics* 20: 449–67.

Straker, A. (1983) *Mathematics for Gifted Pupils.* London: Longman.

Watson, A. and Mason, J. (2004) *Primary Questions and Prompts for Mathematical Thinking.* Derby: Association of Teachers of Mathematics (www.atm.org.uk).

9 Talk

The key to mathematical understanding?

Mike Askew

Introduction

This chapter looks at the importance of talk in mathematics teaching and learning. I argue that effective teaching – that is teaching that helps learners construct mathematical meaning rather than simply learn procedures and routines – rests on a 'teaching tripod' of tasks, tools and talk. Although all three of these are essential elements in mathematics lessons, talk, and productive talk in particular, is the primary means through which learners construct mathematical meaning.

Chapter aims

The aims of this chapter are to:

- Examine why talk is so important in learning mathematics and how it helps learners' construct mathematical meaning
- Provide examples of productive talk
- Present ways to promote and support productive talk in classrooms
- Think about how lessons can best be planned and enacted to bring about productive talk.

The mathematics curriculum and children's learning

Talk and children's development of mathematics knowledge and understanding

As a teacher in training I was brought up on this motto:

I hear and I forget
I see and I remember
I do and I understand.
                    (Nuffield Mathematics Project/British Council 1978)

Complete tosh. How many things have I seen that I no longer remember? When I am awake at three in morning because something someone said to me is playing on a continuous loop in my head, where is that stuff about hearing and forgetting? What is perhaps most striking, though, is that talk is conspicuously missing from this prescription.

While I have no grandiose expectations that what I write will seep into the collective consciousness, I am aware of the possibility of some future historian, looking through quaint artefacts called 'books' ('Curious aren't they, however did they manage before Kindle implants?'), might chuckle at the naivety of my ideas. But anyway I am claiming that

Productive talk is the key to mathematical understanding.

I am not arguing that we throw away the base-ten blocks, burn the exercise books and sit round and chat. Learners of all ages need to be doing things in mathematics lessons, manipulating objects both physical and virtual. They need to be recording in images, symbols and words, on paper and on screens. I'm taking these as necessary givens. The position that I am strongly taking is that talk is what helps learners construct meaning from their actions and records. Doing and recording are the bones and muscles of learning mathematics: talk is the lifeblood that moves them.

One of the difficulties in writing about talk (or dialogue) in mathematics classrooms is that is it not monolithic; dialogue varies across three dimensions – purposes, content and context (Boerst et al. 2011). The purposes of classroom dialogue can be as diverse as examining different representations of a mathematical concept, exploring connections between seemingly different ideas, or sharing different solutions to a problem. The content of the dialogue can range through recall of facts and definitions, describing procedures, sharing different strategies. The context can be in small groups or whole class, with or without designated roles for group members, highly structured or more freewheeling.

There is not enough space here to cover all these possibilities so I restrict the focus to dialogue with the purpose of supporting growth in mathematical meaning through the content of problem solving. Within this purpose and content I look at two contexts in which learners can engage in productive talk: the private talk that takes place in pairs or small groups and the public conversations in whole class settings (Askew

2012). In private talk, learners make sense of problems, try out ideas and risk getting things wrong. In public conversations, learners collectively share and consider different solutions, examine a range of representations, strategies and methods, and connect different ideas, all arising out of their problem-solving activity. A key idea is that the private talks give rise to public conversations that move everyone's mathematical knowledge and understanding forward, rather than simply share different solutions to the problem.

I have chosen this purpose (meaning making), content (problem solving) and these contexts (private talk, public conversations) for several reasons. First, the role of the teacher is subtly different in the two contexts; supporting pairs or small groups of children as they solve problems makes different demands from orchestrating whole class dialogue arising out of these solutions. Second, problem solving is a challenging part of the curriculum, often mistakenly thought of as something children can do only after they have learnt the 'content'. Research demonstrates the power of learning content through problem solving – problem solving as a means to the end of developing mathematical meaning (Fosnot and Dolk 2001). This is difficult to enact in classrooms. Third, if children are really engaged in solving problems – that is, figuring out the mathematics that might be helpful and choosing methods or strategies, as opposed to applying a procedure to a piece of mathematics 'wrapped up in words' – then the ensuing dialogue is contingent upon the strategies and solutions that children produce. The content of such dialogue cannot be completely predicted or controlled and places demands on the teacher in the moment-to-moment unfolding of the lesson. In summary, dialogue around problem solving provides a 'critical case' that can be used to reflect upon dialogue in other parts of the curriculum.

Conceptual and theoretical perspectives

'The importance of discussions in mathematics teaching is rooted in the nature of mathematics as a discipline, the ways in which students learn, and the context of teaching' (Boerst et al. 2011: 2). Boerst and colleagues neatly encapsulate three reasons for the importance of dialogue in mathematics lessons. Let us look briefly at each.

Dialogue and the nature of mathematics

It is tempting to think of the 'canon' of mathematical knowledge existing in books and journals as being different from the mathematics that children have to learn. But it is possible to extend the idea of learning, taking it out of the heads of individuals and thinking of mathematics, as a discipline, as 'learning' (Davis et al. 2000). For example, the history of the development of an idea like zero challenges the popular notion of the isolated mathematician suddenly discovering or inventing an idea that was unequivocally accepted by the community of mathematicians. Mathematical ideas have grown through mathematicians coming together and debating them, following false leads, rejecting and only then subsequently accepting ideas. The idea of zero in western mathematics was not widely accepted before the twelfth century and it took hundreds of years for mathematicians to become fully comfortable with the idea. From this perspective, the growth of knowledge within the community of mathematicians is analogous to the growth of mathematical knowledge within classroom communities. A main difference, however, is the time-scale: what might have taken hundreds of years in the history of mathematics might have the luxury of only a few weeks in school. I am not arguing that children have to reinvent the whole of mathematics – to go through the history of the discipline in weeks rather than centuries. I am pointing to the parallels in the importance of dialogue in each domain – mathematics as a discipline and school mathematics.

Dialogue and how children learn

The 'hear, see, do' slogan was developed at a time when Piaget's theories were influential (although whether they actually changed teachers' practices or were used to justify what was already going on in classrooms is debatable: Valerie Walkerdine (1984) presents a powerful argument in support of the latter position).

The Piagetian notion of 'stages of thinking' was powerful, especially the idea that primary-aged children were mostly in a stage of 'concrete operations' requiring 'hands on' experiences through which they would 'discover' mathematics. Although not so explicitly argued now, the view of children's thinking being qualitatively different from adults' thinking still echoes through much of primary education.

Recent research, however, challenges the 'stages' theory of thinking (Goswami and Bryant 2007), suggesting that the forms of thinking that we use as adults are pretty much in place from birth. Of course children's thinking is different from that of adults, but that is down to lack of experience rather than their thinking itself being essentially different. Young children can, and do, reason about abstract relationships (just as adults can, and do, need concrete materials to help them think). While children's thinking will grow from their direct experiences of the world, talk is a primary means of extending and reflecting on our direct experiences.

Dialogue and teaching

The research into children's thinking suggests that Vygotsky's (1986) theories about learning and development were closer to the mark. Piagetian theories were used to argue that children had to have reached a particular developmental level before certain learning was possible; for example, children could not be introduced to algebra before reaching the formal operations 'level' of development. In contrast Vygotsky (1986) argued that learning leads development; it is through working on algebraic ideas that one becomes able to think about formal relationships. The Piagetian view of the learner was one of inside-out – the child develops (inside) and only then can engage with ideas 'out there'. The Vygotskian view is one of outside-in – through interactions with others, in contexts that the child may not initially fully comprehend, the child grows and develops into that understanding. Again, talk is central to those interactions with others.

But not any old talk will do: it has to be productive in that it builds on and develops the collective understanding. Aspects of being productive can be thought of as similar to the notion of 'accountable talk' that Lauren Resnick (2010) and colleagues introduced to highlight that classroom talk must be judged against something. *Productive classroom talk* can be accountable to three things: building the community, reasoning and knowledge (Michaels et al. 2008).

Resnick's (2010) research shows that developing accountable talk that is directed to building the community is probably the easiest to implement in classrooms. By asking, 'Who agrees with what Lynne has just said?', 'Jennie, you had a different idea, how does that fit?' or 'Who can re-explain in their own words what Russell has just said?' teachers can change the dynamic of classroom dialogue from one of 'show-and-tell' to one of collective engagement with the mathematics.

The talk that then arises also has to be accountable to reasoning: the arguments and ideas children produce must be commensurate with the logic of mathematical argument. And the talk must also be accountable to knowledge: the mathematics that emerges must eventually be correct. Resnick (2010) suggests, perhaps surprisingly, that it is easier to encourage talk that is accountable to reasoning than it is to produce talk that is accountable to knowledge. She bases this claim on the observation that children can produce well-reasoned arguments grounded in mathematical ideas that are incorrect. An example illustrates this.

A boy I once met visiting a lesson was listing even numbers and confident that 2, 4, 6, 8 were correct. He was equally confident that 9 was also even.

MA: How do you know if a number is even?
Jo: It's when you can split it into even towers. Look, six can be split into two even towers (*demonstrating this with interlocking cubes and showing how two towers of three were 'even' by putting his hand flat across the top of them*).
MA: So what about nine?
Jo: You can split this into three even towers (*shows three towers of three with the cubes and their 'evenness' with his hand*).

Jo's logic was not flawed: this is the reasoning behind defining composite numbers (that is, non-prime) numbers, of which the even numbers are a particular subset (those composite numbers with two as a factor). At the same time it is incorrect to say that nine is even.

As this short example shows dialogue that is accountable to the mathematical knowledge makes demands on the teacher that may be more difficult to manage than the accountability to the community or reasoning. Helping Jo make sense of his answer, to value what he had done (rather than simply 'correct' him) and to have a conversation about composite numbers depended on my mathematical understanding. Talk that is accountable to the knowledge is particularly challenging as not only does it have to steer learners' thinking in the right direction, but also at its best it has to do this in ways that still value the learner's thinking even when that thinking is incorrect.

Case studies

So what might all this look like in practice? This section presents two case studies from primary school classrooms. In each case, commentary woven into the account explores and unpicks the nature and purpose of the talk that has taken place, and its role in meaning-making.

Reflection

I invite you to look for similar examples in your own teaching and think about the role of talk.

Case Study 9.1: Division

This case study comes from a lesson with a Year 5 class (9 and 10 year olds) about division problems where the answer has to be rounded down. We (the lesson was team taught by the teacher and me) had previously introduced the children to the T-table to help them keep track of their calculations in multiplicative problems involving simple ratios. For example, putting 7 postcards to a page in an album and figuring out how many postcards would be needed to fill an album of 18 pages might involve recording this as:

Pages	Postcards
1	7
2	14
4	28
8	56
16	112
2	14
18	126

The children were not skilled in dealing with written word problems. In particular they would read the problem but not appreciate the need to go back and reread parts to help them understand it. More often than not, having read the question at the end of the problem they would answer it on the basis of what they thought might be the problem, rather than going back and rereading to check that their interpretation was correct.

We set up problems in a 'deconstructed' way to encourage the children to talk about what the problem meant rather than rush to find an answer. In pairs the children shared a paper with the opening sentence of a problem, the closing question and space for working out. Each child was given a slip with a 'clue' on it. The rule was that they could read out their clue but not show it to their partner (to discourage anyone from putting their paper on the table and opting out of working on the problem). In this particular lesson the children were working on this problem:

Anansi makes shoes for spiders.

How many boxes of spider shoes is Anansi able to fill?

Their two clues were:

Clue 1. Anansi makes 52 spider shoes.
Clue 2. Spider shoes come in boxes of 8.

Commentary

While the pairs were starting on the problem, the teacher and I made two 'tours' around the class. The first tour was to check that everyone had understood the problem correctly; children often claim to be stuck, not because they lack the resources to solve the problem, but because they haven't fully understood what they have been asked to do. If that's the case with several children, then the best thing may be to momentarily bring the class back together to clarify things with everyone.

The second tour round was to monitor everyone's progress on the task, where the teacher's role then includes giving feedback when a line of inquiry looks productive, asking questions to prompt further thinking, and suggesting possible approaches to take.

Private talk

All the children seemed to have understood the problem and were able to start, so I chose to listen in closely to one pair, Dee and Jay. Dee had only recently joined the class and I was interested to learn more about her mathematical thinking.

Dee, on hearing Jay's clue (1), immediately jotted down '52 spider shoes' and drew eight boxes (gleaned (incorrectly) from her Clue 1).

MA: (*to Jay*) Do you agree with what Dee has recorded?

Jay: (*hesitatingly*) Yes.

MA: (*pointing to the eight boxes*) So tell me what these represent?

Dee: The eight boxes.

MA: Oh, OK. Jay, can you remember what Dee's clue was?

Jay: I think it was that there are eight spider shoes in a box.

Dee: (*reading*) 'Spider shoes come in boxes of 8'.

Jay: We don't need eight boxes. We have to find out how many boxes.

Dee: Yeah, boxes of eight (*which she records as B O 8*). It's a divide.

Jay: Yes, divide (*writing down 52/8*).

Dee immediately wrote down this in 'bus stop' notation, but Jay wanted to use a T-table.

MA: Why not do it both ways and see if it works out the same?

Jay set up a table:

Shoes	Boxes
8	1

Reflection

It would be more conventional to have this in the order:

Boxes	Shoes
1	8

I chose not to suggest that they change the order: does that matter?

Together they filled it in, doubling to get two and four boxes and adding one more to find the total for five.

Shoes	Boxes
8	1
16	2
32	4
40	5

Dee: Another box will be 48 shoes, so 7 boxes is 56.
Recording:

Shoes	Boxes
8	1
16	2
32	4
40	5
56	7

MA: So what's the answer?
Both: Seven boxes.
MA: OK, and that fits with your clues?
Dee: (*pointing to the top row of the table*). Yes, eight shoes in a box
Jay: And 52 shoes.
Dee: So 52 shoes, that needs seven boxes.
MA: (*to Jay*) You agree?
Jay: Yes.
Dee: (*reading, as if to make the point clear to me!*) 'How many boxes of spider shoes is Anansi able to fill?'

> **MA:**   OK, so he fills seven boxes. Lovely.
> **Jay:**   (*pausing*) No, he fills six boxes. The last box isn't full.
> **MA:**   What do you think, Dee?
>
> Dee added a final row to the T-table:
>
> | Shoes | Boxes |
> |:---:|:---:|
> | 8 | 1 |
> | 16 | 2 |
> | 32 | 4 |
> | 40 | 5 |
> | 56 | 7 |
> | 48 | 6 |
>
> **Dee:**   There are four left over. It's six full boxes and four shoes over.

Commentary

Teacher inputs in private talk depend on careful listening in on what the children are saying to decide whether or not to join in the conversation. If the children are working productively in a direction that looks likely to yield a solution, then any intervention is likely to be minimal, although some feedback needs to be given on the approach taken and why it seems to be working. This is important not only for the particular learners getting the feedback, but also in terms of the 'cocktail party effect' – that good ideas get shared around the class. Other children will pick up and use ideas that they've heard are successful (and no, it's not cheating, it's effective collaboration).

If a pair are working well but on listening in the teacher decides their approach may be leading them away from a productive solution, then there is no easy answer as to the type of intervention to make; this will depend on many factors including judging how these particular children will cope with possibly spending time on a trail not leading anywhere. Some children are fine with this; they have the resilience to deal with temporary setbacks. If they are confident that they are on the right tracks, then trying to change their approach may not be successful anyway. Others, however, may become frustrated. The danger with stepping in too soon is that the children will stop thinking for themselves and learn to wait for the teacher to bail them out. The danger with waiting too long is that they become discouraged and see themselves as failures and not able to do mathematics. Careful listening is the key – getting the children to explain through in detail what they are doing and thinking often leads to them reappraising their approach for themselves.

In this particular case I held off from indicating whether or not their answer was correct, choosing instead to keep putting it onto the children to check. This was something the class was used to (and Jay in this pair). 'Are you sure?' was a question we regularly asked the children whether or not their answer was correct (often a correct answer is met with 'Fine', so children learn that being asked 'Are you sure?' is code for 'You've got it wrong'!).

In this case the children did self-correct. What if they hadn't? Then I might have asked pairs to join up and share each other's methods and solutions – careful matching up of pairs can lead to groups becoming aware of different answers. Sometimes differences will get resolved in the small groups, sometimes they need to be brought up in the whole class discussion.

Dee was then keen to do the standard algorithm that she had been taught at her previous school. She was able to do this using her fluent number fact knowledge and was pleased to get the same answer. We talked about where the numbers in the standard division were represented in the algorithm and how these related to the figures in the T-table.

I told Dee and Jay that they would be coming to the front to share this second method with the class.

Public conversation

As many of the children had used a T-table to find the answer, we had one pair share this method first. Dee and Jay then came and talked through how to do the standard algorithm method.

Reflection

Some would argue that it is more efficient simply to demonstrate upfront how to do the standard division algorithm and then get the children all using this.

What is gained from working with different representations like the T-table?

Commentary

The majority of children in class were using the T-table as a model for finding the solution to the problem. The conversation with Dee and Jay made clear that they were beginning to use this as a tool for thinking with (Gravemeijer et al. 2000). The layout of the ratios helped them realize that this was a division calculation where the answer needed to be rounded down. Although Dee was confident in her use of the division algorithm, the compact nature of the algorithm means that is can be used in a mechanical way without reading meaning into the numerals. Having the dialogue with Dee about the links with the T-table not only strengthened and confirmed her understanding, but also provided a quick assessment that she could use the algorithm appropriately and not simply as a mindless procedure. It then seemed appropriate to share this with the class.

Conclusion

The private talk in this lesson helped the children to sort out the meaning of a division problem and agree on an appropriate strategy for finding the answer. It was productive talk that was accountable both to reasoning and mathematical knowledge (of division). While the public conversation confirmed these answers it was used to take the lesson beyond simply finding the answer to a particular problem and to use the solutions to that problem as a springboard for beginning to move to using a more formal approach for division calculations. This again was productive through being accountable to the community as well as reasoning and knowledge.

Case Study 9.2: Chopsticks

This lesson was carried out with a Year 2 (6 and 7 year olds) class towards the end of the first term so the majority of children were still aged 6. As in the previous example, the teacher and I team-taught the lesson as part of a project working with a school to raise learners' attainment. The children were a diverse group, including many immigrants, so part of what we were doing was working to build up their ability to talk mathematics (for details, see Askew 2012).

We orally posed a simple problem:

> Some friends go out for a Chinese meal.
> How many chopsticks do they use?

We spent time at the beginning of the lesson playing with pencils to make sure everyone, even if they'd never been to a Chinese restaurant, had a sense of chopsticks coming in twos. Working in pairs, children were given a different number of people in their 'party' so that pairs might share methods but not be able to simply copy from each other.

We were interested in whether the children approached the problem by counting in twos or whether anyone realized that the answer could be found by doubling the number of people. For example, if there were 15 people having the meal, did the children add 15 and 15 or did they count up 15 twos? It turned out the class was fairly evenly split in the two approaches.

Private talk

As the children were working, the teacher and I did our 'tours' of the class. The children were confident in their problem solving and the task was one that they easily understood. So most of our attention was given to discussing which solutions we wanted shared with the whole class.

Commentary

This was the second year of working with this class and the children were confident that they could work in whatever ways they liked and could represent their working in a variety of ways. They were also used to cooperating effectively in pairs. In short, the history of the class contributed to their success. It takes time for good dialogue habits to be built up and we need to take that into account when choosing tasks and expecting children to engage with them productively.

The pairs were fairly evenly split between those doubling the number of eaters and those counting in twos. Children doubling the number of people, in the main, used a number line to find the answer, so we chose a pair whose working was typical. One pair had, however, set out the addition in a traditional column way, so we took this to be an opportunity to explore this with the class.

Several pairs finding the solution by counting in twos represented this in a fashion reminiscent of a double number line (a horizontal T-table). For example, in Figure 9.1 we have the count of the stick figures and the pairs, while Figure 9.2 shows a child's even more iconic version of this. In anticipation of drawing on this in the public conversation, we showed the pair working on Figure 9.2 how to record this as a double number line with the number of children on the top and the number of chopsticks below the line.

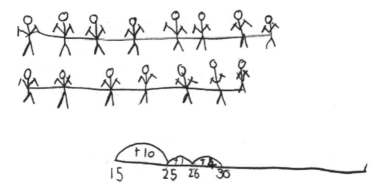

Figure 9.1 Finding the number of chopsticks for 15 people

Figure 9.2 Coordinating chopsticks with people

We told all the children who we had selected to share methods to be prepared to come and address the whole class.

Commentary

Selecting which solutions methods means judging which are most likely to be beneficial to the whole class. The public conversation is not simply a time for 'show-and-tell'; it needs to be organized around mathematical ideas.

Public conversation

The first part of the public conversation was based around a pair of children coming up and sharing their number line solution and then the pair who had used column arithmetic coming and explaining that. With both of these representations on the board, we discussed the similarities and differences.

The second half of the conversation had a different focus. Those children we had primed came and recreated the double number line on the interactive white board (Figure 9.3). The class then engaged in a dialogue about how this double number line could be used to answer a whole range of chopsticks problems, such as:

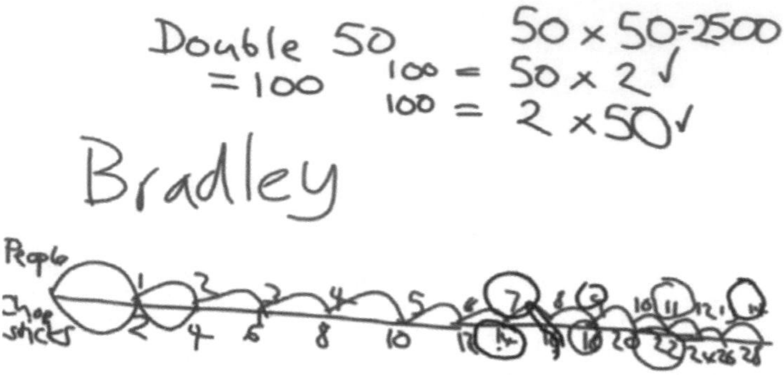

Figure 9.3 Working with a double number line

- If there were 12 people how many chopsticks would they use?
- If 18 chopsticks had been used, how many people was that?

In their pairs the children posed similar problems for each other to share.

In the light of the discussion we were able to 'push' the children's thinking further. Suppose, we said, we could extend the double number line further:

'There's not enough room on the board, but imagine we continued until there were 50 people on the top. How many chopsticks would that be and what mathematical sentence could we use to record this?'

Back to a private talk in pairs, the children quickly figured out that the answer would be 100. Together again as a whole class, we recorded the different ways children thought this could be expressed:

$$50 + 50$$
$$2 \times 50$$
$$\text{Double } 50$$
$$50 \times 50$$
$$50 \times 2$$

Again we gave them a few minutes of private talk to decide which of these would be acceptable. Everyone agreed that they would all be fine except 50 × 50 which was going to be much too big. As we were clearing up, a boy came up and quietly said that 50 × 50 would be 'two thousand five hundred'. Of course we stopped the clearing up so that he could share this answer with the class and how he'd worked it out:

> Well, ten times fifty is five hundred, so twenty times is one thousand, another ten is one thousand five hundred, another ten two thousand so fifty fifties is two thousand five hundred.'

Commentary

The role of the teacher in public conversation is complex. It involves attending to the solution being offered by the children who have come to the front but doing this in such a way as to draw in the rest of the class to be thinking about and engaging with the solution being offered, not simply listening politely in the hope (or fear) that they may be called upon next. The public conversation needs to be crafted around carefully chosen examples, which means not seeking volunteers. The examples may be chosen for a variety of reasons:

- Different representations that can be used to help children make links between
- Different solutions that need reconciling
- Different children having the opportunity to speak and share with the whole class.

Managing this whole class discussion in part involves putting yourself, as the teacher, in the position of being one of the other children and trying to imagine what it must be like to be hearing the solution for the first time; acting as an advocate for these listeners in prompting the children explaining to give an account in such a way that the rest of the class can engage with their solution. This is easier said than done. As teachers, having listened to and talked with the children prior to their presenting makes it easier, to be able to make sense of their explanation through 'filling in the gaps'. But other children in the class may be struggling to make sense of the explanation because they neither have the knowledge of the mathematics nor the benefit of prior conversations.

Public conversation can be less than productive when it turns into a private talk between the teacher and the children presenting. Simple things like moving to the back of the class so that the children have to face the class rather than talk to you at the side of the board can make a big difference.

Finally, in this example, the direction that the public conversation took, together with the support of the introduction of the double number line, enabled one child to demonstrate a sophisticated level of mathematical reasoning that might not otherwise have been revealed.

Conclusion

The whole class discussion plays a key role in crafting and bringing out the methods and making the mathematics collectively 'owned'. The focus on the whole class discussion needs to be on the mathematics, not on particular children. The spirit needs to move from one of this is 'their' solution, to 'how does this help us all with our mathematics?'

Summary

It is tempting to try to 'script' dialogue in advance, particularly by pre-determining the questions that one is going to ask. However, if teaching is going to be truly interactive, then responses (not just from the teacher but from the other children) depend upon what emerges in the lesson and so are not completely pre-scriptable (pre-dictable, literal origin of 'say before'). However, this observation is not a recommendation for 'anything goes'. The lessons from which these cases are drawn were planned with clear intentions; the first in the connection between multiplication and division in the context of division problems that involved rounding down, while in the second to explore the connection between counting in twos and doubling.

As part of this planning the problems that the children were going to engage in were carefully chosen as ones that had 'low thresholds' (McClure 2011) in the sense that we expected that all the children would be able to make sense of the problems and find some way of solving them, even if that was mathematically 'naive'. But the problems also had reasonably 'high ceilings' in that they could lead to some quite sophisticated mathematics. 'Anansi' for some children simply helped their understanding of the nature of division problems, for others it introduced them to a more efficient calculation strategy. For some children 'Chopsticks' would (and indeed did) only provide some consolidation in counting in twos, while others began to make some connections between doubling and counting in twos and so some understanding of the connection between multiplication and division. We could not know in advance, however, which children would learn what. We were, however, confident that everyone would learn something.

Such a view of learning outcomes is different to some popularly held advice that learning outcomes can be closely pre-specified at the beginning of a lesson. This may be possible if children are being trained to do something. I can be reasonably confident that over the course of a lesson I can get most children to learn to measure angles using a protractor. But developing understanding or making meaning of mathematics is not within the control of the teacher and unfolds over time. Good lessons built around problem solving and dialogue works with the fact that in any class there will be a range of understandings (even in the most carefully 'setted' group) and that the rate at which these understandings grow and develop is down to too many factors for a single teacher to control.

In summary, productive classroom talk has to embody at least three things:

- It has to have a clear focus: for example, a solution to a problem, particular representations, and connections between ideas. This focus has to be sufficiently rich to sustain dialogue and to promote collective mathematical activity.
- Everyone has to be involved in speaking and listening – engaging in collective mathematical activity – in pairs, small groups and whole class settings.
- The teacher has a dual role here. The first is to be an active member of the collective – listening, prompting, questioning and manager of the discussion. The second is to provide 'space' for everyone to contribute, judging how 'on board' everyone is, encouraging a productive ethos.

Further reading

Fosnot, C.T. and Dolk, M. (2001) *Young Mathematicians at Work: Constructing Multiplication and Division*. Portsmouth, NH: Heinemann.

Fosnot, C.T. and Dolk, M. (2001) *Young Mathematicians at Work: Constructing Number Sense, Addition and Subtraction*. Portsmouth, NH: Heinemann.

Fosnot, C.T. and Dolk, M. (2002) *Young Mathematicians at Work: Constructing Fractions, Decimals and Percents*. Portsmouth, NH: Heinemann.

There are three titles in the *Young Mathematicians at Work* series. Each book has some detailed case studies of children talking about their solutions to problems, with commentary on the importance of talk in promoting learning and the role of the teacher.

Askew, M. (2012) *Transforming Primary Mathematics*. Abingdon: Routledge. In this book I elaborate on the ideas introduced here. As well as providing further theoretical background, I look at how talk needs to be coordinated with tasks and tools.

References

Askew, M. (2012) *Transforming Primary Mathematics*. Abingdon: Routledge.

Boerst, T.A., Sleep, L., Loewenberg Ball, D. and Bass, H. (2011) Preparing teachers to lead mathematics discussions. *Teachers College Record* 113 (12): 2844–77.

Davis, B., Sumara, D. and Luce-Kapler, R. (2000) *Engaging Minds: Learning and Teaching in a Complex World*. Mahwah, NJ: Lawrence Erlbaum Associates.

Fosnot, C.T. and Dolk, M. (2001) *Young Mathematicians at Work: Constructing Number Sense, Addition and Subtraction*. Portsmouth, NH: Heinemann.

Goswami, U. and Bryant, P. (2007) *Children's Cognitive Development and Learning (Primary Review Research Survey 2/1a)*. Cambridge: Faculty of Education, University of Cambridge.

Gravemeijer, K., Cobb, P., Bowers, J. and Whitenack, J. (2000) Symbolizing, modeling and instructional design. In P. Cobb, E. Yackel and K. McClain (eds) *Symbolizing and Communicating in Mathematics Classrooms: Perspectives on Discourse, Tools, and Instructional Design*. Hillsdale, NJ: Lawrence Erlbaum Associates.

McClure, L. (2011) *Low Threshold High Ceiling Tasks in Ordinary Classrooms*. Available at http://nrich.maths.org/7701 (accessed 15 January 2012).

Michaels, S., O'Connor, C. and Resnick, L.B. (2008) Deliberative discourse idealized and realized: Accountable talk in the classroom and in civic life. *Studies in Philosophy and Education* 27: 283–97.

Nuffield Mathematics Project/British Council (1978) *Mathematics: From Primary to Secondary*. Edinburgh: Chambers/Murray/Wiley.

Resnick, L.B. (2010) Nested learning systems for the thinking curriculum. *Educational Researcher* 39 (3): 183–97.

Vygotsky, L.S. (1986) *Thought and Language*. Cambridge, MA: MIT Press.

Walkerdine, V. (1984) Developmental psychology and the child-centred pedagogy. In J. Henriques, W. Holloway, C. Unwin, C. Venn and V. Walkerdine (eds) *Changing the Subject*. London: Methuen.

Part 3

Developing practice in primary mathematics teaching

A strong element of the chapters in Part 2 was the need for teachers to focus on the children they teach, their voices and their needs. A further thread runs through it, that of the professional development of teachers. All the authors discuss the decisions that teachers make day and daily in their practice, emphazing their nature and significance, and the essential role they play in developing professional practice. In relation to such decision-making, Askew talks of the 'demands on the teacher in the moment-to-moment unfolding of the lesson'.

How do we support teachers in making the best decisions? What is it that best enables them to confidently cope with the moment-to-moment unfolding?

Part 3 takes us through three accounts of ways in which teacher development may occur. Ian Thompson discusses the nature and role of evidence in informing policy and hence practice, and through aligning himself to Grover Whitehurst's (2003) definition of evidence-based education as 'the integration of professional wisdom with the best available empirical evidence in making decisions', brings us to a discussion of the genesis and development of such 'professional wisdom'. Elizabeth Carruthers illustrates, through the example of Karen, one teacher's sustained and personal journey of reflection, and its impact on her own practice and that of her colleagues. The need to 'listen generously' is evidenced throughout. Effie Maclellan's chapter takes us deeper into the very particular and contextualized nature of teacher professional learning and developing, identifying a tripartite relationship between self-knowledge, pupil knowledge and subject knowledge. She reminds us that since teaching is deeply situated in practice and consists of a constant conversation between these elements, expertise is dynamic in nature.

Chapters 10, 11 and 12 therefore take us from the large scale to the small scale, from bringing evidence in to generating our own evidence, and powerfully illustrate that while aspects of practice are often dictated by external and large-scale agendas, it is in the small scale particularity of practice that we can often make real change.

10 Evidence-based mathematics teaching and learning

Ian Thompson

Introduction and context

The aim of this chapter is to consider, in the context of 'evidence-based teaching', some of the extant research into the teaching of the four basic arithmetic operations, and the ways in which this research can inform teachers' practice. At the time of writing, a major debate (some might say 'confrontation') is taking place between those who espouse what can be described as the *traditional* approach and those who prefer a *number sense* approach to teaching arithmetic (Cowan et al. 2011). In this context, it is obviously important that any decisions that are taken are based on evidence rather than on other criteria.

Reading this chapter should raise your awareness of:

- What might be meant by 'evidence-based teaching'
- Some of the research findings associated with the teaching of arithmetic
- Potential implications of this research
- Evidence-informed approaches to teaching the basic operations.

Reflection

Before reading further, you might like to jot down your own interpretation of 'evidence based teaching'.

Evidence-based teaching

Readers will no doubt be familiar with the term 'evidence-based practice' (EBP) in the context of the health service. According to Lester (2007: 1),

'The main principle of EBP is that it involves making decisions based on "evidence" rather than on, for instance, untested theory, customary practice, political dogma or uncritical benchmarking.' In the health service it is not uncommon to find reports of research that has involved randomized control groups, whereas trials of this nature are very rare indeed in mathematics educational research in England.

Despite this, the demand for evidence on which to base educational decisions has become more vociferous of late. For example, the word 'evidence' appears frequently in the remit for the review of the National Curriculum in England (DfE 2011a), and Tim Oates, before he was appointed by the Secretary of State to chair and direct the Expert Panel for this review, wrote: 'we should appraise carefully both international and national research in order to drive an evidence-based review of the National Curriculum' (Oates 2010: 3).

Hammersley (2001: 4), on the other hand, argues that: 'research [in the educational arena] usually cannot supply what the notion of evidence-based practice demands of it – specific and highly reliable answers to questions about what "works" and what does not.'

For the rest of this chapter I hope to be guided – or at least influenced – by the following observations of writers on evidence-based education:

- The request by Nutley et al. (2002: 1–2) for less demanding phraseology, preferring 'evidence-influenced', or even just 'evidence-aware' to reflect a more realistic view of what can be achieved.
- Whitehurst's (2003: 4) definition of evidence-based education as 'the integration of professional wisdom with the best available empirical evidence in making decisions'. This should, I hope, legitimize my capitalizing on my 50-year involvement in mathematics education in order to comment on research evidence that I have encountered during that time.
- Mooney's (2011: 2) observation that 'a large number of psychological studies have shown that people respond to scientific evidence in ways that justify their preexisting beliefs'.

This is not really the place to initiate a detailed discussion of the nature of 'evidence', although I do want to focus on two specific issues in relation to the mathematical content of the 2013 National Curriculum and the various documents commissioned to inform it. These issues relate to the publication of data concerning the mathematical performance of secondary children in the fourth Programme for International Student Assessment (PISA) and to data on 10-year-olds from the Trends in International Mathematics and Science Study (TIMSS).

The selection and interpretation of research evidence

The belief that the 'truth' is out there in the form of research findings is a somewhat naive belief, in that the results and conclusions of one group of researchers occasionally contradict those of a different group. Because of this, there can sometimes be a problem with the selection and interpretation of research findings.

The 'selection' issue

A report entitled *A World-Class Mathematics Education for All our Young People* (the Vorderman Report) was commissioned by the Conservative Party in 2009 and published in August 2011. A key sentence in the report, referring to the secondary PISA data, and repeated on many occasions by Michael Gove, the Secretary of State for Education, and Nick Gibb, the Schools Minister, is: 'In the last decade, we have plummeted down the international league tables ... from 8th to 27th in mathematics' (Conservative Party 2011: iii).

After the publication of this report, the highly emotive word 'plummeted' duly appeared in most of the media's coverage. However, it is a pity that secondary-focused rather than primary-focused research was quoted. For example, if the authors had chosen to analyse the performance of 10-year-olds on successive TIMMS tests, would they have reached the same conclusion? Interestingly, the only mention in the Vorderman Report of these results is the simple statement: 'In TIMSS, England has remained fairly stable' (Conservative Party 2011: 7).

So, what do the actual data tell us? In 1995 England's 10 year olds scored 484 scale points. This was 16 points below the international average – and it placed them seventeenth out of 26 countries. Not a particularly impressive performance. However, in 2003 they managed to score 531 scale points – 36 points above the international average (the mean was 495) – and ranked tenth out of 25 countries. This constitutes a rise of seven places with roughly the same number of participating countries. In 2007 they increased this score by 10 scale points to 541. This was a full 41 points above the international average and placed them seventh out of 37 countries. To contextualize these results by moving closer to home, it is interesting to note that Scotland scored one scale point more than England in 1995. However, in 2003 England made substantial gains on Scotland (531 to 490) and widened the gap even further in 2007 (541 to 494) (see Table 10.1).

Table 10.1 Scores for England and Scotland in three TIMSS surveys

	1995	2003	2007
England	484	531	541
Scotland	485	490	494

The 'interpretation' issue

When different individuals analyse the same piece of research, the question of interpretation of the findings arises. For example, the conclusions of the Vorderman analysis of the PISA data are based on a comparison of the 2000 and the 2009 data, despite the fact that the OECD itself has argued that the 2000 and 2003 results should not be used as comparators because England's response rate was too low and also that our score in 2009 was actually not statistically different from the OECD average (OECD 2009). In addition, Jerrim (2011: 21) argues that his statistical analysis of the PISA data does not support the conclusion that England's secondary children's performance has declined (or improved) in relation to that of its international competitors. He concludes his report by saying: 'The decline seen by England in the PISA international rankings is not, in my opinion, statistcally robust enough to base public policy on' (Jerrim 2011: 21).

Another 'interpretation' problem obtains with reference to the primary TIMSS data and the report of the Expert Panel – commissioned for the review of the National Curriculum. This document argues that the improvement in standards after the introduction of the National Strategies flattened out after a modest increase 'and our comparative international league-table position fell' (DfE 2011b: 37). However, it is interesting to note that the actual document quoted in evidence by the Expert Panel states:

> This improvement (in England's performance from 1995 to 2003) is clearly shown whether the change in England's score over this period is analysed or England's performance is compared with that of other participating countries.
>
> (Whetton et al. 2007: 10)

It is also important to note that in 2003, only six of the participating countries scored significantly better than England, and that in 2007 only the four Pacific Rim countries did significantly better. Also, the official report on England's performance in TIMSS 2007 (NFER 2008: 2) says that 'England's performance in mathematics at year 5 is amongst the best in the world and continues to improve.' This strikes me as a particularly remarkable achievement that contradicts the Vorderman Report's somewhat bland comment that England's results have 'remained fairly stable' and raises serious questions as to how three 'expert' professors could possibly interpret the TIMSS data described above and in Table 10.1 as a 'falling' international league-table position (DfE 2011b: 37).

Reflection

Before reading further, jot down those mental calculation strategies you are aware of for the addition and subtraction of two-digit numbers.

Research on calculation methods

Let us now consider the nature and use of 'evidence' in relation to our own classroom practices as mathematics teachers. The Draft National Curriculum (DfE 2012) is heavily biased towards the teaching and learning of traditional, formal written algorithms. Consequently, the next sections discuss research evidence that might raise questions about this approach. I start by describing three research projects in which I was the lead or sole investigator, and through commentary and reflection points invite you to consider their relationship to your own knowledge, pedagogy and practice.

Research project 1: Mental calculation strategies

In a research project funded by the Nuffield Foundation (Thompson and Smith 1999) we investigated the mental calculation strategies used for the addition and subtraction of two-digit numbers by 144 children from Years 4 and 5 in 18 schools in the north-east of England. In the interviews the children were asked to calculate mentally a graded set of two-digit additions and subtractions at a level commensurate with their age and ability, and were then asked to describe the strategies they had used to generate their answers.

Apart from a small percentage of children who were still using counting procedures, the majority used one of the following strategies: partitioning, sequencing or mixed methods, as illustrated in the following three addition examples:

John (27 + 28) – Partitioning ('split' method)

'55 ... Two 20s are 40 ... 7 and 8 ... If there's 7, take 3 off 8 which would be 10, which would make 50 ... and 3 took off 8 would be 5 ... so the answer would be 55.'

Stacey (27 + 28) – Sequencing ('jump' method)

'55 . . . You take the 7 off the 27 . . . and you add the 28 and the 20 together . . . that makes 48 . . . and then you add the 7 on . . . you take 2 off it and make 50 . . . and then you add the extra 5.'

Kyle (27 + 28) – Mixed method ('split-jump' method)

'55 . . . I did the 20 and the 20 . . . then I did the 8 and which made 2 more to 50 . . . and then I added the two which made 50 . . . and then I added the 5 . . . which made 55.'

Interestingly, 77 per cent of the children used one or more of these strategies for addition and 58 per cent used one or more for subtraction. The important thing to notice is that these three strategies *do not* involve tens and units, i.e. they do not treat 27 as two tens and seven units, but as 20 and 7. Only 10 per cent of the sample used tens and units for addition and 17 per cent did so for subtraction.

Reflection

How would you define 'place value'?

Place value

The Cockcroft Report describes: 'the very important concept of place value (that is, for example, that the 2 stands for 2 units in the number 52, for 2 tens in the number 127 and for 2 hundreds in the number 263)' (Cockcroft 1982: 87).

The Qualifications and Curriculum Authority (QCA 1997: 3) states that: 'A digit can take a range of values according to where it is placed. In the numeral 62 the digit 6 has the value 60 and the 2 has the value 2.'

These two subtly different definitions of place value suggest that we can identify two different aspects of the concept:

- *quantity value*, where, say, 273 is interpreted as 200 plus 70 plus 3
- *column value*, where it is interpreted as 2 hundreds, 7 tens and 3 units (or ones).

The fact that nearly eight times as many children used the *quantity value* aspect of place value for their additions in the research reported above suggests that this aspect appears to be easier for young children to understand. This finding influenced the Year 3 objective in the *National Numeracy Strategy Framework for Teaching Mathematics from Reception to Year 6* (DfEE 1999: 8):

> Respond to such questions as:
> 'Say what the digit 3 in 364 represents. And the 6? And the 4?'
> (They represent 300 and 60 and 4).

Research project 2: Young children's written procedures

This research project (Thompson 1994) investigated the 'natural' written procedures for addition of 117 9- and 10-year-old children who had not been taught traditional paper and pencil methods for the basic operations. The children were asked to try to set out their work so that a friend could understand how they had done their calculations. Three-quarters of the children set them out horizontally (see Figure 10.1), working from left to right rather than by following the standard procedure that operates from right to left.

Twenty-one children (18 per cent) set out at least one of their calculations vertically, mimicking the traditional layout, but thirteen of them consistently added by working from left to right, beginning their calculation with the most significant digit (see Figure 10.2). The other eight attempted the traditional standard algorithm, but often made errors when carrying a 10. The children working from left to right were *always* successful – probably because they were using their own methods: procedures that they fully understood and in which they had confidence.

Notice that in both of the examples shown, which were typical of the sample, the children are using *quantity value* (working with 30, 40 and 50), even though Denise has actually chosen to set her work down in columns (Figure 10.2).

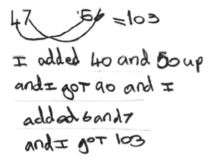

Figure 10.1 Kelly's written procedure

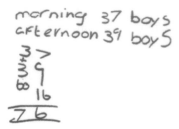

Figure 10.2 Denise's left-to-right addition method

Research project 3: Place value research

The findings of the research projects reported above suggested a third study (Thompson and Bramald 2002), funded by the Nuffield Foundation and with the self-explanatory title *An Investigation of the Relationship between Young Children's Understanding of Place Value and their Competence at Mental Addition.* This study took the form of a series of one-to-one interviews with 144 children from Years 2 to 4 in eight primary schools.

One question asked children to calculate mentally 25 + 23. Of the thirty-one children (21 per cent) who were unable to give an answer or who gave an incorrect one, more than half were from the lowest attaining subgroup of the youngest children, as might be expected. Ninety-one children (63 per cent) gave the correct answer using a *quantity value* procedure (either '20 + 20 = 40; 5 + 3 = 8; 40 + 8 = 48' or '25 + 20 = 45; 45 + 3 = 48').

Two other questions focused specifically on the traditional interpretation of place value – where the 6 in 362 means 'six tens' or 'a 6 in the tens column', and what in this chapter is being called *column value*. The first question was modelled on the one that led the Cockcroft Committee to talk about a 'seven-year gap', meaning that there are concepts understood by some 7-year-olds that are not understood by some 14-year-olds (Cockcroft 1982). This question involved, after a careful build-up, asking individual children to write down what the current milometer of a car (6299) would read after one more mile. Thirty-five children (24 per cent) – mainly from the more able subgroup of the older children – were correct.

The second question was based on one designed by the Assessment of Performance Unit (Apu 1982) to assess place value understanding. This involved explaining, again after a careful build up, how the value of four blocks had changed after they had been moved from the units to the tens column on a hundreds, tens and units baseboard. Only fourteen children (10 per cent) were successful on this item. It was felt that these two questions were testing different aspects of place value, and that any child deemed to have grasped the concept should have been able to achieve success on both of these items. In fact, just *four* children (3 per cent) were successful on both questions. This result of 3 per cent success on questions involving the *column value* aspect of place value compares very unfavourably with the 63 per cent of children who successfully calculated 25 + 23 using methods that involved the *quantity value* aspect.

The findings of the three studies reported above suggest the following:

- Children's two-digit mental calculation strategies are primarily based on left-to-right methods that deal with the multiples of ten before the ones: they partition the numbers (25 is 20 and 5) using the *quantity value* aspect of place value.
- Children who have not been taught standard procedures develop written methods of their own that parallel these mental methods.
- It is clearly possible to perform two-digit calculation successfully without understanding what is traditionally meant by place value (*column value*) by using – with understanding – methods that involve *quantity value*.

Reflection

Do these reports suggest any implications for the teaching of written calculation?

Implications

A consideration of the four written calculation procedures illustrated in Figures 10.3 to 10.6 shows that they all involve *quantity value* rather than *column value*, and all start from the left rather than from the right.

These written methods would appear to constitute a more natural progression from young children's mental calculation strategies and early personal mathematical graphics than do the traditional standard algorithms that are totally dependent on the *column value* aspect. The evidence suggests that it might be sensible to focus on these methods for many primary school children and leave the learning of column methods for the more able children in Years 5 and 6.

$$
\begin{array}{r}
47 \\
+76 \\
\hline
110 \\
13 \\
\hline
123
\end{array}
$$

Figure 10.3 Addition

$$
\begin{array}{r}
326 \\
-178 \\
\hline
22 \quad (\rightarrow 200) \\
126 \quad (\rightarrow 326) \\
\hline
148
\end{array}
$$

Figure 10.4 Subtraction

$$
\begin{array}{r}
38 \\
\times\, 7 \\
\hline
210 \\
56 \\
\hline
266
\end{array}
$$

Figure 10.5 Multiplication

108 ÷ 6

$$
\begin{array}{rl}
108 & \\
-60 & (10 \times 6) \\
\hline
48 & \\
-30 & (5 \times 6) \\
\hline
18 & \\
-18 & (3 \times 6) \\
\hline
0 & \qquad \text{Answer } 10 + 5 + 3 = 18
\end{array}
$$

Figure 10.6 Division

Evidence on the teaching of division

In 2011, ministers asked Ofsted to provide evidence of effective practice in the teaching of early arithmetic. This led to the publication of *Good Practice in Primary Mathematics: Evidence from 20 Successful Schools* (Ofsted 2011). The schools visited – ten maintained and ten independent – all had a strong track record of high achievement. The progress of those pupils in the maintained schools had been significantly above the national average for the last four years in Key Stage 2 mathematics tests.

Sections in the document deal with the actual content of the arithmetic curriculum that the children in these particular schools were taught; the specific procedures they used as a result of this teaching; and those they described in discussion with Ofsted inspectors. On close study, one perceives an undercurrent of negativity whenever phrases such as 'informal procedures' or 'expanded algorithms' are used: methods such as the informal written calculation strategies known as front-end addition, subtraction by complementary addition, grid multiplication and division by chunking – procedures illustrated above in Figures 10.3 to 10.6. Interestingly, the word used most frequently in the document to describe these methods is 'interim' – a somewhat loaded word.

It is also interesting that this negative attitude towards such methods appears to contradict advice given in earlier Ofsted/HMI publications:

> In number, pupils are not always supported well enough in the use of informal methods of calculation when they cannot cope successfully with standard written methods.
>
> (Ofsted 2002: 2)

> There is considerable evidence to indicate that many 'imposed methods', on which much time is spent in schools, are often quickly forgotten, and that pupils or adults revert to their own methods which they understand and in which they are more confident.
>
> (DES 1985: 4)

> In the classes where standards were low, it was frequently the over-emphasis on written recording and computation.
>
> (Ofsted 1993: 10)

I intend to focus here on the algorithm that receives the most adverse criticism in the document *Good Practice in Primary Mathematics: Evidence from 20 Successful Schools* (Ofsted 2011) – namely the written division method known as 'chunking'.

The 'chunking' algorithm

The following section comprises four statements about chunking/division from the Ofsted (2011) document followed by a few thoughts about each one.

1. 'Nearly half of the schools in the survey do not teach "chunking" as a strategy for division. They explained that it confuses pupils, particularly those who are low attaining' (Ofsted 2011: 16).

Let us see what insights research – national and international – has to offer concerning this declared 'confusion'. Anghileri et al. (2002) compared the results of 276 English Year 5 children from ten schools with 259 Dutch children from similar backgrounds on a ten-question division test. In January the English success rate was 38 per cent and the Dutch was 47 per cent. However, on the same ten problems tackled in June the success rate rose to 44 per cent for the English children and 68 per cent for the Dutch children. The researchers concluded that:

> The traditional algorithm was widely used by the English pupils who showed less progress than the Dutch pupils who used written methods based explicitly on repeated subtraction.
>
> (Anghileri et al. 2002: 1)

Anghileri (2006) later compared the written responses of a further 308 Year 5 English students with those of the English cohort in the earlier study on the same ten division problems and found that for the two-digit by two-digit division questions, the success rate had improved from 51.3 per cent to 60.1 per cent. In 1998 no child had used the chunking algorithm, whereas six years later the same percentage used it as used the traditional algorithm. The success rates differed by 23 per cent in favour of the chunking group (55 per cent to 32 per cent).

Unfortunately the Ofsted (2011) document fails to discuss the acknowledged 'confusion' caused by the long division algorithm. All the research from the 1980s and 1990s on the learning, mis-learning and forgetting of such algorithms appears to have been ignored. For example, Hart (1981), when considering the implications of the extensive research of the Concepts in Secondary Mathematics and Science (CSMS) team, concludes:

> The interviews on every topic showed that children for the most part did not use teacher-taught algorithms...To a great extent children adapt the algorithms they are taught or replace them by their own methods.
>
> (Hart 1981: 212)

In 1980 the Cockcroft Committee commissioned a report by the University of Bath on the use of mathematics in employment. The report states that: 'It is interesting that we do not find more evidence of "school methods" in people's arithmetic calculations' (University of Bath 1981: 110).

Also, in a chapter entitled 'Idiosyncratic methods', the authors report observing an example of a real problem dealing with trays of sausages that led to the calculation '2820 divided by 30' (University of Bath 1981: 106). The method illustrated is '40 trays is 1200lbs (40 × 30), so try 80 . . .'. This, of course, is a version of chunking that, more likely than not, had not been taught in school.

2. 'Because they do not spot the larger multiples of the divisor, they tend to work repeatedly in smaller steps of 10 times and 1 times the divisor' (Ofsted 2011: 16).

This 'weakness', of course, depends upon how much work the children have done on multiples. One useful strategy to help them develop confidence in this area, using just the basic skills of doubling, halving and multiplying by ten is to work with what I call 'partial multiple tables'. For example, if dividing by 36 the basic table looks like the one shown in Figure 10.7).

Three or six 36s can be found by addition, and if the dividend is a larger number, the table can be easily extended by multiplying 72 by 10 to find twenty 36s, and so on.

3. 'It is not clear why pupils who are able to understand the short division method seem to become confused when trying to record the same steps in the formal algorithm' (Ofsted 2011: 28).

I would argue that there is a very great difference between being able to correctly execute the short division algorithm and actually understanding it.

$$1 \rightarrow 36$$
$$2 \rightarrow 72$$
$$4 \rightarrow 144$$
$$10 \rightarrow 360$$
$$5 \rightarrow 180$$

Figure 10.7 A 'partial multiplies' table

$$\frac{1\ 3}{8)10^24}$$

Figure 10.8 Short division

Take the calculation $104 \div 8$ (Figure 10.8) where the 'patter' goes something like: '8 into 1 does not go [although it actually does if the one has its real value of 100] . . . 8 into 10 goes one remainder 2 . . . [8 into 10 *what*? One *what*?] . . . Carry the 2 . . . 8 into 24 goes 3.' It is very difficult to give meaning to this procedure; it just has to be learned (and quickly forgotten, as much research in the 1980s showed us). In my own case I successfully learned subtraction by 'equal additions' in primary school, but never came to terms at the time with the apparent unfairness of borrowing from one place (thin air?) and paying back to another!

The document also argues that chunking and short division do not support each other – the implication being that we should not be teaching chunking. I have argued the exact opposite (Thompson 2011) from the perspective of young children's understanding of place value.

4.   'Schools that teach the "chunking" method for long division acknowledge that some pupils have difficulty spotting large multiples and that errors creep in with the repeated subtractions' (Ofsted 2011: 28).

Even as an enthusiast for 'chunking' I have been critical of the emphasis given to '*subtractive* chunking'. The argument often provided in favour of the procedure is about 'choice': the most able child can work with large chunks whereas the less able can use smaller ones. The only problem is that for the less able, this leads to more subtractions, an operation that the child is probably not too proficient at in the first place. For this reason I have argued for 'additive chunking' or 'chunking up' (see Thompson 2005).

A Mathematics Specialist Teacher (MaST) reports on a small-scale research project in which Year 3 children were challenged to use their own written methods to solve simple two-digit by one-digit divisions (Bradford 2011). The vast majority of children solved the problems using multiples of the divisor in a manner similar to that illustrated in Figure 10.9.

This example and many others in the article suggest that working forwards is much easier than working backwards for at least two reasons:

•   Working backwards would give the sequence 31, 27, 23, 19, 15, 11, 7, 3 – an unfamiliar sequence compared to the forward multiples of four.

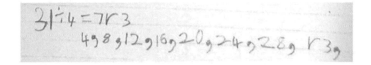

Figure 10.9 Division by counting up in 4s

- It is straightforward in Figure 10.9 to count the number of 4s written down and read off the remainder 3, whereas there is potential for confusion in the subtraction sequence. Do you start the count at 31 when you have not yet subtracted a 4? Do you include the 3 which you might feel you are counting twice if you also count it as the remainder?

This method is obviously more useful when dividing by a single-digit number, however, making use of a 'partial multiples' table (Figure 10.7) enables the procedure to be used for dividing by two- or three-digit numbers. Bradford's (2011) conclusion is that 'This work appears to offer "practical" evidence to back up Thompson's (2005) theoretical arguments concerning "complementary multiplication"' (Bradford 2011: 13).

On the same theme, Borthwick and Harcourt-Heath (2007) analysed the answers of 995 children on four Year 5 Qualifications and Curriculum Authority test questions. They repeated the analysis four years later (Borthwick and Harcourt-Heath 2010) using the same questions with a cohort of 1068 Year 5 children from the same schools. On the second occasion 28 per cent of the children achieved the correct answer on the division question – an increase of 7 per cent over the previous cohort. Also, the number of children successfully using the 'chunking up' strategy was greater by almost 50 per cent than the number of successful children using any other strategy.

Conclusion

This chapter has argued the case for an 'evidence-influenced' approach to the teaching of written calculation methods, and has discussed some of the evidence that might be expected to influence such an approach. Returning to Lester (2007), quoted at the beginning of this chapter, it is very important that all decisions concerning the teaching of written calculation (or anything at all!) are 'based on "evidence" rather than on . . . political dogma or uncritical benchmarking'.

Reflection

- Do you feel that the arguments made in this chapter are robust enough to convince you of the importance of teaching informal methods of calculation?
- What evidence do you, or could you, use to inform your practice in teaching mathematics?

Further reading

Thompson, I. (ed.) (2010) *Issues in Teaching Numeracy in Primary Schools* (2nd edn). Maidenhead: Open University Press.

The five chapters in the 'calculation' section of this book cover mental methods; the empty number line; and written methods for the four basic operations.

Guidance Paper – Calculation

This brief paper produced by the Primary National Strategy in 2006 is a useful document for planning a school calculation policy in that it illustrates progression in the teaching of written calculation algorithms for the four basic operations. Available at http://webarchive. nationalarchives.gov.uk/20110202093118/http:/nationalstrategies. standards.dcsf.gov.uk/node/47364?uc=force_uj (accessed 17 March 2012).

References

Anghileri, J. (2006) A study of the impact of reform on students' written calculation methods after five years' implementation of the National Numeracy Strategy in England. *Oxford Review of Education* 32 (3): 363–80.

Anghileri, J., Beishuizen, M. and van Putten, C. (2002) From informal strategies to structured procedures: Mind the gap! *Educational Studies in Mathematics* 49 (2): 149–70.

Assessment of Performance Unit (APU) (1982) *Mathematical Development: Primary Survey Report No. 3*. London: HMSO.

Borthwick, A. and Harcourt-Heath, M. (2007) Calculation strategies used by Year 5 children. *Proceedings of the British Society for Research into Learning Mathematics* 27 (1): 12–17.

Borthwick, A. and Harcourt-Heath, M. (2010) Calculating: What can Year 5 children do? *British Society for Research into Learning Mathematics (BSRLM) Informal Proceedings,* 30–3. Available at www.bsrlm.org.uk/ IPs/ip30-3/BSRLM-IP-30-3-03.pdf (accessed 30 January 2012).

Bradford, K. (2011) Division – forwards or backwards? *Primary Mathematics* 15 (2): 9–13.

Cockcroft, W.H. (1982) *Mathematics Counts: Report of the Committee of Inquiry into the Teaching of Mathematics in Schools* (Cockcroft Report). London: HMSO. Available at www.educationengland. org.uk/documents/cockcroft (accessed 31 January 2012).

Conservative Party (2011) *A World-Class Mathematics Education for All our Young People* (Task Force Report chaired by C. Vorderman). Available at www.conservatives.com/News/News_stories/2011/08/~/media/ Files/Downloadable%20Files/Vorderman%20maths%20report.ashx (accessed 30 January 2012).

Cowan, R., Donlan, C., Shepherd, D.-L., Cole-Fletcher, R., Saxton, M. and Hurry, J. (2011) Basic calculation proficiency and mathematics achievement in elementary school children. *Journal of Educational Psychology* 103 (4): 786–803.

Department for Education (DfE) (2012) *National Curriculum for mathematics Key Stages 1 and 2 – Draft.* Available at http://media .education.gov.uk/assets/files/pdf/p/draft%20national%20curriculum %20for%20mathematics%20key%20stages%201%202%20primary% 20%20%20%2011%20june%202012.pdf (accessed July 2012)

Department for Education (DfE) (2011a) *Review of the National Curriculum in England: Remit.* Available at www.education.gov.uk/schools/ teachingandlearning/curriculum/nationalcurriculum/b0073043/ remit-for-review-of-the-national-curriculum-in-england (accessed 30 January 2012).

Department for Education (DfE) (2011b) *The Framework for the National Curriculum: A Report by the Expert Panel for the National Curriculum Review.* London: DfE. Available at www.education.gov.uk/publications/ standard/publicationDetail/Page1/DFE-00135-2011 (accessed 30 January 2012).

Department for Education and Employment (DfEE) (1999) *The National Numeracy Strategy Framework for Teaching Mathematics from Reception to Year 6.* London: DfEE.

Department of Education and Science (DES) (1985) *Mathematics from 5 to 16.* HMI Curriculum Matters 3. London: HMSO.

Hammersley, M. (2001) Some questions about evidence-based practice in education. Paper presented at the symposium on Evidence-Based Practice in Education at the Annual Conference of the British Educational Research Association, University of Leeds, 13–15 September.

Hart, K. (1981) *Children's Understanding of Mathematics 11–16*. London: John Murray.

Jerrim, J. (2011) *England's 'Plummeting' PISA Test Scores between 2000 and 2009: Is the Performance of our Secondary School Pupils Really in Relative Decline?* London: Department of Quantitative Social Science, Institute of Education, University of London.

Lester, S. (2007) *Evidence-Based Practice: A Resource Paper*. Available at www.sld.demon.co.uk/ebp.pdf (accessed 30 January 2012).

Mooney, C. (2011) *The Science of Why We Don't Believe Science*. Available at http://motherjones.com/politics/2011/03/denial-science-chris-mooney (accessed 30 January 2012).

National Foundation for Educational Research (NFER) (2008) *England's Achievement in TIMSS 2007: National Report for England*. NFER: Berkshire.

Nutley, S., Davies, H. and Walter, I. (2002) *Evidence Based Policy and Practice: Cross Sector Lessons from the UK*. St Andrews: ESRC UK Centre for Evidence Based Policy and Practice Research Unit for Research Utilisation.

Oates, T. (2010) *Could Do Better: Using International Comparisons to Refine the National Curriculum in England*. Cambridge: University of Cambridge Examinations Syndicate. Available at www.cambridge assessment.org.uk/ca/digitalAssets/188853_Could_do_better_FINAL _inc_foreword.pdf (accessed 30 January 2012).

Office for Standards in Education (Ofsted) (1993) *The Teaching and Learning of Number in Primary Schools*. London: HMSO.

Office for Standards in Education (Ofsted) (2002) Ofsted Invitation Conference for Primary Teachers, Brunel University, 20 March. Available at www.ofsted.gov.uk/resources/ofsted-subject-conference-reports-200102 (accessed 30 January 2012).

Office for Standards in Education (Ofsted) (2011) *Good Practice in Primary Mathematics: Evidence from 20 Successful Schools*. London: Ofsted. Available at www.ofsted.gov.uk/resources/good-practice-primary-mathematics-evidence-20-successful-schools (accessed 30 January 2012).

Organization for Economic Cooperation and Development (OECD) (2009) *Viewing the United Kingdom School System through the Prism of PISA*. Available at www.oecd.org/dataoecd/33/8/46624007.pdf (accessed 30 January 2012).

Qualifications and Curriculum Authority (QCA) (1997) *Mathematics Year 4 Assessment Unit: Place Value*. London: DfEE.

Thompson, I. (1994) Young children's idiosyncratic written algorithms for addition. *Educational Studies in Mathematics* 26 (4): 323–45.

Thompson, I. (2005) Division by complementary multiplication. *Mathematics in School* 34 (5): 5–7. Available at http://www.ianthompson.pi.dsl.pipex.com/index_files/division%20by%20complementary%20multiplication.pdf (accessed 30 January 2012).

Thompson, I. (2011) Are we selling the children short? *Primary Mathematics* 15 (3): 3–4.

Thompson, I. and Bramald, R. (2002) *An Investigation of the Relationship between Young Children's Understanding of Place Value and their Competence at Mental Addition* (Final report submitted to the Nuffield Foundation). Newcastle upon Tyne: Department of Education, University of Newcastle upon Tyne.

Thompson, I. and Smith, F. (1999) *Mental Calculation Strategies for the Addition and Subtraction of 2-Digit Numbers* (Report for the Nuffield Foundation). Newcastle upon Tyne: Department of Education, University of Newcastle upon Tyne.

University of Bath (1981) *Mathematics in Employment (16–18)*. Bath: University of Bath.

Whetton, C., Ruddock, G. and Twist, L. (2007) *Standards in English Primary Education: The International Evidence* (Primary Review Research Survey 4/2). Cambridge: Faculty of Education, University of Cambridge.

Whitehurst, G.J. (2003) The Institute of Education Sciences: New wine, new bottles. Paper presented at the annual meeting of the American Educational Research Association, Chicago, IL, September.

11 Are the children thinking mathematically?

The pedagogy of children's mathematical graphics

Elizabeth Carruthers

Introduction and context

This chapter discusses some of the pedagogy that supports children's own ways of writing down their mathematical thinking. It is based on a case study of a teacher, drawing on her perspectives and reflections, as she described how she started to uncover children's mathematical graphics. 'Children's mathematical graphics' is a term first used by Worthington and Carruthers (2003) to describe the many ways that children put their own mathematical thinking on paper as they work out *their* mathematics.

The aims of this chapter are to:

- Uncover the pedagogy behind children's own ways of representing their mathematical thinking
- Highlight key pedagogical strategies
- Explain some of the challenges of introducing children's mathematical graphics throughout the primary school
- Illustrate an expert teacher's reflections and new thinking as she developed her understanding about children's mathematical graphics.

Children's mathematical graphics and the curriculum

The mathematical curriculum in England threads, at times, a positive and open approach to children's own ways of thinking about mathematics. It is these nuggets of enlightenment that teachers can use to justify their practice in supporting young children's own choices and thinking in mathematics. For example the *Practice Guidance for the Early Years Foundation Stage* (DfES 2007b: 61) states: 'value children's own graphics and practical explorations of problem solving'. This is vital in creating an environment that encourages and supports children's own mathematical graphics.

The following statements are also sprinkled through the mathematics sections (DfES 2007b: 61; DfE 2011):

- 'Look at how children are creating and experimenting with marks and symbols'
- 'Note the context in which young children use marks and symbols'
- 'Sharing children's thinking makes adults aware of children's interests and understandings and enables them to foster development of knowledge and ideas'
- 'Choose sensible calculation methods to solve whole-number problems drawing on their understanding of the operations'
- 'Explaining methods is an important foundation for reasoning and proof in later key stages'

Two government documents give further guidance on this. First, *Mark Making Matters* (DCSF 2008) places the emphasis on children and their own free graphicacy and meanings they are making in all curriculum areas. This important change in the curriculum clarifies that graphicacy is not just literacy related, and gives teachers freedom to think more widely about its development.

Second, the government document *Children Thinking Mathematically* (DCSF 2009) concentrates mainly on children's mathematical graphics and explores the range of graphics children use and the mathematical environments that encourage this.

While these examples do seem to encourage teachers to listen to and value children's own methods, there are also some rather less clear pointers such as 'communicate in spoken, pictorial and written form, at first using informal language and recording, then mathematical language and symbols' (DfE 2011: 21).

This statement could mean that the children use their own informal methods and then progress to standard methods, whereas Carruthers and Worthington (2006, 2011) report that children move *between* standard methods and their own methods, if given the freedom. This is an important transition period.

Hoyles (2009) writes that the taught procedures supporting calculation can often be taught without children grasping why they work. She continues that pupils prefer to use a common-sense approach but because they feel teachers seem to value standard approaches more, they forego their own methods in order to gain the teacher's approval. Hoyles (2009) reminds us that teachers should be mindful of children's fragility and appreciate their mathematical argument. It is advisable therefore to encourage reasoning rather than 'answer getting' (Hoyles 2009: 12).

An Ofsted (2011) survey of the teaching methods of twenty high achieving schools in mathematics offers insight into the difficulties teachers face with written methods. In congruence with Hoyle's (2009) work, even in schools where long division methods had changed to one of jottings rather than the traditional algorithm, pupils (especially low attainers) were hesitant to use jottings, perceiving this as a weakness. Interestingly, the Ofsted (2011) study reports that difficulties lie more in formal recording than in understanding.

Children's mathematical graphics

The case study featured in this chapter is based on our work (Carruthers and Worthington 2005) exploring children's mathematical graphics. When children were given open opportunities to use their own mathematical graphics, they chose to use a range of graphics including their own invented symbols and standard symbols. This is different from standardized prescribed ways of written mathematics where all of the written mathematics is school derived and the children are confined to definite ways of representing and they are also restricted to using graph paper or worksheets where they fill in boxes.

Our pedagogical perspective is a Vygotskian sociocultural one. Children's mathematical graphics are cultural tools (Vygotsky 1978) that children choose to use and make meaning within their mathematics. These graphics are representations of their thinking. Ernest (1991), Cobb et al. (1992), Pimm (1995) and Thompson (2008) have acknowledged the significance of children's own representations. Van Oers' (2000) work has also highlighted the importance of children as symbol users and symbol inventors, arguing that 'the efforts of the pupils to get a better grip on symbols in a meaningful way should be considered one of the core objectives of education, especially the domain of mathematics' (van Oers 2000: 126).

Children's mathematical graphics are derived from their own rich and diverse cultural experiences from home, community and school. Cullen and Jordan (2004) emphasize the importance of the relationships within and beyond the school for the child's intellectual growth.

> Teachers' responses to what they notice children engaged with also depend on their learning more about those interests in which children themselves could already be well informed, so that the

children will be able to co-engage in developing ever greater complexity and breadth of understanding about the topic area.

(Jordan 2010: 99)

Vygotsky (1978) sees the teacher as mediator co-constructing learning
with the child. His concept of the zone of proximal development is familiar to most teachers as that 'space' between the known and still unknown
which is ripe for development (Vygotsky 1978). In the view of Scrimsher
and Trudge (2003), the zone of proximal development

> is not some clear cut space that exists independently of the pro-
> cess of joint activity itself (i.e. between the child and knowledge-
> able other) despite the fact that many authors write as though
> the teacher's role is to identify the space between what the child
> currently knows and what the teacher can help him to know.
> Rather the zone of proximal development is *created* in the course
> of collaboration as an emergent property of teacher–child or peer
> interaction.
>
> (Scrimsher and Trudge 2003: 300)

Scrimsher and Trudge (2003) also describe the Russian word *obucherie* as
meaning teaching *and* learning together and therefore they are not seen
as isolated units. They explain the importance of the word *obucherie*.
'The more accurate interpretation of the word [*obucherie*] as teaching
and learning connotes highly interactive relations involving all participants in creative activity and growth' (Scrimsher and Trudge 2003:
298). The teacher is therefore involved in a shared understanding and/or
learning from the child about the child's thinking and contexts. From
a Vygotskian sociocultural perspective, individual factors, such as children's interests and background histories, should be interwoven with
teachers' motivations and together make not a zone but zones of proximal
development.

Case study: Karen's story

In the following case study I explore the ways in which Karen, a reception/
nursery teacher, had changed her own understanding and perception of
the importance of listening to the children's thought processes as they
developed their mathematical understanding. Having improved her own
knowledge of early mathematical graphicacy, and hence become more
sensitized to the ways in which children make and communicate meaning, she found her own practice and, indeed, that of colleagues in her
school in the classroom changing.

Case Study 11.1: Children's learning, teachers' learning – a two-way process

Karen had attended a course on *Children's Mathematical Graphics* (Carruthers and Worthington 2005) which proved a catalyst in changing her thinking on classroom practice. Six months after the course Karen agreed to take part in a research project. This was designed to analyse aspects of the pedagogy of children's mathematics that she had personally identified as being pivotal in changing her practice in mathematics. The following is an account of a two-hour conversation with Karen in which she talks freely about changes in her thinking and practice and the impact it was having in the wider context of the school. The conversation unfolded and the topics arose naturally; there was no fixed agenda. I asked questions responding to what she had said and, at times, confirmed or clarified her narrative.

I have organized the data into themes derived from the conversation itself and the meanings we were uncovering. The rest of this chapter presents a discussion of Karen's changing perspectives in relation to these themes.

Karen and personal change

Karen had enthusiastically recalled her first attempt to open up the mathematics and challenge the children. She wanted to offer a challenge beyond what she thought they could do (echoing Vygotsky's (1978) view that useful instruction is in advance of development).

Karen recalled that she read a book to the children, *One is a Snail, Ten is a Crab* (Pulley Sayre and Sayre 2004); the book uses pictures of animals, highlighting their feet to support counting and calculating. She suggested that each child choose a number and then work out which combination of creatures would have feet totalling that number.

All the children chose a different number; many chose larger numbers than they would normally work with in the classroom. For example Roxy chose 67, Tyree chose 800 and Jamie chose 100 because he said 'that is massive'. Each child chose different animals to represent the feet and all the graphics were different.

> Karen said this was a real 'eye-opener' and children's self-challenges and their individual problem solving was, for her, 'remarkable'.

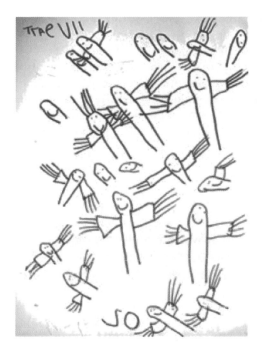

Figure 11.1 Travell's drawing

Each child had a different strategy. For example Travell (4 years, 11 months) had decided to find out 'What is 40'. His first attempt was to draw lots of people and say to the adult nearby, 'Is that 40?' He had used a common-sense and age-appropriate strategy; he had a go. The adult sensitively said, 'I don't know. How can you find out?' Travell then counted in twos to 20 and then looked at the '100 square', continued counting in twos to 32. He had counted all the people he had drawn. Finally he drew four additional people and counted the total, writing: '20 people makes 40' (see Figure 11.1). (Based on an extract from Carruthers and Worthington 2011.)

> Karen emphasizes:
>
> For children to use their own mathematical graphic, give them a real challenge, it will uncover their strategies, thinking and ways of working.

This episode had uncovered that able children were probably not challenged enough in their mathematics. It also had a huge impact on Karen's drive to want to know more about children's own mathematics. This openness of a teacher to experiment in her own classroom is a highly personalized form of professional development. Karen constantly came back to the fact that she had not noticed or uncovered the mathematics the children were capable of. Furthermore, as she walked around her classroom, she observed that there were lots of opportunities in mark making and graphics in literacy but not for mathematics.

Karen commented:

> When I thought about it, it does not make any sense, why would we have done that, but it was because we were not thinking about mark making in mathematics. I am now seeing it in a different way and that is the big change. I now know what it means.

This perhaps relates to what Carruthers and Worthington (2006) emphasize when they say that having an abundance of graphic materials freely available makes a huge difference to the children. They should have the opportunity to choose to use paper and pencils or pens or other graphic materials if they wish. Children cannot be spontaneous with their mathematical graphics if there are no graphic tools at hand.

It is clear that the knowledge that Karen had gained from the course had made a big difference to reflection on and understanding of her practice as a teacher of mathematics. It is also possible that her gains were in part due to her own personal theories of learning. She explained to me how, even before the start of the course, she already had an understanding that children are capable of more than the set and often narrow tasks schools give them, explaining that in her first year of teaching she had often been surprised by their organization and logic, confirming Tizard and Hughes' (1984) findings that even very young children are logical thinkers.

Karen's recognition of this, supported by her own developing expertise, allowed her to begin to change her pedagogy. As Fleer (2010) points out, it is how we view children that determines the way we teach.

Reflection

What is your personal theory of how children learn mathematics?

Karen related a story about a child and their mathematics:

> We introduced the book *How Big is a Million* (Milbourne and Riglietti 2007) which is about a penguin who wants to know how big a million is. We asked the children how big a million is and we went outside and inside. Then we [the staff] just stood back and looked at what the children were doing. We had put out calculators and clipboards, paper, pencils, pens everywhere and I walked past and I just saw this piece of paper on the clipboard. Usually I would not have paid very much attention to it but I stopped and I asked the children around, 'Who did this', and Thomas said, 'Me, I did this' and I said to Thomas, 'Could you tell me what you were doing?' Thomas said, 'I was trying to see what a hundred looks like', and I said, 'Right, so what did you do?' Thomas said, 'I did lots of circles and I got to 95 and ran out of space, I know that a hundred is a bit bigger than that' [the circles on the page].
>
> So I was just amazed because he had sat there and decided...and he said 'I had to do circles inside circles because I had no space on the page'.
>
> Before I had attended that course I would not have really paid any attention to that piece of paper unless I had seen him doing it in front of me. I just felt that I came away knowing more about that one child and what he was thinking. He knew what 95 is, he has just turned 5 and he said 95 is near 100. From just one piece of representing I learned so much about that child (see Figure 11.2).

I asked Karen if, as she said, she previously would not have paid attention to a child's marks that appear scribble-like, how would she have reacted?

Karen responded:

> If I had watched a child doing it and they had explained it there and then I would have been more interested – but if I had just seen it I would have left it and it would have been tidied away. I would not have thought that represented mathematical thinking. I have done a lot around mark-making and writing but not maths and I am now really valuing what children are doing in maths.

Figure 11.2 I tried to make 100 circles but I only got to 95 and ran out of space (Thomas, 5 years, 1 month)

Karen agreed that this listening to children's own explanations of their mathematical graphics had been a huge conceptual shift for her. Salmon and Kohler Riessman (2008: 32) reflect that young children need adults who 'listen generously'. Wells's (1986) study reported that children become more competent if they have an attentive, listening adult who is genuinely interested in what they say. In Karen's case, listening attentively also contributed to the enhancement of her professional knowledge and practice.

Reflection

Consider ways you can give children opportunities to use their own mathematical graphics.

Exploring children's mathematical graphics and taking risks

Karen then described another mathematics story. She had given the children a moderate challenge about one more and one less and thought they would be able to do this easily, but many of them had difficulties.

Karen said:

> Olivia (5 years, 5 months) was really interesting; she picked the number 20 and said to me I don't know that [what one less than 20 is]. I said, 'Well maybe you could use the paper to help you'. 'Can I write all the numbers?' [the child said]...and I said, 'Please do', so she wrote out all the numbers to 20. Then I said, 'What are you going to do now?' and she pointed to 20 and said that if you go that way, that is one less so the answer is 19. Every time she picked a card she used her number line (see Figure 11.3).

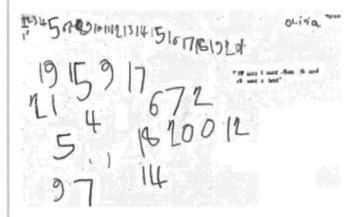

Figure 11.3 Olivia (5 years, 5 months) made her own number line to work out the subtraction.

I asked Karen if Olivia had been making an aide memoir. I suggested that she had also been organizing her own resources, meaning that she needed a number line and instead of relying on the teacher she used her own initiative.

Karen agreed and explained:

> I have never seen her make her own number line before; I was blown away. She is not somebody who I have seen problem solving. She would be happy to copy my examples before but not think for herself. She could explain exactly how she did it and I said so what if you picked up 14 and she immediately went to the number line and told me the answer. When she said I am going to write down the numbers, I did not know where she was going with this.

Karen trusted the children, even though at the time she did not understand their reasoning. Karen was in what Gooche (2010: 42) describes as a 'risky space for teachers to occupy', not knowing where this was going, but her developing expertise and confidence allowed her to take the chance. Such a space leads to 'huge rafts of possibilities' (Gooche 2010: 56).

From the children's perspective, there was also the power of using a number line, obviously a useful strategy, especially when they had their own personal one.

Karen said that she had noticed that children were explaining their own methods to other children:

> Tyree picked number 9 – and said, 'I do not know what one less than 9 is.' I said to her, 'Do you need any thing to help you?' She drew circles and crossed one off and she counted them and said, '8.' I said, 'Then what is one more?' and she said, 'I know one more, because I can just put nine in my head and count up so that is 10 . . .' So she knew what one more was and she needed the graphics to work out one less. It just shows you where she is – one more, fine, and one less, she needs additional support.
>
> At the end of the session I asked the class if they would like to share their learning. Tyree showed her friends on the board exactly what she did.

Tyree was using her graphics as a tool to support her thinking. Carruthers and Worthington (2006) clearly make the distinction between what teachers refer to as recording their mathematics (where the children already know the answer) and children's own mathematical graphics that support their thinking in uncovering the answer. Tyree also had been able to show children how she did it because it was her own way and she understood it. I asked Karen if Tyree had shown everybody her very own way of solving the problem.

Karen replied:

> Yes, and that is exactly what I did not give children the opportunity to do before.

It was clear Karen thought this was extremely significant and helpful to all the children and this was powerful; children explaining their graphics to other children. This is what is described by Carruthers and Worthington (2006) as peer modelling; a crucial pedagogical strategy to support children's mathematical thinking. There are many different ways to tackle a mathematics problem, ways that we, as adults, have not thought of. Taking time to allow such peer modelling in classrooms can help both the children's and the teacher's learning.

Reflection

- In what ways do you think children sharing their mathematical graphics with their peers will support their mathematical thinking?
- How do you think it will support the teacher's mathematical thinking?

Influencing others

Karen's personal deliberation and reflection not only led to a shift in her own professional learning and practice, but also began to impact on colleagues in her immediate team and beyond.

A huge and difficult change for her team was understanding the difference between recording and children's mathematical graphics. In schools in England, 'recording mathematics' is something children do after they have used practical apparatus to solve a mathematics problem. They write the answer and often draw the apparatus they used. They already know the answer before they record it. In contrast, however, children use their mathematical graphics to work out a mathematics problem that they do not know the answer to. The graphics helps them think through their mathematics.

> Karen articulates the challenge that faces them:
>
> > If it is recording, why are we doing it? And that has been a really difficult thing for us to think about.

This is a key question for their team. It has been particularly difficult for them because, as Karen says, it challenges their understanding of the purpose of recording:

> > We still catch ourselves asking the children to record. What is the point of recording if they already know the answer? We have really tried to stop the recording with no purpose; it was not driving their learning in any way. It was just evidence for a book...what is the point in it, why are they doing it? I know he can do 5 add 1 equals 6 so writing it down is not going to help because he already knows this.

Another significant change in pedagogy is that Karen and her team are actively looking for children's own mathematical graphics, perhaps because they know the children can do their own thinking in mathematics now.

> Karen agreed:
>
> > Yes, and I just feel that is where this [children's mathematical graphics] is now being valued and I am actively looking for it and that is the big difference.

Influencing the rest of the school

> Karen explained:
>
> > We have just started talking about children's mathematical graphics in Year 1. One of the Year 1 teachers, who is new to teaching in Year 1, invited me in to see what I thought. He was doing a maths

session, and straightaway I thought, if I had looked at this before I had attended the maths graphics course, I would have looked at it totally differently. In another Year 1 class I discovered that one child was expected to write in neat boxes when he knew the answer in his head. I discussed this with the Year 1 teacher. So we are beginning to really challenge the teaching. I have been put on to the maths team to influence the rest of the school.

Karen has managed to introduce elements of supporting children's mathematical graphics throughout the school. There is a real tension in the school between making children write neatly in squared paper books (from Year 1) and uncovering the children's own mathematical thinking through their own graphics. At the time of the conversation Karen's school was in special measures and this brought with it a lot of outside influence that may have been at odds with the developing practice of the school. (It is now out of special measures in Ofsted category 'Good'.)

Karen was tense and forceful as she explained what was expected by Ofsted:

We are being battered to make sure our books are neat. So we talked and there is now a real recognition that graphics to support thinking is not neat and we all support that. So we are finding a way to ensure that, without compromising the neatness in the book. So that is where we are at, at the moment. We are happy that the question has been raised and we are thinking about it . . . and generally it is recognized . . . children using their own method is an issue throughout the school and we are all in agreement about that. Representing thinking is not neat, it is not in boxes, we are not going to do it this way. If you have children sitting at a table putting numbers in boxes the expectation is more about putting the numbers in the boxes. We need to be thinking about what we are wanting children to do and get out of it. The focus should be on the mathematics not the recording, not 'Is it on the line?' but 'What is the maths?' Is there mathematical thinking going on?

Reflection

What do you think is the purpose of neat presentation in mathematics?

Support staff in change

Karen reflected:

> It is such a different way of thinking [supporting children's mathematical graphics] to what people are really used to – people have to be passionate about it and buy into it, see the value of it, because to change your way of thinking that much, people really need to understand why. With my team, we have developed a really open dialogue. They are confident to speak out and question, otherwise people pay lip service to things and go 'Oh yeh' and they have not actually engaged with it to any real level.

Karen reflected that professional reading seemed to have helped:

> My team have borrowed the book we got on the course and I have not seen it for some time as it has been borrowed by nearly all the staff and there has been impact. People have been coming at it from reading the same thing. My Foundation Stage team say here come and see this and they talk about mathematical graphics and we look together. We have given ourselves the flexibility to have a go.

Back and Joubert (2009) in their study of effective mathematical professional development reported that reading and reflecting on research findings were valuable in supporting teachers' thinking.

Children and change

I asked Karen what change, if any, she could see in the children.

Karen expressed that she was not sure the children had changed:

> The opportunities I provide have changed and my thinking and understanding of children's development has changed.

It seems as a result of this personal change she has uncovered children's mathematical thinking that perhaps lay hidden. A very poignant discovery for Karen was that the children who sometimes may be 'invisible' within a class are noticed for their abilities.

Karen said:

It brings out those that are almost missed as able mathematicians.

There was some kind of barrier before, and now, because of the change in teacher attitude towards mathematics, the children are showing what they can do. Karen now knows that all these drawings and marks have meaning, even in mathematics. Class culture in mathematics has moved to *a culture of mathematical enquiry* (Carruthers and Worthington 2011). Children are now organizing themselves and seeing what they need to solve their problems and now choose their own methods.

Karen explained:

The children are now more used to me valuing what they have done and what they have to say about their mathematics; they talk about what they have done much more — they are more engaged in graphicacy for maths as well as for writing. They do more maths now.

And we as teachers are engaged in dropping the mathematical graphics in as a model, not for them to copy but for them to think about, not to do the teachers way but find the way that makes sense to them.

Karen and the foundation staff used informal modelling as a teaching strategy. This is when mathematical methods both formal and informal are presented to children flexibly throughout the week. Mostly they relate to real contexts, for example, different ways to represent the register or data collecting for a school trip. At this time children's own methods are also shared with the class. The children are not pressurized to use the method demonstrated but instead it is used as a discussion point. Children might draw on this knowledge at a later date and choose to use the methods modelled by the teacher or the children (Carruthers and Worthington 2011).

The imposed curriculum

I asked, 'You said that you could see the children's own graphics in literacy but not in the maths. Do you think that might be to do with the curriculum, for example, the Foundation Stage document in literacy is full of communication statements but not so in mathematics.'

> Karen talked about the Foundation Stage Profile (DfES 2007a). She said that Problem Solving, Reasoning and Numeracy (PSRN) does not involve a huge amount of deliberation:
>
> > It is clear cut in PSRN it is not about representing their thinking but in CLL [Communication Language and Literacy] it is huge. In PSRN what we are assessing against is a tick list.

I agreed but I also said FSP point 8 in mathematicss is about problem solving and that is about thinking.

> Karen agreed but she said teachers do not understand it, their expectations are too low, and it often goes no further than 'How many milks do we need? They do that in the nursery'. Karen felt strongly that the statement in the Foundation Stage Profile (DfES 2007a) 'Count to ten reliably' was a low expectation for nearly all her children. She said that her children were now doing complicated mathematics and that did not register anywhere in the foundation mathematics assessment criteria. The content of the expected mathematics curriculum to her was sparse and did not help teachers understand children's mathematics.

The NCETM (2009) study also reported on a reception class that had displays of mathematical graphics on the wall: 'The standard of the mathematical understanding, thinking and reasoning that the displays revealed was far higher than the specified curriculum objectives for children this age' (NCTEM 2009: 64).

The evidence seems to emphasize there is general low expectation and paucity of challenge for children in school mathematics. Teachers may need to think beyond the restrictions of the current mathematics curriculum if they want to offer teaching opportunities that match children's true mathematical ability.

Conclusion

The pedagogy of children's mathematical graphics is complex and, as Karen identifies, challenges and changes thinking. Karen's collaborative discussions with her colleagues brought them to a willingness to discuss ways to change their pedagogy.

Karen, the Foundation Stage staff and the children were also becoming interdependent (Rogoff 1990: 39) rather than dependent. The teaching staff were finding ways to share understanding about the children's mathematical thinking. In an environment that encourages children's own thinking, socially inclusive relationships are part of the ethos (Lancaster 2003). These relationships mean that the adults understand how to share power so that children can take part fully and be able to access opportunities and real choices. Children's ideas and thoughts are central to this environment. Chambers (1994) explains that children need to be active participants in their own learning and not passive receivers of knowledge.

Summary

Karen's reflections brought to the fore some key points about mathematical graphics that can make a difference to teaching and learning:

- A need to know more, try out ideas and take risks
- Providing:
  - o open challenges that stretch children's thinking
  - o graphic materials and resources in abundance
  - o easily readable references, for example one hundred squares and number lines
- Trusting the children
- Having open honest dialogues with colleagues
- Modelling teacher and child mathematical methods in flexible ways
- Valuing all children's mathematical graphics
- Sensitively asking the children about their graphics.

Karen had a deep insight into children and their learning before the mathematics course; the main change was that she now looks at the children being equally as creative and able in mathematics as well as in literacy. Thinking was a thread that ran through the whole interview; teachers' thinking about children's mathematical thinking and striving for that knowledge.

Further reading

Carruthers, E. and Worthington, M. (2011) *Understanding Children's Mathematical Graphics: Beginnings in Play*. Maidenhead: Open University Press.
This book illustrates the mathematical practice of early years teachers with case studies and reference to the theory and pedagogy of children's mathematical graphics.
Pound, L. (1999) *Supporting Mathematically Development in the Early Years*. Maidenhead: Open University Press.
This has a general early years mathematical focus but with an emphasis on children as mathematical thinkers.

References

Back, J. and Joubert, M. (2009) Reflecting on practice in early years' settings: Developing teachers' understanding of children's early mathematics. *Proceedings of the British Society for Research into Learning Mathematics* 29 (1): 13–18.

Carruthers, E. and Worthington, M. (2005) Making sense of mathematical graphics: The development of understanding abstract symbolism. *European Early Childhood Education Research Association Journal* 13 (1): 57–79.

Carruthers, E. and Worthington, M. (2006) *Children's Mathematics: Making Marks, Making Meaning* (2nd edn). London: Sage.

Carruthers, E. and Worthington, M. (2011) *Understanding Children's Mathematical Graphics: Beginnings in Play*. Maidenhead: Open University Press.

Chambers, P. (1994) The origins and practice of participatory rural appraisal. *World Development* 22 (7): 953–69.

Cobb, P., Yackel, E. and Wood, T. (1992) A constructivist alternative to the representational view of mind in mathematics education. *Journal for Research in Mathematics Education* 23: 2–33.

Cullen, J. and Jordan, B. (2004) Our elusive dream: Towards an early years (birth to eight) curriculum approach. Paper presented at New Zealand Association for Research in Education (NZARE) conference, Wellington, 24 November.

Department for Children, Schools and Families (DCSF) (2008) *Mark Making Matters: Young Children Making Meaning in All Areas of Learning and Development*. Nottingham: DCSF.

Department for Children, Schools and Families (DCSF) (2009) *Children Thinking Mathematically*. London: DCSF.

Department for Education (DfE) (2011) *Key Stage 1 MA2 Number*. London: DfE.

Department for Education and Skills (DfES) (2007a) *The Foundation Stage Profile*. London: DfES.

Department for Education and Skills (DfES) (2007b) *Practice Guidance for the Early Years Foundation Stage*. London: DfES.

Dreyfus, S. and Dreyfus, H. (1980) *A Five-Stage Model of the Mental Activities Involved in Directed Skill Acquisition*. Berkeley, CA: Operations Research Center, University of California.

Ernest, P. (1991) *The Philosophy of Mathematics Education*. London: Falmer.

Fleer, M. (2010) *Early Learning and Development: Cultural-Historical Concepts in Play*. Melbourne, VIC: Cambridge University Press.

Gooche, K. (2010) *Towards Excellence in Early Years Education: Exploring Narratives of Experience*. Abingdon: Routledge.

Hoyles, C. (2009) Understanding mathematics learning. *Better: Evidence Based Education* Autumn: 12–13. Available at www.ncetm.org.uk/public/files/573534/Understanding_mathematics_learning.pdf (accessed 30 May 2012).

Jordan, B. (2010) Co-constructing knowledge: Children, teachers and families engaging in a science rich curriculum. In L. Brooker and S. Edwards (eds) *Engaging Play*. Maidenhead: Open University Press.

Lancaster, L. (2003) Moving into literacy: How it all begins. In N. Hall, J. Larson and J. Marsh (eds) *Handbook of Early Childhood Literacy*. London: Sage.

Milbourne, A. and Riglietti, S. (2007) *How Big is a Million?* London: Usborne.

National Centre for Excellence in Teaching Mathematics (NCETM) (2009) *Final Report: Researching Effective CPD in Mathematics Education*. London: DCSF.

Office for Standards in Education (Ofsted) (2011) *Good Practice in Primary Mathematics: Evidence from 20 Successful Schools*. London: The Stationery Office. Available at www.ofsted.gov.uk/resources/good-practice-primary-mathematics-evidence-20-successful-schools (accessed 23 May 2012).

Pimm, D. (1995) *Symbols and Meanings in School Mathematics*. London: Routledge.

Pulley Sayre, A. and Sayre, J. (2004) *One is a Snail, Ten is a Crab*. London: Walker.

Rogoff, B. (1999) *Apprenticeship in Thinking: Cognitive Development in Social Contexts*. Oxford: Oxford University Press.

Salmon, P. and Kohler Riessman, C. (2008) Looking back on Narrative Research: An exchange. In M. Andrews, C. Squire and M. Tamboukou (eds) *Doing Narrative Research*. London: Sage.

Schrimsher, S. and Trudge, J. (2003) The teaching/learning relationship in the first years of school: Some revolutionary implications of Vygotsky's theory. *Early Education and Development* 14 (3): 293–312.

Thompson, I. (2008) What do young children's mathematical graphics tell us about the teaching of written calculation? In I. Thompson (ed.) *Teaching and Learning Early Number* (2nd edn). Maidenhead: Open University Press.

Tizard, B. and Hughes, M. (1984) *Young Children Learning: Talking and Thinking at Home and at School*. London: Fontana.

van Oers, B. (2002) Teachers' epistemology and the monitoring of mathematical thinking in early years classrooms. *European Early Childhood Education Research Journal* 10 (2): 19–30.

Vygotsky, L.S. (1978) *Mind in Society: The Development of Higher Psychological Processes*. Cambridge, MA: Harvard University Press.

Wells, G. (1986) *The Meaning Makers: Children Learning Language and Using Language to Learn*. Portsmouth, NH: Heinemann.

Worthington, M. and Carruthers, E. (2003) *Children's Mathematics: Making Marks, Making Meaning*. London: Sage.

12 Teaching mathematics

Self-knowledge, pupil knowledge and content knowledge

Effie Maclellan

Introduction

Mathematical learning is significantly influenced by the quality of mathematics teaching (Hiebert and Grouws 2007). In spite of the evidence for teachers seeking to do what they believe to be in the best interests of their learners (Schuck 2009; Gholami and Husu 2010), research and policy reports (within the UK and beyond) draw attention to insufficient mathematical attainment (Williams 2008; Eurydice 2011). Why is there this discrepancy? On the one hand, teachers are open to improving their professional practices (Escudero and Sánchez 2007), and on the other, the findings of mathematical education research make little or no impact on teachers' practice (Wiliam 2003), even though teachers themselves think that they are enacting new or revised practices (Speer 2005).

This chapter seeks to address this discrepancy not through offering advice on what works in classrooms (because such advice rarely has the same meaning for all classrooms) but through causing teachers to reflect on their own expertise. Because teaching is understood not only as overt behaviour but also as the teacher's thinking – precipitated by the situational, developmental and contextual needs of particular learners (Shulman 1988) – this chapter explores three dimensions of the teacher's thinking: teachers' self-knowledge, pupil knowledge and content knowledge. Since dialogue, reflection and discussion are central to teacher learning, the chapter is structured to stimulate readers to think about their own practices as well as discussing practices with peers. The rationale for this approach is twofold. First, regardless of whether one is teaching at early or later stages of school, profound mathematics teaching involves learners constructing understandings of mathematics (Ginsburg and Amit 2008). Second, as teachers talk and work together on matters that are deeply situated in practice, they share and attempt to understand how each deals with specific concepts and procedures, they identify inconsistencies in their collective knowledge and they consult authoritative sources. Further, they set goals, monitor collaborative effort, and negotiate future courses of action. In so doing, they steer and organize the construction of their corporate knowledge, through taking account of different contributions in the context of their own teaching (Hurme et al. 2006; Damşa et al. 2010).

It is teachers' lived professional experience that on a daily basis they will be met with learners who vary in their prior mathematical experience and their motivation to learn. Because classes are constructed according to chronological age, this variation can include learners who are advanced, who underachieve, who grapple with the language of instruction, who come from diverse cultural and/or economic backgrounds, and who have learning problems. Indeed some learners may fit into more than one of the categories. The variation of some learners performing at, some performing below and some capable of performing well above, stage-level expectations is demanding in any curricular area, but teachers are particularly challenged by the mathematics curriculum because of learners' lack of expected progression and failure to achieve stage-level standards (Miller and Hudson 2007).

How teachers respond to this variation and capitalize on professional support to maximize their own learning can be understood in terms of teachers' expertise. Some will be overwhelmed by the vast amount of mathematics research information that is 'out there'. At the other end of the continuum will be teachers who will evaluate that information and select from it in ways that are fit-for-purpose. When people work in any domain they are constantly in the process of developing expertise. Through sensitizing ourselves to notice what was previously taken-for-granted or unnoticed, our observations can inform action in the future. By becoming aware of how our attention shifts, we can learn, intentionally, from experience. Dreyfus characterized this growth of expertise through five different stages (Dreyfus and Dreyfus 1980), which represent qualitatively different forms of learning behaviour (Berliner 1994; Flyvberg 2001).

Reflection

Consider the novice-to-expert levels in Table 12.1 and also think of a mathematical topic that you teach.

- How expert do you consider yourself to be in teaching that topic?
- What implications for your continuing professional development arise from your earlier judgement?

Table 12.1 Novice-to-expert levels

	Knowledge	Coping with complexity	Perception of context
Novice	Minimal or 'textbook' knowledge without connecting it to practice	Little or no conception of dealing with complexity	Tends to see actions in isolation
Beginner	Working knowledge of key aspects of practice	Appreciates complex situations but only able to achieve partial resolution	Sees actions as a series of steps
Competent	Good working and background knowledge of area of practice	Copes with complex situations through deliberate analysis and planning	Sees actions at least partly in terms of longer term goals
Proficient	Depth of understanding of discipline and area of practice	Deals with complex situations holistically, decision-making more confident	Sees overall 'picture' and how individual actions fit within it
Expert	Authoritative knowledge of discipline and deep tacit understanding across area of practice	Holistic grasp of complex situations, moves between intuitive and analytical approaches with ease	Sees overall 'picture' and alternative approaches; vision of what may be possible

Source: Adapted from Lester (2005)

What has been considered as particularly significant in the Dreyfus model is that the development of proficiency and expertise is marked by an abandonment of the rule-based thinking which underpins the thinking of the first three levels (Dreyfus and Dreyfus 1980). Rather, expertise is characterized by an extensive, well-organized and flexibly accessible domain-specific knowledge base. Further, this knowledge base is one to which experts add all the time as they reflect on previous teaching episodes and strive to ensure greater refinement in subsequent episodes.

.c characteristic of expertise is consistent with the evidence
_ teachers' mathematical knowledge is an important aspect of
e teaching (Hill et al. 2005), it is not of itself sufficient (Shechtman
. 2010). In addition to, and in interaction with, teachers' mathemat-
_l knowledge, proficient and expert teachers are both highly motivated
and self-regulating.

Teachers' self-knowledge

The professional status of teachers requires them to initiate, control and
manage teaching episodes by themselves; in other words that they be self-
regulating. Such autonomy is very necessary because the sheer complexity
of the mathematics classroom means that there can be no algorithmic response available for every problem that presents itself. Not only do teachers need to be aware of and monitor their own thinking, understanding
and knowledge about teaching but also they need to be sensitive to the different kinds of knowledge which they can draw upon to help develop their
practice (Parsons and Stephenson 2005). Such self-regulation is defined as:

> the self-conscious monitoring of one's cognitive activities, the ele-
> ments used in those activities, and the results educed, particularly
> by applying skills in analysis and evaluation to one's own infer-
> ential judgments with a view toward questioning, confirming,
> validating, or correcting either one's reasoning or one's results.
>
> (Facione 1990: 10)

Self-regulation is commonly understood as being an iteratively phased
activity. Teacher thinking in relation to teaching episodes can readily
map on to the different phases (see Table 12.2).

Reflection

Consider a mathematics teaching episode which has depended on your self-
regulation. Map onto the framework below the Planning you did in advance
of the lesson, the Monitoring and Control in which you engaged during
the lesson and your Reflections after the lesson. This mapping is unlikely to
be the same for different teachers and unlikely to be the same for different
lessons. If you are working with others, compare your responses. If working
on your own, compare your self-regulation for two different mathematics
teaching episodes. In either event, try to tease out the implications of your
analyses for your further development.

Table 12.2 Teachers' cognitive self-regulation

Phase	Teacher cognitive self-regulation in relation to a teaching episode	Other considerations which arise from, and feed into, teachers' regulation
Planning	• Determines targets and standards; sets out objectives • Considers the prior knowledge learners need to have in order to benefit from teaching episode • Anticipates potential obstacles in the resources to be used by learners	• Time and effort needed by teacher for planning • Judging how self-efficacious learners may be to episode • Judging how interested learners may be in episode
Monitoring	• Formal/informal judgements of learning, of task appropriateness and of contextual conditions • Self-assessment of one's own planning	• Skill in diagnosing moment-to-moment interactions between and among learners and their context • Determining if and when to act in relation to indicators of learning
Control	• Adjusting episode to 'repair' what is going wrong • Adapting episode to accelerate learning when it is evident that planning underestimated learner competence	• Options for changing/renegotiating task • Selection/adaptation of strategies to promote learning and manage motivation
Reflection	• Judges whether episode did or didn't work using predetermined criteria • Considers why/offers explanation of, the task 'worked' or didn't 'work'	• Teachers' knowledge of attribution, motivation, self-efficacy • Autonomy to modify subsequent teaching episode

In teaching, these phases of self-regulation need constant adaptation because of the dynamics of the environment and the social relationships of the classroom. Thus it is through the many cycles of planning, monitoring, controlling and reflecting that practice develops, and it is through deliberate practice that expertise develops, although the practice may be neither enjoyable nor easy.

The importance of teacher self-regulation is evidenced in learners who are self-regulating since their initiative, motivation and personal responsibility are mirrored in academic success (Nota et al. 2004). Space limitations here prevent adequate consideration of how self-regulation develops, but the more teachers are aware of both cognitive factors (developmental differences in learners' working memory; the role of prior knowledge; self-awareness; awareness of task's constituent demands; feelings of familiarity, difficulty, confidence, satisfaction) and motivational factors (judgements of learning; competence; interest and value; goal orientation; self-efficacy and volition) (Pintrich and Zusho 2002) the more autonomous teachers can be in using their adaptive expertise (Berliner 2001) to enable learners' deeper understanding of the subject-matter. Expert teachers pay close attention not only to the factual accuracy of learners' responses but also to the logical persuasiveness of the learners' reasoning (Sato et al. 1993). If teachers are unaware of learners' thinking, they are less likely to engage learners in self-regulating activities (Parsons and Stephenson 2005) thereby inhibiting the acceleration of learning which is available even to low-achievers when self-regulation is deployed (Zohar and Ben David 2008; Zohar and Peled 2008). The reality of self-regulation is in the strong linguistic component which characterizes many classrooms and which provides the mechanism for learners to negotiate how they make rules, draw conclusions, approach/solve a task, justify choices, and evaluate the advantages/disadvantages of different strategic behaviour. It is through consciously embedding these opportunities in all teaching episodes that teachers can support learners' self-regulation (Carr et al. 2011).

Pupil knowledge

Concerns about mathematical achievement centre on learners' understanding (Hiebert and Lefevre 1986). Learning with understanding is increasingly coming into sharper focus through the realization that the memorization of facts or procedures without understanding often results in fragile learning. This is not to say that factual accuracy and procedural facilitation are unimportant: just that they are insufficient of themselves. Understanding is mental activity which makes use of knowledge: facts, concepts, principles, procedures and phenomena which each individual stores in memory as a connection or network. This knowledge varies from person to person as do the unique ways in which each individual forms connections between pieces of knowledge. The different pieces of knowledge are representations which are (unique-to-the-individual) configurations of symbols, real objects or events and mental images (Janvier 1987). So, for example, one can 'picture in one's head' what a cat is through a picture, or a verbal description, or a recent visit to the zoo. Thus individual understanding of 3 might be linked to a number of representations: such as the counting sequence 1, 2, 3; to the numeral 3; to three fingers; to 3 being 1 less than 4; and/or to other experiences that individuals have had. Constructing representations can be complex. To solve word problems learners must create different mental representations: they need to understand the numerical values and the quantitative relations between them (mathematical understanding) and they need to understand what information is essential and what information is less important (contextual/situational understanding). They then mathematize the situation: lock the two representations together in terms of previous mathematical knowledge, to determine how to proceed. Appropriate operation(s) can then be enacted and results interpreted in terms of both the mathematics and the situation described in the problem. But if learners, instead, use a meaningless strategy (perhaps identifying salient words such as 'more' or 'less' with particular operations) without regard for the situation, they do not fully understand either what the problem asked or how good their solution is (Thevenot et al. 2007). Understanding is thus the process of constructing networks of meaning between existing bits of knowledge and integrating new representations. Although it is never complete, understanding is said to develop as representations are connected in progressively more elaborate networks.

Individual internal representations of any idea are extremely important, but being internal are not visible to others; they have to be brought into a form which others can see. To express any mathematical concept or problem, a representation must necessarily be used (Dreyfus and Eisenberg 1996). Symbols, pictures, language, counters, number lines, fraction bars, cubes, graphs, tables or formulae are common external representations. Being able to 'see' or identify the same mathematical concept or problem in different representations (and thereby move fluently among representations) indicates stronger understanding (Dufour-Janvier et al. 1987). This is analogous to travelling to a new destination. The traveller may have a set of directions listing street names and turns to follow, which is perfectly adequate albeit limiting. If, additionally, the traveller has a map of the area, he/she can determine the most efficient route among neighbouring streets, and accommodate road closures. In other words, understanding of navigation is strengthened by having more than one representation. Because any single external representation cannot describe fully a mathematical construct, the limitations of any particular representation can be overtaken by using multiple representations (just as a map is another resource to support the traveller), which help learners to construct a better picture of a mathematical concept.

Learners are presented regularly with representations since these are what teachers and learners use as carriers of knowledge and as thinking tools to describe or explain a concept, a relationship, or a problem. External representations are important because they interact with learners' internal representations and help the learner to make more sense (Greeno 1991). But learners tend to discount their common-sense knowledge of the real world and view mathematics as artificial and disconnected from reality (Greer et al. 2002). So the richness of available representations and the facility to 'translate' between them need to be an explicit focus of teaching if learners are to avoid confusing external representations of concepts with the concepts themselves (Janvier 1987; Greeno 1991). In other words external representations mustn't be privileged to the point of being manipulated without reference to the internal representation that the learner is using. Neither is it helpful to impose external representations or coerce learners to use particular external representations. Teachers therefore have to elicit learners' existing thinking and ideas so that new knowledge is not isolated from existing knowledge. The mechanism for this is discussion which allows:

- Teachers to identify what strategies learners are using (and thereby decide how to respond and/or whether to build on that particular learner's suggestion)
- Learners to share their thinking with the other members of the class
- Others to comment, question, elaborate on the suggestion.

A prototypical sequence for such discussion might be:

- Teacher poses a question or problem to the class (possibly making three or four answers available for consideration).
- Learners have time to think of answers or responses individually.
- Learners discuss possible responses (in groups of four or fewer).
- Individual learners 'vote' for an answer or a preferred solution.
- Teacher tallies and displays distribution of votes to the class.
- Class discussion ensues, with learners justifying their answers.
- Teacher moderates discussion to allow closure.

Reflection

The following three aspects of the significant concept, place value, are ones that you might, at times, want to emphasize in a teaching episode. Consider how much emphasis you put on the different representations which together constitute a robust understanding of the concept.

1. The relationship between the oral name and the numeral. Perhaps the easiest of the representations is the connection between what we call 'numbers' and their written form. Tasks such as 'Can you read these numbers: 17, 39, 50, 56, 71?' and 'Circle numbers on the chart as I read them: 14, 25, 42' focus on this relationship. Our 'twelve' in some other cultures is 'ten-two', and our 'forty-seven' is 'four-ten-seven'. We use 'ty' to mean 'ten', but 'twen', 'thir' and 'fif' don't sound like 'two', 'three' and 'five'. Finally, teen numbers are reversed. 'Seventeen' can be misunderstood as '71'.

2. The relationship between the oral name and the quantity. While counting in ones may be secure, learners need to appreciate that counting in groups – 2s, 5s, 10s – is more efficient. From a display of bundles of ten and a large collection of single counters, what are the learners doing when you pose tasks such as the following: 'Show me thirty', 'Show me thirty-five', 'Look at this collection of thirty-five. If we count them by ones, how many will we get?', 'If we count them by tens, what answer do we get?' and 'Show me seventy. How many tens is that?'

3. The relationship between the numeral and the quantity. Here the task is to emphasize the relationship of the written symbol with the numerosity, so the same type of tasks as above can be used.

Is it your practice to deal with these relationships explicitly and discretely? Do you give equal attention to each or put more emphasis on one? Although only an initial understanding of place value has been illustrated, analogous relationships have to be constructed for more advanced concepts to allow profound understanding of the relationship between a digit's place and its value.

Content knowledge

As has been argued throughout this chapter, knowledge is not a collection of static gobbets but the thinking and reasoning that people draw upon (and construct) when solving problems and engaging in non-routine activity. Furthermore the importance of understanding is irrefutable. Key mathematical understandings appear to coalesce round additive and multiplicative reasoning (Nunes et al. 2009) which can be most economically illustrated through the range of mathematical problems that are used in primary school (Carpenter et al. 1999).

Additive reasoning focuses on the sums of, and differences between, quantities and in part develops intuitively. Nevertheless, addition and subtraction as reflected in different types of problems are experienced variously by learners (see Table 12.3).

Table 12.3 Types of addition and subtraction problems

Problem type			
Join	*Result unknown* May has 5 apples. John gives her 8 more. How many apples does May have altogether?	*Change unknown* John has 5 marbles. How many more does he need to have 13 marbles altogether?	*Start unknown* May has some hoops. John gives her 5 more. Now she has 13 hoops. How many did she have to start with?
Separate	*Result unknown* John has 13 jigsaws. He gives 5 to the boy next door. How many does he have left?	*Change unknown* May has 13 flowers. She planted some, now she is left with 5. How many did she plant?	*Start unknown* John has some grapes. He gives 5 to May and now has 8 left. How many did he have to start with?
Part-part-whole	*Whole unknown* May has 5 pink shirts and 8 blue ones. How many shirts does she have?	*Part unknown* John has 13 pens. 5 are red and the rest, blue. How many blue ones has he got?	
Compare	*Difference unknown* John has 13 arrows. May has 5. How many more arrows does John have?	*Compare quantity unknown* May has 5 books. John has 8 more. How many books has John got?	*Referent unknown* May has 13 hats. She has 5 more than John. How many hats has May got?

Source: Adapted from Carpenter et al. (1999)

These problems contain the same key words but the structure of each is unique and influences how easy or how difficult learners may find them. A major task for many learners is to appreciate that these are alternative representations of additive reasoning.

Multiplicative reasoning, on the other hand, does not develop intuitively and requires formal instruction (Sowder et al. 1998). Multiplicative reasoning is what underpins understandings of common and decimal fractions, percentages, proportion and ratio, all critically important ideas for us to develop. While additive reasoning is a necessary first stage, it is important to enable learners to restructure their concept of number to understand the unit of quantification is not one but a set (such as a pair, a trio, or other composite unit) or a fractional quantity (such as one-quarter, one-third). There is now a new variable, the multiplier, which counts sets. Learners need to be able to understand a collection of items as a set (the multiplicand) which is operated on by the multiplier to result in product. Equally they need to understand the relationships of dividend, divisor and quotient (see Table 12.4).

Again, while these problems appear to be the same, their structural differences are mirrored, initially, in very different problem solutions by learners.

Reflection

Consider how much emphasis you put on these different representations of additive and multiplicative reasoning.

- Do you expect that having taught one representation of an operation that learners will automatically or easily generalize to others?
- Are there some problem types you shy away from?
- What changes to teaching the 'four rules' might you now consider, in the light of reading this chapter?

Conclusion

This chapter has been written for readers who strive to be experts in mathematics teaching and so has primarily been concerned with how teachers think about themselves, their practices and their learners' thinking. Teachers' own complex reflections on practice are important because it is through these that they implement change meaningfully in their

Table 12.4 Types of multiplication and division problems

Problem type	Multiplication	Measurement division (quotitive division)	Sharing division (partitive division)
Grouping/ partitioning	Jack has 4 tomato plants. There are 6 tomatoes on each plant. How many tomatoes are there altogether?	Jack has some tomato plants. There are 6 tomatoes on each plant. In total there are 24 tomatoes. How many plants does Jack have?	Jack has 4 tomato plants, with the same number of tomatoes on each. There are 20 tomatoes altogether. How many are there on each plant?
Rate	Jenny walks 3 miles an hour. How many miles does she walk in 5 hours?	Jenny walks 3 miles an hour. How many hours will it take to walk 15 miles?	Jenny walked 15 miles. It took her 5 hours. What is her average hourly walking speed?
Price	Comics cost £2.00. How much do 12 comics cost?	Comics cost £2.00. How many comics can you buy for £24.00?	Mum bought 12 comics, spending £24.00. If each comic was the same price, what did it cost?
Multiplicative comparison	The tree is 3 times as tall as the house. The house is 9 feet high. How tall is the tree?	The tree is 27 feet tall. The house is 9 feet high. The tree is how many times taller than the house?	The tree is 27 feet high, 3 times as tall as the house. How high is the house?

Source: Adapted from Carpenter et al. (1999)

classrooms. The explicit opportunity to think about, question and elaborate on different perspectives of problem solving, both as learners and as teachers, allows teachers to focus more on deep understanding of task demands and on learner-centred teaching (Kramarski and Revach 2009). As well as questioning and reviewing one's practices, it can at times be helpful to resource one's reflections through further reading. The research literature in mathematics education is vast but two relatively recent publications (noted below) stand out because they have been written with practising teachers in mind.

Further reading

Nunes, T., Bryant, P. and Watson, A. (eds) (2009) *Key Understandings in Mathematics Learning*. London: Nuffield Foundation.
This publication synthesizes the recent research literature of mathematics learning by children (aged 5–16 years). It explores issues such as the insights learners must have in order to understand basic mathematical concepts; the sources of these insights and how informal mathematics knowledge relates to learning mathematics in school; and the understandings learners must have in order to build new mathematical ideas using basic concepts. The publication is presented in a set of eight papers, all of which are available from the funder of the study, the Nuffield Foundation (www.nuffieldfoundation.org).
Carpenter, T., Fennema, E., Franke, M., Levi, L. and Emspon, S. (1999) *Children's Mathematics: Cognitively Guided Instruction*. Portsmouth, NH: Heinemann.
Cognitively Guided Instruction (CGI) is a professional development programme for teachers which started in the United States at the beginning of the twenty-first century and continues to develop. CGI is an approach to teaching mathematics rather than a curriculum programme and at its core is the practice of listening to learners' mathematical thinking and using this as a basis for teaching. Research into CGI shows that expert teachers use a variety of practices to extend learners' mathematical thinking; and that their professional judgement is central to making decisions about how to use information about children's thinking. See http://ncisla.wceruw. org/publications/reports/NCISLAReport1.pdf

References

Berliner, D. (1994) Expertise: The wonder of exemplary performance. In J. Mangieri and C. Block (eds) *Creating Powerful Thinking in Teachers and Students*. Fort Worth, TX: Harcourt Brace College.
Berliner, D. (2001) Learning about and learning from expert teachers. *International Journal of Educational Research* 35 (5): 463–82.
Carpenter, T., Fennema, E., Franke, M., Levi, L. and Emspon, S. (1999) *Children's Mathematics: Cognitively Guided Instruction*. Portsmouth, NH: Heinemann.

Carr, M., Taasoobshirazi, G., Stroud, R. and Royer, J. (2011) Combined fluency and cognitive strategies instruction improves mathematics achievement in early elementary school. *Contemporary Educational Psychology* 36 (4): 323–33.

Damşa, C., Kirschner, P., Andriessen, J., Erkens, G. and Sins, P. (2010) Shared epistemic agency: An empirical study of an emergent construct. *Journal of the Learning Sciences* 19 (2): 143–86.

Dreyfus, S. and Dreyfus, H. (1980) *A Five-Stage Model of the Mental Activities Involved in Directed Skill Acquisition*. Berkeley, CA: Operations Research Center, University of California.

Dreyfus, T. and Eisenberg, T. (1996) On different facets of mathematical thinking. In R. Sternberg and T. Ben-Zeev (eds) *The Nature of Mathematical Thinking*. Hillsdale, NJ: Lawrence Erlbaum Associates.

Dufour-Janvier, B., Bednarz, N. and Belanger, M. (1987) Pedagogical considerations concerning the problem of representation. In C. Janvier (ed.) *Problems of Representation in the Teaching and Learning of Mathematics*. Hillsdale, NJ: Lawrence Erlbaum Associates.

Escudero, I. and Sánchez, V. (2007) A mathematics teacher's perspective and its relationship to practice. *International Journal of Science and Mathematics Education* 6: 87–106.

EURYDICE (2011) *Mathematics in Education in Europe: Common Challenges and National Policies*. Brussels: Education, Audiovisual and Culture Executive Agency (EACEA). Available at http://eacea.ec.europa.eu/education/eurydice/documents/thematic_reports/132EN.pdf (accessed 30 May 2012).

Facione, P. (1990) *Critical Thinking: A Statement of Expert Consensus for Purposes of Educational Assessment and Instruction: The Executive Summary of the Delphi Research Report*. Millbrae, CA: California Academic Press.

Flyvberg, B. (2001) *Making Social Science Matter*. Cambridge: Cambridge University Press.

Gholami, K. and Husu, J. (2010) How do teachers reason about their practice? Representing the epistemic nature of teachers' practical knowledge. *Teaching and Teacher Education* 26: 1520–9.

Ginsburg, H. and Amit, M. (2008) What is teaching mathematics to young children? A theoretical perspective and case study. *Journal of Applied Developmental Psychology* 29 (4): 274–85.

Greeno, J. (1991) Number sense as situated knowing in a conceptual domain. *Journal for Research in Mathematics Education* 22 (3): 170–218.

Greer, B., Verschaffel, L. and De Corte, E. (2002) The answer is really 4.5. In G. Leder, E. Pehkonen and G. Törner (eds) *Beliefs: A Hidden Variable in Mathematics Education?* Dordrecht: Kluwer Academic.

Hiebert, J. and Grouws, D. (2007) The effects of classroom mathematics teaching on students' learning. In F. Lester (ed.) *Second Handbook of*

Research on Mathematics Teaching and Learning. Reston, VA: National Council of Teachers of Mathematics.

Hiebert, J. and Lefevre, P. (1986) Conceptual and procedural knowledge in mathematics: An introductory analysis. In J. Hiebert (ed.) *Conceptual and Procedural Knowledge: The Case of Mathematics*. Hillsdale, NJ: Lawrence Erlbaum Associates.

Hill, H., Rowan, B. and Ball, D. (2005) Effects of teachers' mathematical knowledge for teaching on student achievement. *American Educational Research Journal* 42 (2): 371–406.

Hurme, T., Palonen, T. and Järvela, S. (2006) Metacognition in joint discussions: An analysis of the patterns of interaction and the metacognitive content of the networked discussions in mathematics. *Metacognition and Learning* 1: 181–200.

Janvier, C. (1987) Representation and understanding: The notion of function as an example. In C. Janvier (ed.) *Problems of Representation in the Teaching and Learning of Mathematics*. Hillsdale, NJ: Lawrence Erlbaum Associates.

Kramarski, B. and Revach, T. (2009) The challenge of self-regulated learning in mathematics teachers' professional training. *Educational Studies in Mathematics* 72 (3): 379–99.

Lester, S. (2005) *Novice to Expert: The Dreyfus Model of Skill Acquisition*. Available at www.sld.demon.co.uk/dreyfus.pdf (accessed 28 May 2012).

Miller, S. and Hudson, P. (2007) Using evidence-based practices to build mathematics competence related to conceptual, procedural, and declarative knowledge. *Learning Disabilities Research and Practice* 22 (1): 47–57.

Nota, L., Soresi, S. and Zimmerman, B. (2004) Self-regulation and academic achievement and resilience: A longitudinal study. *International Journal of Educational Research* 41 (3): 198–215.

Nunes, T., Bryant, P. and Watson, A. (eds) (2009) *Key Understandings in Mathematics Learning*. London: Nuffield Foundation.

Parsons, M. and Stephenson, M. (2005) Developing reflective practice in student teachers: Collaboration and critical partnerships. *Teachers and Teaching* 11 (1): 95–116.

Pintrich, P. and Zusho, A. (2002) The development of academic self-regulation: The role of cognitive and motivational factors. In A. Wigfield and J. Eccles (eds) *Development of Academic Motivation*. London: Academic Press.

Sato, M., Akita, K. and Iwakawa, N. (1993) Practical thinking styles of teachers: A comparative study of expert and novice thought processes and its implications for rethinking teacher education in Japan. *Peabody Journal of Education* 68 (4): 100–10.

Schuck, S. (2009) How did we do? Beginning teachers teaching mathematics in primary schools. *Studying Teacher Education* 5 (2): 113–23.

Shechtman, N., Roschelle, J., Haertel, G. and Knudsen, J. (2010) Investigating links from teacher knowledge, to classroom practice, to student learning in the instructional system of the middle-school mathematics classroom. *Cognition and Instruction* 28 (3): 317–59.

Shulman, L. (1988) The paradox of teacher assessment. Paper presented at the New Directions for Teacher Assessment. *Proceedings of the Educational Testing Service (ETS) Invitational Conference*, New York, October.

Sowder, J., Armstrong, B., Lamon, S., Simon, M., Sowder, L. and Thompson, A. (1998) Educating teachers to teach multiplicative structures in the middle grades. *Journal of Mathematics Teacher Education* 1 (2): 127–55.

Speer, N. (2005) Issues of methods and theory in the study of mathematics teachers' professed and attributed beliefs. *Educational Studies in Mathematics* 58: 361–91.

Thevenot, C., Devidal, M., Barrouillet, P. and Fayol, M. (2007) Why does placing the question before an arithmetic word problem improve performance? A situation model account. *Quarterly Journal of Experimental Psychology* 60 (1): 43–56.

Wiliam, D. (2003) The impact of educational research on mathematics education. In A. Bishop, M. Clements, C. Keitel, J. Kilpatrick and F. Leung (eds) *Second International Handbook of Mathematics Education* (Vol. 2). Dordrecht: Kluwer Academic Publishers.

Williams, P. (2008) *Independent Review of Mathematics Teaching in Early Years Settings and Primary Schools: Final Report*. London: DCSF. Available at http://dera.ioe.ac.uk/8365/1/Williams%20Mathematics.pdf (accessed 10 December 2011).

Zohar, A. and Ben David, A. (2008) Explicit teaching of meta-strategic knowledge in authentic classroom situations. *Metacognition and Learning* 3: 59–82.

Zohar, A. and Peled, B. (2008) The effects of explicit teaching of meta-strategic knowledge on low- and high-achieving students. *Learning and Instruction* 18: 337–53.

13 Transforming primary mathematics teaching through professional development

Mary McAteer

This, the final chapter of the book, draws together some of the issues presented earlier through a narrative which focuses on how teachers learn to become better teachers of primary mathematics. It begins by giving a brief introduction to the concept of good mathematics teaching (in primary schools), and from that, discusses how teachers *become* good mathematics teachers. At the time of writing, primary school teachers in the United Kingdom generally do not have a mathematics specialism, nor had the option to select such a route through their initial teacher education; thus the focus of the discussion will be on models of effective professional development, evaluations of their effectiveness and impact, and experiences and reflections from professionals engaged in such programmes. (It is worth noting, however, that pilot schemes to provide mathematics and other specialisms during the postgraduate training year in the United Kingdom are planned for a September 2014 commencement.)

Good mathematics teaching: what is it and what does it look like?

In a report commissioned by the (then) Teacher Training Agency (TTA), Askew et al. (1997) identified a range of characteristics of good mathematics teaching in primary schools. Effective teachers had, they found, a particular set of beliefs and values in relation to mathematics teaching which informed their conceptual understanding and impacted on their practice. Furthermore, while not necessarily correlated with high levels of subject qualification, effective teaching was predicated on a connectionist concept of mathematics. The use of effective assessment and monitoring techniques was also a key characteristic of effective teachers. In addition, it was noted that

> Highly effective teachers were much more likely than other teachers to have undertaken mathematics-specific continuing professional development over an extended period, and generally perceived this to be a significant factor in their development.
>
> (Askew et al. 1997: 5)

Anthony and Walshaw (2009), drawing on the New Zealand Iterative Best Evidence Synthesis Program, offer ten principles of effective teaching of mathematics. Again, the identification of curriculum structures and processes, an appropriate range of teaching and assessment strategies, and sound teacher knowledge and understanding grounded in a connectionist approach resonate strongly with earlier work in the United Kingdom. The need for effectively resourced and supported professional development opportunities for teachers is also identified.

Other reports since the early 1990s, in both the United Kingdom and other parts of the world, present broadly similar findings.

Following the Williams Report (2008), a number of surveys have been undertaken in order not only to identify good practice but also to make recommendations to policy-makers and school leaders. In their report, *Good Practice in Primary Mathematics: Evidence from 20 Successful Schools*, the Office for Standards in Education, Children's Services and Skills (Ofsted 2011) in the United Kingdom presented the findings from a survey of 20 schools who were successful (in terms of pupil attainment and progress) in the teaching of mathematics. From the data collected, they identified a set of 10 key features of successful mathematics teaching in primary schools. These features can be loosely classified into four broad categories:

- Teachers' subject knowledge
- Teaching and assessment strategies
- Curriculum coherence
- School leadership and management.

It is clear from the report that Ofsted perceives effective mathematics teaching as providing pupils with both conceptual understanding and mathematical fluency. In successful schools, problem solving in mathematics is effectively integrated throughout the curriculum, drawing on and developing both understanding and fluency, relating effectively to other curricular areas. This effective curriculum planning and coherence is emphasized also through their recognition of clear coherence calculation policies and guidance in many maintained schools, and the way in which they 'ensure consistent approaches and use of visual images and models that secure progression in pupils' skills and knowledge lesson by lesson and year by year'. Further, these effective schools 'recognise the importance of good subject knowledge and subject-specific teaching skills and seek to enhance these aspects of subject expertise' (Ofsted 2011: 7).

A later report in 2012, *Mathematics: Made to Measure*, described within the text as 'schools' perceptions of, and reaction to, the pressures to raise standards' (Ofsted 2012: 7), presents a set of key findings relating to mathematics education within the 3–16 age range. Of particular interest to many teachers might be their finding that

> While the best teaching developed pupils' conceptual understanding alongside their fluent recall of knowledge, and confidence in problem solving, too much teaching concentrated on the acquisition of disparate skills that enabled pupils to pass tests and examinations but did not equip them for the next stage of education, work and life.
>
> (Ofsted 2012: 9)

In its identification of some less effective teaching as the acquisition of disparate skills, there are resonances with the connectionist approach advocated by Askew et al. (1997). Once again, the identification of a need for a more integrated approach to problem solving, and a need for clear and coherent curriculum policies and guidance underpinned by 'professional development that focused on enhancing subject knowledge and expertise in the teaching of mathematics' (Ofsted 2012: 9) reiterates previous findings and analyses. Their recommendations to the Department for Education include that they should 'promote enhancement of subject knowledge and subject-specific teaching skills in all routes through primary initial teacher education' (Ofsted 2012: 9).

While plans are in development for subject specialized initial teacher education routes, primary schools at present must rely on professional development opportunities to provide and further enhance subject knowledge and specific pedagogies. Ofsted (2012) recommendations suggest that schools should, among a range of other actions,

develop the expertise of staff:

- in choosing teaching approaches and activities that foster pupils' deeper understanding, including through the use of practical resources, visual images and information and communication technology
- in checking and probing pupils' understanding during the lesson, and adapting teaching accordingly

- in understanding the progression in strands of mathematics over time, so that they know the key knowledge and skills that underpin each stage of learning
- ensuring policies and guidance are backed up by professional development for staff to aid consistency and effective implementation

(Ofsted 2012: 10)

There are common themes emerging from this (and other) reports. It seems clear that in a period when primary school teachers are not required to be specifically qualified in mathematics, nor are many likely to be in the foreseeable future, there is a clear need for high quality and effective professional development which addresses subject knowledge, teaching learning and assessment, and school organization.

Let me start then by exploring continuing professional development in recent years, examining its nature, and the ways in which its effectiveness has been identified and assessed.

Improving primary mathematics teaching and learning through effective professional development

It is common practice in many parts of the world to provide further, enhanced development and learning opportunities for teachers after they have qualified and are in post. Variously identified by terms such as INSET or In-Service and (continuing) professional development, it covers a range of types of provision from short to longer courses, and from those which are award-bearing to those which are not. In this chapter, I will use the term continuing professional development (CPD) to cover all these modes and models.

It is helpful first of all to further explore the range of modes and models, and their purposes.

Kennedy (2005: 236–7) identifies (in broad terms) nine models, categorized as follows:

- The training model
- The award-bearing model
- The deficit model
- The cascade model
- The standards-based model
- The coaching/mentoring model

- The community of practice model
- The action research model
- The transformative model.

In her article, Kennedy (2005) discusses each in turn, asking what its characteristics are, exemplifying it in practice (in Scotland), and finally, using five key questions to consider the interrelationships between the models, she analyses their appropriateness as models of transformation. In keeping with the focus of this book, the improvement in teaching and learning primary mathematics, I will focus on the ways in which she identifies those models best fitted to transformation. How might we best provide the type of CPD which has the capacity to transform?

Kennedy's analysis provides a continuum of purpose from transmission, through transitional to transformative, articulating an increasing capacity for professional autonomy as it moves to transformative. Describing *action research* in Somekh's words as 'the study of a social situation, involving the participants themselves as researchers, with a view to improving the quality of action within it [Somekh 1988: 164]' (cited in Day 1999: 34), and *transformative CPD* as the 'effective integration of the range of models described above, together with a real sense of awareness of issues of power, i.e. whose agendas are being addressed through the process' (Kennedy 2005: 247), Kennedy suggests that only these two models have the capacity to bring about transformation.

As well as providing a typology of CPD purpose, it is also important that we find ways of assessing the quality of provision. In the recent climate in England, CPD opportunities have been many and varied, but costly. For most teachers, engagement with good quality CPD makes quite a hole in their school's budget. For this reason alone, it is imperative that the opportunities they do avail of are high quality, providing value for money – something which is pragmatically interpreted on two levels by most schools. Teachers' own initial reports of their experiences, positive or otherwise, are often the first indicators noted. However, the need for that experience to translate into positive outcomes for pupils is paramount in an era of performance comparisons. On that basis, judgements of quality and value for money are made over periods of time. Schools may have their own processes for monitoring the subsequent impact of CPD courses, and teachers who have availed of such opportunities are expected to make a positive contribution to the school improvement agenda. This brings us to two key questions. The first of these relates to the nature of high quality professional development, while the second brings this to bear on the concepts of school improvement and impact.

What then are the characteristics of high quality professional development?

The educational Partnership for 21st Century Skills (2012) in the United States suggests that high quality CPD should, among other things:

- Focus on twenty-first-century skills and content
- Illustrate how a deeper understanding of subject matter can actually enhance problem solving, critical thinking, and other twenty-first-century skills
- Cultivate teachers' ability to identify students' particular learning styles and intelligences
- Help teachers develop their abilities to use various strategies (such as formative assessments) to reach different students as well as create environments that support differentiated teaching and learning
- Provide models of instruction that show what twenty-first-century skills look like in real classrooms and allow ample time for teachers to observe and learn from them
- Highlight ways teachers can seize opportunities for integrating twenty-first-century tools and teaching strategies into their classroom practice
- When appropriate, take advantage of twenty-first-century tools to support twenty-first-century skills
- Encourage knowledge sharing among communities of practitioners, using face-to-face, virtual and hybrid exchanges
- Be scalable and sustainable.

This would suggest that high quality professional development should update and up-skill teachers in a way that helps improve outcomes for pupils.

Work in recent years in the United Kingdom has focused more on how the effectiveness of existing CPD programmes can be evaluated, and through this, characteristics of good professional development can be extrapolated. A range of typologies for the evaluation of continuing professional development currently exists, with that of Harland and Kinder (1997) still being considered seminal. Building on the Joyce and Showers (1980) model they proposed a nine-point typology of outcomes identifying the following key evaluation categories:

- Material and provisionary outcomes
- Informational outcomes
- New awareness
- Value congruence

- Affective outcomes
- Motivational and attitudinal outcomes
- Knowledge and skills
- Institutional outcomes
- Impact on practice.

Ofsted (2010) present a number of recommendations (which can be inferred to be indicators of quality) to schools in order to ensure the effectiveness of their professional development. These recommendations include the need for a school-based focus, monitoring and evaluating impact, ensuring that teachers are regularly in receipt of subject knowledge updating, developing expertise in coaching and mentoring, and ensuring sufficient time for staff to discuss and reflect on what they have learned.

The review conducted by Cordingley et al. (2004) for the (then) National College of School Leadership identified similar characteristics, adding to 'reflection', the need for CPD to be sustained over a period of time to allow embedment. They also suggested that their evidence indicated positive links between teacher development and its impact on student outcomes which included motivation, achievement, attitudes to and organization of study, and general academic skills.

The identification of 'impact' is not without some controversy however. There are questions about the difficulty in establishing causal relationships between teacher professional development and improved pupil achievement. Powell and Terrell (2003) question the appropriateness of many definitions of impact, claiming that teachers' own judgements are just as important as externally determined measures. The disjuncture between externally assessed measures of impact and teachers' own perceptions has been reported by Hustler et al. (2003) and Muijs et al. (2004) among others, and could be thought to indicate an 'inaccuracy' of sorts in teachers' own perceptions. Robinson and Sebba (2006) report the work of Muijs et al. (2004), 'suggesting that there is little relationship between teachers' reports of their use of specific practices and the actual occurrence of these practices' and advise the need for caution in using professional perception-based evidence.

Despite the difficulties in assessing the quality of professional development, the review of postgraduate professional development, commissioned by the then Teacher Training Agency (TTA) to inform the development of a proposed new programme, reported findings under a series of key headings, suggesting effective programmes should:

- Lead to recognized qualifications at master's level or above
- Improve pupils' performance through the improvement of knowledge, understanding and practice of teachers, and by embedding improved practice in schools

- Develop teachers' research and problem-solving skills by integrating within it the critical evaluation of evidence and research from a range of sources, including academic research and other data available in schools
- Be shaped by, and adapted to, the needs of schools, teams of teachers and individual teachers in the region(s) where the provision is offered
- Directly involve teachers, schools and other local and regional stakeholders in effective partnerships for planning and developing its content and means of participation
- Contribute to an increase in teachers' participation in postgraduate professional development
- Take account of barriers to participation in CPD
- Be subject to internal and external quality assurance procedures
- Provide for the gathering of operational data, and monitor and evaluate the programme's impact on practice in schools.

Williams (2008: 24), in his review of mathematics teaching in Early Years settings and primary schools, recommended the provision of CPD 'of high academic quality' for specialist teachers who would then become 'the pathfinders for the profession'. His review made clear that not only should teachers receive such high quality CPD, but it should be structured and supported in such a way as to make significant and positive impact on schools and settings, and hence on pupils' learning and achievement. Kennedy (2005) cautions that the capacity for transformation is simply that – capacity. The question as to how this can be translated into action is vital and merits further exploration.

The question of impact: how can CPD effect positive change in schools?

If we consider the work of Newmann et al. (2000), we get an idea of how the staff members in a school can effectively bring about whole school improvement. He suggests that this improvement is enabled by

> the collective competency of the school as an entity to bring about effective change. This implies four core components: knowledge, skills and dispositions of individual staff; a professional learning community in which staff work collaboratively; programme coherence; technical resources.
>
> (Newmann et al. 2000, cited in Hopkins and Jackson 2003)

Thus, in this interpretation, effective professional education (and I would argue that this is the case both pre-service and in-service) would enable the development of, or further enhance, knowledge and skills, while also fostering certain attitudes, and in particular, those of community and collaboration. Other analyses – such as that of Cordingley et al. (2003) and of Jackson and Street (2005) – similarly identify collaborative practices as central in effecting positive outcomes for schools. Suggesting that collaborative enquiry, which while highly contextualized, challenges the 'taken-for-granted' in everyday practice, is supported by higher education processes and is rigorous and disciplined, is core in the quest for authentic school improvement (and they make a clear distinction between 'authentic' and other surface-level interpretations of improvement), they provide a possible insight into why such approaches may work. The ability of teachers to bring their professional learning back to practice can clearly be enhanced if that learning has taken place with colleagues, with the support of a school leadership team, or the support and facilitation of an external 'expert' (all ways in which Cordingley et al. (2004) define collaboration). Clearly a supportive school leadership and a culture of openness and shared learning will further enhance the potential for impact.

The particular qualities of effective CPD for primary mathematics teachers

In relation to primary mathematics teaching, a synthesis of these features would suggest that effective professional development for teachers should provide:

- The development of mathematics subject knowledge
- Expertise in a range of pedagogical practices
- Support for the needs of the individual school
- Quality assurance processes
- Planned opportunities to collaborate (in a range of ways)
- Access to external expertise
- Adequate time to both reflect on and embed learning.

McNamara et al. (2002), in their research monograph *Developing Mathematics Teaching and Teachers*, review models of professional development in the UK over the previous 20 years provided by universities, mathematics associations, curriculum development projects and initiatives, national strategies and local authorities. Drawing on findings of 'what works', and (critically) identifying and discussing weaknesses in models (something which they had found to be underrepresented in the literature they reviewed), they distil a set of three key messages in relation to ensuring the effectiveness and hence impact of CPD. The programmes they reviewed were all focused specifically on mathematics subject knowledge and pedagogies, and within these parameters they found that, first of all, adequate time coupled with teachers' own involvement in the management of the process was seen as effective in changing beliefs and practices. Secondly, models where one teacher was 'trained', and then expected to cascade that training to colleagues, were consistently identified as ineffective due in considerable part to the lack of both time and supportive culture in which such cascading would occur. Finally, a model of 'diffusion' rather than 'dissemination', similar to that of Japanese Lesson Study, was identified as potentially very highly effective. Citing Earl et al. (2000: 10) they advocate the creation of 'strong professional learning communities at school level' (McNamara et al. 2002).

The Researching Effective CPD in Mathematics Education (RECME) project, set up by the National Centre for Excellence in the Teaching of Mathematics (NCETM) in their 2009 report, cited five key factors in effective mathematics professional development for teachers, namely, leadership, practical approaches, stimulation, challenge and enjoyment, time and reflection and networking. In particular it is noted that following effective CPD, teachers reported, in addition to positive changes in their attitude, enthusiasm and energy, learning in three main areas; 'mathematical knowledge for teaching, increased awareness both of their own classroom practice and of their students' responses, and learning new information' (NCETM 2009: 94).

Oates (2010: 11) identifies strengths in the much praised Singapore system, while cautioning the 'limited examination of only selected aspects of a system'. Examination of their national CPD framework however does provide some useful insights and identifies similarities with findings elsewhere. The National Institute of Education, Nanyang Technological University (NIE/NTU), Singapore (n.d.) describes the key functions of its professional development programme as a course which will:

- Upgrade content knowledge of teachers
- Update teachers with pedagogical innovations in subject teaching
- Equip teachers with new competencies in response to societal needs and demands
- Keep teachers abreast of new developments and initiatives in education
- Educate teachers with research and management skills
- Enhance their teaching effectiveness through life-long learning.

A study in the United States found that

> teaching mathematics teachers deeper content and how to use an inquiry-based approach to deliver that content does indeed translate into greater student proficiency in mathematics. Doing more of such PD with teachers confers greater effects on the students they teach.
>
> (Sample McMeeking et al. 2012: 176)

Studies from other parts of the world bring some different qualities to light. The Japanese Lesson Study approach is much written about at present, and presents a model of collaborative planning, practice and practice review, not dissimilar to collaborative action research. It is a time and energy intensive process, but one which is supported by reduced teaching loads and structures which enable such practices to occur. Pockets of Lesson Study approaches exist in the United States and the United Kingdom at present, but its use is not extensive, nor well resourced.

The current picture in the United Kingdom: stories of change and development

The teacher professional development initiatives in the United Kingdom in recent years have focused increasingly on a number of specialist skill or subject knowledge areas. Some of the larger scale initiatives such as the postgraduate professional development (PPD) programme and the Mathematics Specialist Teacher programme (MaST) have been developed with specific aims in mind, in particular, that of making an impact on pupil achievement as well as teacher learning. The MaST programme, as identified in Chapter 1, was started in 2010 to provide high quality, high impact professional development for primary teachers. Developed in response to Recommendation 3 of the Williams Report (2008), that

> There should be at least one Mathematics Specialist in each primary school, in post within 10 years, with deep mathematical subject and pedagogical knowledge, making appropriate arrangements for small and rural schools. Implementation should commence in 2009 and be targeted initially to maximise impact on standards and to narrow attainment gaps

it was organized by universities (either alone or in consortia) in partnership with local authorities across England.

Predicated on a three strand model (subject knowledge, pedagogy, and working with others) it was delivered by a unique combination of local authority mathematics consultants and university staff. Taking a total of two academic years, it provides a sustained, network-based approach to teacher development and school improvement. The programme outcomes at an operational level are the conferral of Mathematics Specialist Teacher status, and the award of a postgraduate certificate (which can contribute to the completion of a full master's award). Teachers on the programme receive a mixture of theoretical and practical input, and have opportunities to work collaboratively in schools in practice-development mode. Assessment for the programme focuses on practice-based inquiry reports.

While no formal evaluation of the MaST programme has as yet been published, there are significant indicators of impact emerging from ongoing studies conducted by a number of the university providers. The final section of this chapter reports on one such study conducted by Edge Hill University as an exemplar of impact across the sector. A total of 215 programme participants completed questionnaires relating to their (changed) practice after participation, and its impact on their pupils. There was an overwhelming indication of change in pedagogy which in some cases was the development of *replacement* pedagogies (in which previous approaches were substantially replaced by new approaches) but in most cases was the development of complementary pedagogies, thus increasing the range of strategies at their disposal. The pedagogy showing the highest level of 'new use' was guided reasoning, with 60 per cent of the respondents indicating its adoption as a result of the programme. Problem posing approaches and the use of models, images and manipulatives also featured more highly after the programme. While there was very little reduction in the use of algorithmic strategies after the programme, there was a greatly increased (34 per cent) use of supplementary and complementary informal strategies.

Some 95 per cent of respondents also noted an improvement in children's attainment (classroom-based, school-based or at national testing level), and 99 per cent of these respondents reported that they believed the improvements to have been brought about by their participation in the programme. The further along they were in the programme, the more likely they were to report improvements in national tests. While this is obviously an area for further exploration, and there is of course the recognition that effects such as these are both complex and susceptible to time-lag, it would seem that early indicators strongly suggest a positive impact on pupil attainment.

From the sample of 215 teachers who responded to the questionnaires, a stratified sample of nine participants took part in loosely structured interviews. Data were coded through thematic analyses approaches, and overall, their identification of the impact of the programme falls into three categories:

- Improvements in pupil attainment
- Change in teaching practices/improvements in teacher knowledge (pedagogic knowledge and subject knowledge)
- Sharing knowledge.

Improvements in pupil attainment

While many teachers in interview identified significant improvements in pupil attainment after their teacher had been on the programme, some, like Joanne, also explained why she believed the improvement had occurred, explaining that:

> We are trying to encourage a lot more talking about what they are doing, identifying patterns and rules and the children are very good at reasoning and looking into applying skills now as opposed to just following a given rule.

Likewise, Sunita mentioned the way in which changed practice impacted not only on pupil understanding, but also on their enjoyment:

> maybe they were just doing things more by rote and now they are understanding more... it's that understanding that they now have and I think it is that, that they really enjoy. They can now really do it and understand it and that is where the enjoyment comes from.

The issue of enjoyment was mentioned by a number of teachers both in relation to their own engagement with mathematics and that of their pupils. As John said, 'a great range of teaching strategies is key to really engaging children'. Rosie explained further that 'anything that involves a practical aspect they really enjoy and they are learning through that enjoyment'.

In a context where there is concern about public perceptions of and attitudes to mathematics, the promotion of children's enjoyment, while at the same time developing conceptual and procedural knowledge would seem to be an important positive outcome. Teachers who demonstrate their own positive attitudes and enjoyment would seem an important part of this process.

Change in teaching practices/improvements in teacher knowledge (pedagogic knowledge and subject knowledge)

Teachers all articulated significant changes in their *pedagogic knowledge*, explaining how they now had both a great range of teaching approaches at their disposal, and also were more skilled in assessing the fitness for purpose of such approaches. While a number of teachers talked of an increase in their range of pedagogical strategies, some developed this further to include ways in which they had learned to make appropriate pedagogical selections. John elaborated on his improved range of teaching strategies, saying that:

> ...the models and images, the games they all help to get the knowledge across and the children, they learn in different ways and it's identifying what clicks with them. The more methods you have to draw upon the better really.
>
> (John)

Kate explained how:

> The course really highlighted how individualised learning is and what works for one child might not work for another... the greater range of strategies you have to teach with, the more chance you have of tapping into what actually works for each child.
>
> (Kath)

This new learning had an impact on their forward planning, as they began to realize that the pre-prepared plan might not be appropriate to suit the needs of their pupils. For Aiya, that meant the ability and confidence to adapt mid-lesson, describing her lesson planning as a process that had become 'more fluid'. Josie explained how her forward planning had now changed significantly as she became more aware of the need to provide for ongoing pupil need:

> [Now] I can't plan for a topic two weeks in advance until I have found out what my group need from me... actually finding out where the children are at or how well they seem to be picking something up and then using that as a basis for how I am going to go about teaching the topic.

Changes in *subject knowledge* were articulated clearly, and often associated with a commensurate improvement in confidence of the teacher. This improved subject knowledge was described in terms of the ability to now teach the full age range, or enhanced conceptual understanding, with Suraya saying that it had given her confidence in her understanding of 'the application of the subject'. Natalie further linked this to her role as a mathematics specialist in her school:

> I think the whole package over the two years covered most areas of maths. I think it has provided me with the knowledge that I required to do this role effectively and that is what I wanted to get out of it really.

Sharing knowledge

It was clear that participant teachers found the 'working with colleagues' aspect of the programme highly useful in their settings. While it was the case that pedagogic knowledge was shared more than subject knowledge, the reach of this sharing process extended to teaching assistants, class teachers, school heads and maths coordinators. In most cases, pedagogic knowledge sharing was done informally through one-to-one opportunities during teaching or discussion and planning sessions. Some however used the opportunity to put in place a series of more formal internal staff development events focusing on both pedagogic and subject knowledge. One woman noted that despite her own increased knowledge and expertise, she had needed to learn the art of sensitively working with her colleagues:

> You just have to be so careful, you know, you can't just go in there and say, 'you should all be teaching maths like this', you just have to you know bring it to their attention that there are a wide range of approaches out there and that it is worth trying them out because the children could really benefit from them.

A number of participants made similar statements, adding that the structure of the programme had provided highly effective support for them in this undertaking through its 'working with others' strand.

Other impacts of the programme

It was clear from the interviews that there were other outcomes also. On the whole, these related to the networking opportunities afforded by the nature and structure of the programme, the opportunity to hear leading experts in the field present their research, to have thinking challenged and stretched, and rather unexpectedly, to have the opportunity to complete assessment tasks. Teachers valued the opportunities to 'meet other colleagues and to kind of discuss what they had tried' and how 'lecturers that have challenged our thinking . . . just really inspiring us to go back and try different ways of teaching'. It was evident also that the mix of practice and theory was appropriate to their needs, although it was noted by some participants that while the theoretical perspectives helped develop their own thinking and understanding, writing 'academic' assignments was not always enjoyable. That said, a number of interviewees indicated that they had found this aspect enjoyable, or useful. One woman indicated that it was only when she started 'writing it all down' that she realized how much she had learned and that for her, writing it helped consolidate her learning.

If we return to indicators of effective mathematics CPD (subject knowledge, pedagogy, contextualized support, rigour, collaboration, external expertise, time-resourced), it seems evident that these teachers have indeed been experiencing such a process, and that its impact on practice is high and positive. The weakness identified in 'cascade' models of CPD seems to have been ameliorated somewhat by providing explicit support for leadership development, and by requiring participants to undertake a (supported) collaborative endeavour during the second year of the programme. The outcomes would also seem to support those of Cordingley et al. (2003), whose review of collaborative CPD

> offers detailed evidence that sustained and collaborative CPD was linked with a positive impact upon teachers' repertoire of teaching and learning strategies, their ability to match these to their students' needs, their self-esteem, confidence and their commitment to continuing learning and development. There is also evidence that such CPD was linked with a positive impact upon student learning processes, motivation and outcomes.
>
> (Cordingley et al. 2003: 8)

End words

In the introduction to this book, I stated my hope that we would present a text that was not only a guide to practice, but also a 'guide to understanding and developing practice' through the presentation and discussion of case studies from practice-based research in primary mathematics teaching. The realization of this hope however depends as much on the way in which the book is read, as it does on how it is written. Throughout the text, we offer opportunities for you to question, reflect, challenge and review practice. Sharing these deliberations with colleagues can help make such a process richer and more rewarding.

Part 2 presents case studies from practice, from teachers' desires to question and thus know and understand their practice better, and from their willingness and openness to listen to children's own articulations of their learning needs. These are presented not as examples of how things should, or indeed could, be done, but as prompts for your own thoughts and reflections. While they may provide you with some answers, it is hoped that they provide you with more questions. The art and practice of teaching is complex, dynamic and unpredictable. So too are changes in practice. It can be tempting to look for causality and certainty, but it is seldom a fruitful quest. It is in the questioning, the troubling through that we begin to understand both our contexts and our actions. It is in the understanding that we can begin to make sound professional judgments.

In Part 3, the chapters explore and articulate more fully the ways in which practitioners develop that understanding and capacity for judgment through the relationship they develop with theoretical perspectives, whether that be through applying and testing theory in their own contexts, or by attempting to theorize their practice in context. This relationship with educational theory gives practitioners the ability to recognize, and then question the 'taken-for granted' in practice, and to understand how best to respond to change and challenge, and how to support pupil learning by understanding our own. Just as the art and practice of teaching is complex, so also is the art and practice of learning. For teachers, undertaking professional learning poses the challenges of developing of self and pupil knowledge, as well as professional and academic knowledge. In the current culture of pupil assessment, accountability for pupil achievement, the search for self-knowledge can be coloured by the needs of a performativity culture. So too can the search for pupil knowledge. Knowledge of the self in relation to beliefs and values, and of pupils in relation to more than curriculum attainment, are, as Maclellan suggests in Chapter 12, what enable teachers to make meaningful changes in practice.

While this is not a book on 'reflective practice', *per se*, it becomes evident as we reflect on the book's chapters, both individually and collectively, that the sustained inquiry and reflection processes of teachers, the meaningful development activities they engage in, and the networking opportunities they have, all help teachers develop their own professional knowledge, understanding and judgment. The dynamic and moment-to moment unfolding nature of practice requires that this is underpinned by a willingness and openness to engage in a way that is at times challenging, that gives voice to their concerns, to those of their colleagues and pupils, that relates their developing understanding to broader contexts, yet still translates it into improved local practice. This process of changing practice is a subtle and nuanced one, predicated on principles rather than procedures. Its genesis is a desire to do right, founded on what MacIntyre (1984: 150) has described as the moral consciousness that leads us to do 'the right thing in the right place at the right time in the right way'. It is this desire to do right, perhaps, which most closely characterizes and underpins the inquiries and research presented in this book.

References

Anthony, G. and Walshaw, M. (2009) Characteristics of effective teaching of mathematics: A view from the West. *Journal of Mathematics Education* 2 (2): 147–64.

Askew, M., Brown, M., Rhodes, V., Wiliam, D. and Johnson, D. (1997) *Effective Teachers of Numeracy: Report of a Study Carried Out for the Teacher Training Agency*. London: Kings College, University of London.

Cordingley, P., Bell, M., Rundell, B. and Evans, D. (2003) The impact of collaborative CPD on classroom teaching and learning. In EPPI-Centre, *Research Evidence in Education Library*. London: Evidence for Policy and Practice Information and Coordinating Centre (EPPI-Centre), Social Science Research Unit, Institute of Education.

Cordingley, P., Rundell, B., Temperley, J. and McGregor, J. (2004) From transmission to collaborative learning: Best evidence in continuing professional development. Paper presented at International Congress for School Effectiveness and Improvement (ICSEI) Conference, Rotterdam, January.

Day, C. (1999) *Developing Teachers: The Challenges of Lifelong Learning*. London: Falmer.

Earl, L., Fullan, M., Leithwood, K. and Watson, N. (2000) *Watching and Learning: OISE/UT Evaluation of Implementation of the National Literacy and Numeracy Strategies*. Toronto: Ontario Institute for Studies in Education, University of Toronto.

Harland, J. and Kinder, K. (1997) Teachers' professional development: Framing a model of outcomes. *Journal of In-service Education* 23 (1): 71–84.

Hopkins, D. and Jackson, D. (2003) *Networked Learning Communities: Capacity Building, Networking and Leadership for Learning*. Available at http://networkedlearning.ncsl.org.uk/knowledge-base/think-pieces/capacity-building-2003.pdf (accessed 21 March 2012).

Hustler, D., McNamara, O., Jarvis, J., Londra, M., Campbell, A. and Howson, J. (2003) *Teachers' Perspectives of Continuing Professional Development*. DfES Research Report 429. London: DfES.

Jackson, D. and Street, H. (2005) Collaborative enquiry: Why bother? In H. Street and J. Temperley (eds) *Improving Schools through Collaborative Inquiry*. London: Continuum.

Joyce, B. and Showers, B. (1980) Improving in-service training: The messages of research. *Educational Leadership* 37: 379–85.

Kennedy, A. (2005) Models of continuing professional development: A framework for analysis. *Journal of In-service Education* 31 (2): 235–50.

MacIntyre, A. (1986) *After Virtue*. London: Duckworth.

McNamara, O., Jaworski, B., Rowland, S., Hodgen, J. and Prestage, S. (2002) *Developing Mathematics Teaching and Teachers: A Research Monograph*. Available at www.maths-ed.org.uk/mathsteachdev/pdf/mdevrefs.pdf (accessed 30 January 2012).

Muijs, D., Day, C., Harris, A. and Lindsay, G. (2004) Evaluating continuing professional development: An overview. In C. Day and J. Sachs (eds) *International Handbook on the Continuing Professional Development of Teachers*. Buckingham: Open University Press.

National Centre for Excellence in Teaching Mathematics (NCETM) (2009) *Final Report: Researching Effective CPD in Mathematics Education*. London: DCSF.

National Institute of Education, Nanyang Technological University (NIE/NTU) (n.d.) *Professional Development Programmes and Courses*. Available at www.nie.edu.sg/studynie/professional-development-programmes-and-courses (accessed 30 May 2012).

Newmann, F., King, B. and Young, S.P. (2000) Professional development that addresses school capacity: Lessons from urban elementary schools. Paper presented to Annual Meeting of the American Educational Research Association, New Orleans, 3 April.

Oates, T. (2010) *Could Do Better: Using International Comparisons to Refine the National Curriculum in England*. Cambridge: University of Cambridge Examinations Syndicate. Available at www.cambridge assessment.org.uk/ca/digitalAssets/188853_Could_do_better_FINAL_inc_foreword.pdf (accessed 30 January 2012).

Office for Standards in Education (Ofsted) (2010) *Good Professional Development in Schools*. Available at www.ofsted.gov.uk/resources/good-professional-development-schools (accessed 21 March 2012).

Office for Standards in Education (Ofsted) (2011) *Good Practice in Primary Mathematics: Evidence from 20 Successful Schools*. London: The Stationery Office. Available at www.ofsted.gov.uk/resources/good-practice-primary-mathematics-evidence-20-successful-schools (accessed 23 May 2012).

Office for Standards in Education (Ofsted) (2012) *Mathematics: Made to Measure*. London: Ofsted. Available at www.ofsted.gov.uk/resources/110159 (accessed 30 May 2012).

Partnership for 21st Century Skills (2012) *A Framework for 21st Century Learning*. Available at http://p21.org/ (accessed 11 April 2012).

Powell, E. and Terrell, I. (2003) Teachers' perceptions of the impact of CPD: An institutional case study. *Journal of In-service Education* 29 (3): 389–404.

Robinson, C. and Sebba, J. (2006) *A Review of Research and Evaluation to Inform the Development of the New Postgraduate Professional Development Programme*. Available at www.tda.gov.uk (accessed 21 March 2012).

Salmon, P. and Kohler Riessman, C. (2008) Looking back on Narrative Research: An exchange. In M. Andrews, C. Squire and M. Tamboukou (eds) *Doing Narrative Research*. London: Sage.

Sample McMeeking, L., Orsi, R. and Cobb, R.B. (2012) Effects of a teacher professional development program on the mathematics achievement of middle school students. *Journal for Research in Mathematics Education* 43 (2): 160–82.

Somekh, B. (1988) Action research and collaborative school development. In R. McBride (ed.) *The In-Service Training of Teachers*. London: Falmer.

Williams, P. (2008) *Independent Review of Mathematics Teaching in Early Years Settings and Primary Schools: Final Report*. London: DCSF. Available at http://dera.ioe.ac.uk/8365/1/Williams%20Mathematics.pdf (accessed 10 December 2011).

Index